TOURISM AND SOCIAL IDENTITIES

GLOBAL FRAMEWORKS AND LOCAL REALITIES

ADVANCES IN TOURISM RESEARCH

Series Editor: **Professor Stephen J. Page**
University of Stirling, UK
s.j.page@stir.ac.uk

Advances in Tourism Research series publishes monographs and edited volumes that comprise state-of-the-art research findings, written and edited by leading researchers working in the wider field of tourism studies. The series has been designed to provide a cutting edge focus for researchers interested in tourism, particularly the management issues now facing decision-makers, policy analysts and the public sector. The audience is much wider than just academics and each book seeks to make a significant contribution to the literature in the field of study by not only reviewing the state of knowledge relating to each topic but also questioning some of the prevailing assumptions and research paradigms which currently exist in tourism research. The series also aims to provide a platform for further studies in each area by highlighting key research agendas, which will stimulate further debate and interest in the expanding area of tourism research. The series is always willing to consider new ideas for innovative and scholarly books, inquiries should be made directly to the Series Editor.

Published:

Benchmarking National Tourism Organisations and Agencies
LENNON, SMITH, COCKEREL & TREW

Extreme Tourism: Lessons from the World's Cold Water Islands
BALDACCHINO

Tourism Local Systems and Networking
LAZZERETTI & PETRILLO

Progress in Tourism Marketing
KOZAK & ANDREU

Destination Marketing Organisations
PIKE

Indigenous Tourism
PAGE, RYAN AND AICKEN

An International Handbook of Tourism Education
AIREY & TRIBE

Tourism in Turbulent Times
WILKS, PENDERGAST & LEGGAT

Taking Tourism to the Limits
RYAN, PAGE & AICKEN

Forthcoming:

Micro-clusters & Networks – The Growth of Tourism
MICHAEL

Tourism and Politics
BURNS & NOVELLI

Tourism and Small Businesses in the New Europe
THOMAS

Hospitality: A Social Lens
LASHLEY, LYNCH & MORRISON

For other titles in the series visit: www.elsevier.com/locate/series/aitr

Related Elsevier Journals — sample copies available on request
Annals of Tourism Research
International Journal of Hospitality Management
Tourism Management

TOURISM AND SOCIAL IDENTITIES

GLOBAL FRAMEWORKS AND LOCAL REALITIES

EDITED BY

PETER M. BURNS
University of Brighton, UK

MARINA NOVELLI
University of Brighton, UK

ELSEVIER

Amsterdam • Boston • Heidelberg • London • New York • Oxford
Paris • San Diego • San Francisco • Singapore • Sydney • Tokyo

Elsevier
The Boulevard, Langford Lane, Kidlington, Oxford OX5 1GB, UK
Radarweg 29, PO Box 211, 1000 AE Amsterdam, The Netherlands

First edition 2006

British Library Cataloguing in Publication Data
A catalogue record for this book is available from the British Library

Library of Congress Cataloging-in-Publication Data
A catalog record for this book is available from the Library of Congress

ISBN-13: 978-0-08-045074-2
ISBN-10: 0-08-045074-1

For information on all Elsevier publications
visit our website at books.elsevier.com

Printed and bound in The Netherlands

06 07 08 09 10 10 9 8 7 6 5 4 3 2 1

Working together to grow
libraries in developing countries

www.elsevier.com | www.bookaid.org | www.sabre.org

ELSEVIER   BOOK AID
International   Sabre Foundation

Contents

Section II: Local Realities: Post-Industrial World and Transitional Economies

List of Figures

List of Tables

Contributors

Peter M. Burns (PhD) is a professor of International Tourism and Development and director of the Centre for Tourism Policy Studies (CENTOPS) at the University of Brighton. He is former director of the Fiji Hotel School and head of the department and of Sport, Leisure and Tourism, The Business School, University of Luton. He is a consultant anthropologist specialising in strategic policy-making/implementation for tourism's human resources and identifying insightful solutions to the cultural impacts of tourism. He has extensive international experience in institutional strengthening and working with communities helping them to achieve better education, participation and training opportunities. He was the founding chair of the Association of Tourism and Leisure Studies (ATLAS) special interest group on Tourism and Social Identities, vice chair of the ATLAS committee, member of the World Tourism Organization Education Committee and one of the first tourism scholars to be elected as an academician of the Academy of Learned Societies for the Social Sciences.

Marina Novelli (PhD) is a senior lecturer in Tourism Development and Management at the Centre for Tourism Policy Studies (CENTOPS), University of Brighton. Her main research interests include regional development and tourism, tourism planning and management, niche tourism and rural tourism markets development and management. She recently edited the volume "Niche Tourism: contemporary issues, trends and cases" (2005, Oxford: Elsevier) and completed a monograph commissioned by the Italian Ministry of Environment on the "Gargano National Park, Apulia – Italy". Her most recent research activity focuses on consumptive vs. non-consumptive tourism, Community Based Tourism and Tourism Cluster Development. She has been previously involved in a variety of European regional planning and tourism management consulting projects and is currently co-ordinator of the special interest group "*Tourism and the Local Economy*".

Patrícia de Araújo Brandão Couto is a doctoral student in Anthropology at Federal Fluminense University, Brazil and recipient of the CAPES-COFECUB research grant from the Sociology Department of Paris X-Nanterre University. Her fieldwork in Bahia, Brazil is uncovering several layers of complex relationships between insiders and outsiders and contributing significantly to the study of tourism (among other influences) upon remote, restructuring microeconomies.

David Dunn (PhD) worked as a television programme maker for 30 years, producing and/or directing a range of dramas and documentaries for STV, ATV, Central and BBC, before becoming an University lecturer in Media and Television Production in 1997, first at Salford and subsequently at Paisley. He now works at Queen Margaret University College, Edinburgh as Head of Drama and Performance. His research interests, on which he has published in journals and edited collections, include: The Tourist Gaze and the Television Camera's Gaze; Consumption of Marginal Places; Gaelic Television in Scotland; and Soap Opera: Place and Gendering.

Jennie Germann Molz is a postdoctoral research fellow in the Centre for Mobilities Studies at Lancaster University. Her interests revolve around mobile information and communication technologies, travel and tourism, consumption, globalization, citizenship and belonging. In addition to publishing articles in journals such as Citizenship Studies and Environment and Planning A, she has authored chapters in several edited collections including Culinary Tourism (University of Kentucky Press, 2004), Tourism Mobilities (Routledge, 2004) and Emotional Geographies (Ashgate, 2005).

Frank Go is a professor and the Bewetour chair at the Rotterdam School of Management, Erasmus University of the Netherlands. His research interests focus on the role of information in choice and sense making, also on brand identity and image, innovation and sustainable tourism business development. He serves on the board of several organizations, the editorial board of eight international journals and formerly worked in the USA, Canada and Hong Kong.

Freya Higgins-Desbiolles is a lecturer in Tourism with the School of Management of the University of South Australia. She is also completing a PhD thesis on the topic of "Tourism, Globalisation and the Responsible Alternative" with the School of International and Political Studies of Flinders University of South Australia. She has taught and researched on the topic of Indigenous tourism for four years and has won the University of South Australia's Equity Award for her efforts in working with Indigenous communities in the development of appropriate curriculum on Indigenous issues. She has worked with the Ngarrindjeri community of South Australia for a number of years and it is their work through Camp Coorong, which inspires her hope for a more just form of tourism.

Janne J. Liburd is an associate professor and head of research and education in International Tourism and Leisure Management at the University of Southern Denmark. She is a cultural anthropologist and her research interests are in the field of sustainable tourism development. She has published on cruise tourism, national park development, heritage tourism, tourism innovation, NGOs and democratic accountability in the Eastern Caribbean. Dr. Liburd is the chair of the B.E.S.T. Education Network.

Donald V. L. Macleod (PhD) is a Minton lecturer in Scottish Heritage and Tourism at the University of Glasgow. He trained as an anthropologist at the University of Oxford, and has taught at the universities of Oxford, London, Glasgow, and Macalester College USA. He has conducted field research in the Caribbean, the Canary Islands and Scotland. Dr Macleod has published widely in journals and edited collections, and produced books including the monograph *Tourism, Globalisation and Cultural Change* (Channel View Publications, 2004), and the edited collections *Niche Tourism In Question* (University of Glasgow Crichton Publications, 2003 – editor) and *Tourists and Tourism* (Berg 1997 – co-editor). His current research interests are embraced within the broad areas of the anthropology of tourism, sustainable development, cultural heritage and identity.

Duncan Marson is a lecturer in Adventure Tourism at the University of Derby Buxton. His ongoing doctoral research focuses on the development of recreational sub-cultures and the use of space and place. His research interests include issues surrounding the cultures of adventure and recreation. Recent research conducted includes visitor experience of rural space, attitude and conflict resolution in the Peak District National Park.

Scott McCabe (PhD) is a senior lecturer in tourism with the Centre for Tourism and Cultural Change at Sheffield Hallam University. His major research interests are in the tourist experience and tourist's everyday language practices. He has published numerous articles and book chapters, which specifically deal with tourist's use of spatial language to make identity claims. He is also interested in non-participation in tourism and teaches tourism-marketing planning.

Linda K. Richter (PhD) is a professor of political science at Kansas State University in the U.S. where she teaches public policy and gender politics. She has authored Land Reform and Tourism Development: Policymaking in the Philippines, The Politics of Tourism in Asia, and has published widely on tourism politics both in the US and abroad. She was the academic representative to the U.S. Travel and Tourism Administration, an associate editor of the Annals of Tourism Research and the Encyclopedia of Tourism. She was a member of International Academy for the Study of Tourism. She received graduate degrees from the East-West Center of the University of Hawaii and the University of Kansas. She has done field research in India, the Philippines and Pakistan and has lectured on international tourism in 19 countries. Her current research concerns international health, security and tourism policies.

James Tunney studied law at Trinity College Dublin (TCD), qualified as a barrister, took a masters in Commercial Law at the University of London and is a senior lecturer in law based at Dundee Business School, although he also lectures part time at St. Andrews in International Business and in International Relations as well as having worked elsewhere, such as the University of Orleans as a visiting professor in Competition law. As well as writing about the legal regulation of travel and tourism and working in consultancy for bodies such as the World Tourism Organisation and UNDP he writes and teaches on competition law, IP law, EU law, China and World Trade.

Gerard van Keken is an independent consultant/projectmanager and working on his PhD at Erasmus University Rotterdam. After several years of travelling the world and working as a consultant, he started working as a project manager at the Tourist Office Zeeland, in the Netherlands. His research interests are coastal tourism, culinary tourism,

tourism event management, research on identity and image in particular and in general the liminal space between theory and practice of tourism.

Johan van Rekom (PhD) is an assistant professor of Marketing Research at the Erasmus University at Rotterdam (the Netherlands). His research interests include identity, in particular the effect of organizational identity on the thinking and motivation of organization members, and branding, in particular the effect of a brand's essence on the positioning opportunities for brands. Before becoming an academic he worked as a tour guide and operated a travel agency.

Philip Feifan Xie (PhD) is an assistant professor in the Sport Management, Recreation, and Tourism Division, Bowling Green State University. He holds a M.A. in Recreation and Leisure Studies and a Ph.D. in Planning from University of Waterloo, Canada. His academic interests are tourism planning and recreation. These include cultural tourism, recreation geography and event management.

Acknowledgements

A number of people have contributed significantly to the realisation of this book. First of all, we would like to thank Mercedita Hoare for her assistance in the completion of the manuscript, and Mary Beth Gouthro and Michael O'Regan for their editorial assistance.

We are particularly grateful to all those colleagues who have refereed the chapters contained in this volume, whose names remain anonymous for the purpose of maintaining integrity.

Tourism and Social Identities: Introduction

Peter M. Burns and Marina Novelli

Social Identity

At first glance, the notion of 'social identity' could be an easy concept to understand. Leaving aside for the moment the idea that our movements in and out of various groups that have various labels attached to them might be quite fluid (Bauman, 2005), according to will and situations, it can mean simply that we belong to a group from which we draw a sense of 'who we are': our identity. The corollary is that we also derive this identity by comparisons with those not in our group, but who belong to other groups: the so-called 'out-groups' interrogated by Henri Tajfel and John Turner (1986) in their work on inter-group discrimination. Tajfel and Turner were interested in a range of interconnected aspects of behavioural psychology that centred on how individuals identified with social groupings, how loyalty to that group is expressed by aggression to out-groups and so on. In a sense, the system can be summarised as 'us' versus 'them' or 'self' versus 'Other' (Said, 1978), and in more recent times Roger Scruton's 'The West and the Rest' (2002). Underpinning Tajfel and Turner's work is that of 'social comparison' (Festinger, 1954) in which we judge our sense of worthwhileness (positive self-perception) by comparing ourselves against others, and how we see others as part of the disruptive pressures characteristic of life in the early 21st century. Examples to illustrate these points can come from almost any direction. Taking a little diversion into 20th century social history (and a little reflective personal narrative), the English seaside resorts of Clacton, Brighton, Hastings and Margate public disorder in the form of street riots broke out in the summers of 1964 and 1965 between two different social groups of youths with diametrically opposed attitudes towards dress, music and lifestyles: Mods and Rockers. In that case trouble flared up, probably encouraged by the sensation-seeking print media, into scuffles and broken shop windows and not much more. However, it caused something of a moral panic and suddenly these groups of youths were seen as representing a disobedient and dark side of society: unruly youths who had never had the discipline of military service (as perhaps their older siblings or uncles may have done via National Service) or the hardships of war that their parents and previous generations had endured.

It was over in a flash and can be explained as an illustration of inter-generational mis-understanding, an assertion of group identity and an early manifestation of consumer culture (where group identity was closely linked to fashion and style commodities and objects).

However, the same cannot be said of a parallel phenomenon that has lasted much longer and has been the subject/object of sustained study: football hooligans (Armstrong, 2003). Here, group identity, rigidly enforced by extremes of loyalty towards each other and their club, modes of dress, and attitudes towards out-groups (sometimes underpinned by right-wing fascist political ideology), has led to serious and violent confrontation, including deaths, across national borders. The football example is useful because it introduces the idea of national identity into the discussion. Where national borders are disputed, shows of nationalism and national identity veer towards the extreme. Examples can be seen in Northern Ireland, Basque regions of Spain, the deconstructed former Yugoslavia and so on. In the Kashmir region of South Asia, on the Wagah border between India and Pakistan, highly ritualised military ceremonies take place during sunset as the border is closed for the night. The aggressive performance, which includes exaggerated marching, eyeball staring and barking of orders, provides an extraordinary visual manifestation of the troubles in that region and seems somehow to act as a surrogate battle egged on by enthusiastic crowds including tourists. The irony is that the uniforms and indeed the whole ceremony 'Beating the Retreat' have their roots in the Colonial era and British army occupation.

These proxy battles draw us through the paradoxes of social identity versus national identity and into ethnocentrism, a concept that frames the debate about ethnicity, inter-ethnic relations and similar social issues. The most common use of the term is as a descriptor for 'thinking your own group's ways as being superior to others' and 'judging other groups as inferior to your own'. The difficulty of course is that ethnocentrism seems to be a common trait, almost nature, among most peoples of the world. It does not take much imagination to see the Greeks or Southern Italians smiling at a British academic's obsession with timekeeping at a conference. Or that same British academic feeling completely out of character when being invited out for an evening meal at 10 p.m. when custom 'at home' dictates going to bed with a nice cup of cocoa at that late hour! These are light-hearted feelings of difference and discomfort. But of course, things can become more serious when groups believe that they are morally or intellectually superior: therein lies the roots of racism and inter-group violence, characterised by the ritualistic game-playing over places next to the pool in Spanish, Greek and Turkish resorts between British and German tourists, or on a more serious note, racism and power can morph into sexual exploitation as noted in the online magazine, *The New West Indian*:

> Jamaica, the Dominican Republic and Cuba, like other economically underdeveloped holiday destinations, are marketed as culturally different places and all tourists are encouraged to view this 'difference' as a part of what they have a right to consume on their holiday. The construction of difference takes place around ideas such as 'natural' vs. 'civilised', leisure vs. work and exotic vs. mundane, rich vs. poor, sexual vs. repressive, powerful vs. powerless (Anon, 2001).

The binary differentiations might seem less than elegant to poststructuralists but nonetheless capture one aspect of identity, power and tourism in a very forceful way. It can be seen, then, that part of tourism's supply-side will include localised culture and people: in other words social identity becomes a commodity. This commodification invokes a controversy about people and their culture by providing the backdrop for leisured relaxation and recreation (Burns & Holden, 1995). Paradoxically, on the consumption side, customer reaction against the McDonaldization of services (cf. Ritzer, 1993), whereby packaged destinations and their social identities are reduced to marketing benefits for consumers, is emerging via a postmodern cynicism against the ubiquitous 'friendly natives' of tourism promotion and where 'everything somehow appears predestined' (Adorno cited in Bauman, 2005, p. 141).

Culture, Globalisation and Tourism

With growing sophistication in market segmentation and the rise of both consumerism and green awareness, there is recognition that tourists themselves are not a particularly homogeneous group and may drift in and out of various touristic social identities (one time at play, another as serious sightseer, clubber, etc.) during the course of their vacation.

The complexity of tourism's social and economic relationship with the receiving destination, both as performance and impact, means that it should not be perceived as an integrated, harmonious and cohesive 'whole'. Understanding the cultural systems and structures that make meaning between visitors and the visited possible is important for at least three reasons. First, culture (especially culture that is understood to be unique or unusual by actors including marketing specialists and planners) can be seen as a commercial resource, an attraction. Second, and arising from this is the idea that an understanding of the complexities and integrity of social identities might help deflect or ameliorate simplistic images of a host culture occurring through the act of receiving tourists. Third, tourism literature rarely acknowledges the world as a system of relations wherein the properties of a 'thing' (in this case, culture) derives meaning from its internal and external relations.

These three items are reflected in Wood's (1993) finely tuned perspective on the issue of tourism, identity and impacts. In discussing tourist and development discourses, his analysis of culture and tourism relies on identifying and understanding systems. He argues that 'The central questions to be asked are about process, and about the complex ways tourism enters and becomes part of an already on-going process of symbolic meaning and appropriation' (Wood, 1993, p. 66).

Insofar as looking for an analytical tool for tourism, Wood's 'process' and 'systems' discussed by Burns (1999a) are synonymous. While Wood (1993) gives a generalised account of cultural impact systems, Greenwood (1989) offers a more specific sense of the cultural problematic encountered by those who study tourism:

> Logically, anything that is for sale must have been produced by combining the factors of production (land, labor, or capital [and enterprise?]). This offers no problem when the subject is razor blades, transistor radios, or hotel accommodations. It is not so clear when the buyers are attracted to a

place by some feature of local culture, such as an exotic festival (Greenwood, 1989, p. 172).

Underpinning Greenwood's insights on local culture is the notion that place and space are inexorable elements of culture, and thus identity, that cannot be separated from the local environment where it develops (though this local environment will have global perspectives). If Greenwood's central concern, the commoditisation of culture for tourism, is to be addressed then a deeper analysis becomes essential. Proponents of 'Tourism First'[1] (cf. Burns, 1999b) tend to see culture from a supply-side point of view framed by the notion of social identity as an attraction. Thus, while attractions may vary (an obvious point) for many destinations, cultural elements, including social identities, will almost certainly be included as part of the 'product mix' (Ritchie & Zins, 1978, p. 257). The extent to which these components of culture are adapted by the local population and offered to tourists for consumption is likely to be framed by at least two factors. First, the relative difference and thus the relative novelty between cultural components of the visitors and the visited, and second, by the type and number of visitors.

Defining Culture within a Tourism Context

Culture is about the interaction of people and results in learning, and that such learning can be accumulated, assimilated and passed on. The point being that culture is observed through social relations and material artefacts and manifested, *inter alia*, by social identity. Culture and identity consists of behavioural patterns, knowledge and values, which have been acquired and transmitted through generations, 'an organised body of conventional understandings manifest in art and artefact, which, persisting through tradition, characterises a human group' (Redfield, cited in Ogburn & Nimkoff, 1964, p. 29).

Descriptions of a specific culture are necessarily static snapshots at a given moment. Culture and the identities that it comprises should be seen as dynamic: a society that does not take on board new ideas, or adapt to changing global conditions is in danger of cultural retrocession. To underline the complexity of thinking about these matters, the following caveat should be acknowledged: 'To speak unproblematically of "traditional" culture is not permissible. All cultures continually change. What is traditional in a culture is largely a matter of internal polemic as groups within a society struggle for hegemony' (Greenwood, 1989, p. 183).[2]

Greenwood was right in his concerns about cultural expropriation. His warning also serves as a reminder of the hypocrisy and paradoxes that surround attempts at cultural

---

[1]The notion of 'Tourism First' and 'Development First' approaches to social development of potential destinations summarizes the development debate as it pertains to tourism. Is it better to develop tourism and allow trickle-down economics and multipliers to spread the benefits or is it better to use tourism as a tool for development? (This matter is discussed in detail in Burns, 1999).

[2]It is reasonable to speculate that Greenwood was in reflective mood in writing this, given that new evidence meant that he had to completely reinterpret his classic essay on culture written up as 'Tourism as an Agent of Change: A Spanish Basque case (1972)'.

'preservation'. Traditional definitions of culture that have been subjected to a sustained attack over the past decade or so: an attack that has meant that the early cultural anthropologists have been dealt with a blow from postmodernism wherein 'culture-is-nothing'. While it is not our intention to discuss postmodernism at length, it is worth undertaking a brief examination of the changing perceptions of culture and social identity as they occur in late capitalist society, so an excursion into the phenomenon of postmodernism is inevitable.

Postmodernism

As indicated above, a few observations about postmodernism is called for in order to identify (but not resolve) some ways in which this interpretation of culture and social identity affects the analysis of tourism within its global context. The dramatic social changes that have been undertaken in the name of 'rationalisation', 'efficiency', 'privatisation' and 're-engineering' have meant the fragmentation of 'culture as a whole way of life' (During, 1993, p. 4) i.e., from the locally organised and easily understood to 'culture as organised from afar, both by the state through its education system, and by ... the "culture industry" ' (During, 1993, p. 4). It is not difficult to ascribe tourism to this 'culture organised from afar' notion.[3] As Huyssen puts it, 'No matter how troubling it may be, the landscape of the postmodern surrounds us. It simultaneously delimits and opens our horizons' (1990, p. 375). The characteristics of this fragmented, schizophrenic of society has been manifested in many ways, but perhaps rise of postmodernism is its most vocal and pervasive demonstration. Again, turning to During (1993), who claims that there are three grounds for suggesting that we live in a postmodern era. First, he notes that modernity can no longer be legitimised by the Enlightenment ideas of progress and rationality 'because they take no account of cultural differences'. Second, he continues with an assertion that 'there is no confidence that "high" or avant-garde art and culture has more value than "low" or popular culture', and finally he asserts that: 'It is no longer possible securely to separate the "real" from the "copy", or the "natural" from the "artificial", in a historical situation where technologies ... which produce and disseminate information and images ... have so much control and reach' (During, 1993, p. 170).

This fragmentation, which may also be described as the 'tabloid' or 'celebrity' society in which emotion and feeling take precedence over content and substance, has led to a confusion about life for those in the de-industrialised countries of the North. MacCannell poses a conundrum reflective of these postmodern times 'In the context of a cannibalistic desire to possess *everything*, it is not especially bizarre for capitalists to want what only

---

[3]These organisers from afar will include powerful producers of cultural forms such as franchised fast foods and sugar-soda beverages that have led to, for example, Ritzer's essay on 'The McDonaldization of Society' which asserts that bureaucratic structures, previously providing the model for rationalisation, essentially Weber's 'theory of rationalisation' (Ritzer, 1998, p. xiii) have been replaced by an even more efficient 'rational system' — the fast food chain — with McDonald's being its most important and powerful manifestation. For Ritzer, McDonald's and its like have become the new social institutions that were formerly thought to consist of family, church, government and the like, their 'rational' approach to production, as Ritzer asserts, has even impacted upon hospitals and governments.

socialists can have, universal brotherhood in a life free of material want and social contradiction' (MacCannell, 1992, p. 100). Paul Sutton and Joanna House take this a little further with an online discussion in which they assert that

> The postmodern is characterised by a 'preoccupation with identity' (Sarup, 1996, p. 97). As outlined above, New Age tourism destinations offer a variety of self development activities and experiences ranging from alternative therapies to self development workshops, and from intellectual courses offered by visiting scholars to art and craft production and alternative lifestyle courses all of which can and have become a tourism commodity ... This [commodification] process is double edged: it opens up many new horizons but also stimulates a profound sense of insecurity. Postmodern cultural pluralism threatens individuals' sense of their own 'ontological security' (Giddens, 1991) and has stimulated an egocentric preoccupation with identity. Individuals no longer find identities based upon nation, ethnicity, gender or class credible. Such incredulity has encouraged a narcissism in which the hyperreal becomes the frame of reference for all activities and experiences

Postmodernism has been described as 'the realization of the capitalist fantasy of the socialist goal of a classless society ... an imagined bourgeois revolution' (MacCannell, 1992, p. 100), wherein 'classlessness' is achieved by excluding the working classes by the creation of communities where there is no place for them, in a sense itself a reflection of Thompson's notion that: 'Fragmentation of the old working-class proletarian culture meant that a politics based on a strong working-class identity was less and less significant [with] people decreasingly identifying themselves as workers' (During, 1993, p. 4). In his discussion on consumerism, Lee (1992) is also critical of the manifestation of postmodernism and describes postmodern as

> Being inadequately adapted to deal with true legitimate cultural forms, however, this ... semi-intellectualised mode of production is more often than not turned upon those forms still in the process of a cultural consecration: 'jazz, cinema ... avant-garde underground (Bourdieu, 1984, p. 360). Such symbolic forms of course have the substantial advantage over fully legitimised forms of being generally far less demanding of their audience's interpretative capacities (Lee, 1992, p. 170).

However, Lee's reflections need to be contextualised within a certain reality: vast parts of the world, including many that are emerging tourist destinations, that is to say only just engaging in the global tourism nexus, two major aspects of postmodern life (i.e., consumerism and tourism) have no relevance for day-to-day existence, which may well be dominated by survival and coping. Even so, given that most tourists come from the North, both consumerism and commoditisation inform, shape, create and recreate social identities as destination, and residents respond economically and psychologically to the demands made by consumers and the companies that deliver them (MacCannell captures it wonderfully with his evocative phrase 'being themselves for others').

Consumerism impacts destinations through tourists bringing with them the urban (and urbane?) attitudes of the consumer society that they live in, such as expectations of service levels, and that 'things have their price', 'time is money' etc. The postmodernism controversy lies at the intersection of contemporary cultural change and the political economy of commodity exchange (Shields, 1991, p. 2).

In the above, it can be seen that places of consumption are far more than accidental mixes of geographic locations and attractions (indeed this is Shields' basic thesis). They represent both postmodern social dynamics and symbolic edifices, wherein everything (including social identity) is for sale: a commodity.[4]

Conclusion

The matters raised above, in-groups and out-groups, social identity, nationalism, ethnocentrism, postmodernism, culture, etc. have great resonance for tourism studies on both sides of the 'host' — 'guest' equation (or with increased mobility perhaps we should call it a continuum). That tourism is a profoundly important economic sector for most countries and regions of the world is widely accepted even if some of the detail remains controversial (how readily we accept UNWTO and WTTC data that tourism is the world's largest industry, or that it accounts for 10 per cent of the global job market!). However, as tourism matures as a subject, the theories underpinning it necessarily need to be more sophisticated; tourism cannot be simply 'read' as a business proposition with a series of impacts. Wider questions of power and identity need to be articulated, investigated and answered. The making and consuming of tourism takes place within a complex social milieu, with competing actors drawing into the 'product' peoples' history, culture and lifestyles. Culture and people thus become part of the tourism product. The implications are not fully understood, though the literature ranges the arguments along a continuum with culture, on the one hand, being described as vulnerable and fixed, waiting to be 'impacted' by tourism (from earlier, more naïve times, see Greenwood, 1978; Farrell, 1974; Turner & Ash, 1975 and more recently Boissevain, 1996; Wyllie, 2000), while on the other, it has been seen as vibrant and perfectly well capable of dealing with whatever changes globalisation and modernity are likely to throw at it (Wood, 1993; Franklin, 2004).

---

[4]As Lee (in his discussion on the postmodern symbolic meaning of commodities) asserts: 'Commodities were used [in the 1980s] to help construct a wide variety of identities, to confirm memberships of particular cultural communities and to signify invidious and often antagonistic social and cultural differences between groups. Endorsed by their advertising and marketing, commodities were used as objects to make visible personal affluence, to suggest sexual potency and physical attraction and, perhaps more than ever before, to function as the index of intelligence, education and social literacy' (Lee, 1993, p. xi).
The dualism here becomes more evident when Lee (in a later discussion on 'decay and rejuvenation') talks about the contradictions of capitalism, signifying that there is an interesting discourse awaiting to be developed on the paradox between what Lee (1993, p. 106) describes hedonism and obsolescence as a corollary of capitalism, a 'throwaway ethic in order to operationalise a greater acceleration of commodity and value turnovers that is ... the principle of mass consumption'. The beginnings of this debate (not to be explored here) are neatly captured by Jean Luc Godard, who described modern youth consumers as 'the children of Marx and Coca Cola' (cited in Lee, 1993).

Social identity has captured the imagination of mainstream sociologists for some decades, and they generally hold that individuals conceptualise self and Other at the level of both the individual and wider society. Given that (a) mobility is central to tourism and (b) social identity in the form of culture is an essential part of many tourism products, the present collection of essays will help problematise tourism by casting light on the relationships between how identity is configured in a variety of circumstances and how such configurations are framed by Orientalism, post-colonialism and commercialism. The consequences of these multiple configurations are significant ranging from outright hostility towards tourism to using it as a way to reinvent or at least reinvigorate declining cultural values and components — especially in a globalising world. Our position is that a social identity perspective on tourism helps provide a platform for a more nuanced understanding of nationalism, self versus Other, and tourism in a fragmenting yet paradoxically homogenising world.

Organisation of the Book

In order to guide the reader through some of the complexities discussed above and to fulfil to human desire for order, the book starts with a general context setting by Peter Burns on the cultural politics of tourism and is then divided into two parts: Global Frameworks and Local Realities each of which is discussed below.

Section 1: Global Frameworks: Theoretical and Comparative Perspectives

The six chapters comprising this section each tackle part of the larger picture of social identity. Linda Richter starts by drawing on her extensive oeuvre to discuss the political environment that makes the travel industry vulnerable, leading her to conclude that while there exists 'no single template for negotiating cultural issues', a plethora of practical examples and case studies provide the raw data for analysing what is happening in the tourism-identity arena. Jennie Germann-Molz provides some real insight into the thinking and therefore identity of 'round-the-world' travellers in her chapter on conflicting experiences about 'the size of the world'. She skilfully weaves several narratives together to provide an idea of how individuals in this niche see themselves. It is most instructive to learn that her work reinforces the view that 'tourists' are not a homogenous group, but have multiple identities: an idea that helps demolish simplistic typology models that for too long have dominated and diminished thinking about tourists and tourism. Her conclusions are many but a rather poignant phrase she uses strikes a chord and helps us to keep things in perspective: 'In a big world, a sense of belonging is derived from being made to feel small.' Gerard van Keken and Frank Go's essay on the 'role of culinary tourism and festival' also hones in on the ideas of contradictions. In their case it is, on the one hand, the speed compression and utility obsession to be found in metropolitan centres characterised by what Ritzer (1998) famously called 'The McDonaldization Thesis' resulting in 'speedy production and consumption ... resulting in a culture of homogenization [and] standardization' and on the other a 'static' position of peripheral regions (though no-one is claiming homogeneity here) which are 'struggling to maintain their unique identity'. They too, make the point about connectivity not geographic distance as being the key element in such discussions. Taking culinary events as their theme, they propose that emphasising the historic basis of regional food and local producers can play a part in resisting the homogenisation of identity and creates genuine opportunities for 'hosts' and 'guests' to interact while at the same time helping local economies and traditions. They make the point that 'culinary tourism is strongly connected with a region's identity' and that 'Festivals can be used to represent the host community's sense of itself.'

James Tunney picks up on the 'host community' in his discussion of the murky world of travel regulation commencing with a provocative piece on 'the knowledge challenge' between law and tourism going on to emphasise the cosmopolitan nature of the enterprise. In a sense, his chapter throws into confusion the nature of identity when he asserts that 'there is no real evidence of a single conception of the traveller or tourist in legal discourse' and with this in mind he draws on Kant to link hospitality, the position of strangers and host–guest relations in an industry increasingly affected by world trade regulations.

Johan van Rekom (with Frank Go) makes a powerful argument about the role of new developments in tourism and what they call an 'identity-enhancing' effect. Using case studies from Bali and Mexico they claim that the status of a region is uplifted in many ways after its 'discovery' for tourism. Addressing concerns of how local identities can 'survive' in an increasingly globalising world, they illustrate how one response to tourism could be the collective emancipation of local culture (a trend identified by Picard, 1995, a decade ago as a kind of resistance but never really developed by colleagues) in circumstances where dominant cultures pertain. This intriguing idea is strengthened by their thoughts on policy implications. Finally, Scott McCabe and Duncan Marson present us with certain theoretical aspects on the social construction of place and space in which they argue, based on Lefebvre (1991) that social space is continually being re-imagined and re-engineered. Their work is particularly important in understanding how tourists make sense of their experiences.

Section 2: Local Realities: Post-Industrial World and Transitional Economies

Part two of the book places some of the global concerns raised above into localised contexts. Donald Macleod starts this process off from two contrasting destinations linked by a colonial Spanish history, Bayahibe (Dominican Republic) and La Gomera (Canary Islands). His examination of how identities are changed by tourism, links modes of livelihoods, traditions and gender roles with local democracy on the one hand and enforced movement of populations on the other. Philip Xie takes inspiration from cultural geography to locate iconography in a tourism context. His idea is that culture markers (as seen through iconography) can help create a deeper understanding of the meaning of events and in turn, this knowledge can help with marketing. Using the Canadian–American festival held annually in Myrtle Beach, South Carolina, showed that tourists treated the event as an opportunity not only to learn something but also to spend a little money on souvenirs of a cultural nature. Increased cultural marker recognition and improved knowledge of Canadian tourist idiosyncratics have helped the US businesses regain some lost ground but further work needs to be done to bring the festival back to its former glory. For those of us familiar with the work of Freya Higgins-Desbiolles, it comes as no surprise that the chapter on tourism conflicts in Australian Aboriginal lands is iconoclastic: with characteristic style, she unfolds a fascinating narrative of local events in what she terms 'reconciliation tourism'. The complexities of utilising social identity, with, *inter alia*, its elements of kinship, relationships with the land, and a variety of formal and informal social institutions are explored ending with a challenge laid out for tourists and tourism entrepreneurs alike. Janne Liburd's chapter on national park development in St. Lucia makes a powerful case for the need to understand socio-cultural and identity perspectives, including cultural practices, in planning for tourism development in transitional economies. The chapter takes us through attempts at community and collaborative management, decentralization and the importance of NGOs in achieving socially responsible business goals. Patrícia Couto's report on her fieldwork in Brazil makes delightful reading for an anthropologist with her clear-cut mission to make sense of the social relationships in a town that is suffering the misfortunes of declining commodity process and paradoxical approaches to tourism. In particular, her distinctive classification of names given to tourists gives us great insight into local situations, and they tackle global forces largely outside of their control. The final chapter of this section is David Dunn's close examination of two 'reality' TV shows that purport to 'settle' tourists as castaways into new surroundings of a supposedly idyllic nature. With Greece and the Scottish island of Taransay in the frame (so to speak), Dunn proceeds to make connections between identity, mythology and (in effect) micro-colonisation of place and space: making the strange to be familiar. His chapter represents an interesting new angle on tourist studies.

Final Considerations

The chapters in this book clearly illustrate the complexities of tourism in the 21st century and the need for qualitative research to help us make sense of it. It is no good in repeating the mantra that 'tourism is the world's biggest industry' if no serious attempts are made to understand what it all means. In effect, you cannot have mobility, performance, co-presence of people at play and people at work, transnational connections, and the mobilization of culture as part of a commercial product without some pretty serious consequences. The present chapters highlight a number of serious issues related to how the presence of 'people on the move' influences identities at destinations through changed business practice, exposure to different values and ideas, and interaction with the world about them.

References

Anon (2001). Tourisme Sexuel dans la Caraïbe. *The New West Indian* no. 5 2001, http://www.awigp.com/default.asp?numcat=sextour

Armstrong, G. (2003). *Football hooligans: Knowing the score*. Oxford: Berg.

Bauman, Z. (2005). *Liquid life*. Cambridge: Polity Press.

Boissevain, J. (Ed.). (1996). *Coping with tourists: European reactions to mass tourism*. Oxford: Berghahn.

Bourdieu, P. (1984). *Distinction: a social critique of the judgment taste*. London: Routledge.

Burns, P., & Holden, A. (1995). *Tourism: A new perspective*. Hemel Hemstead: Prentice Hall.

Burns, P. (1999a). *An introduction to tourism and anthropology*. London: Routledge.

Burns, P. (1999b). Paradoxes in planning: Tourism elitism or brutalism?. *Annals of Tourism Research*, *26*(2), 329–349.

During, S. (Ed.) (1993). *The cultural studies reader*. London: Routledge.

Farrell, B. H. (1974). The tourist ghettos of Hawaii. In: M. Edgell, & B. Farrell (Eds), *Themes on pacific lands*. Western Geographical Series (Vol. 10, pp. 181–221). British Columbia: Department of Geography, University of Victoria.

Festinger, L. (1954). A theory of social comparison processes. *Human Relations*, *7*, 117–140.

Franklin, A. (2004). Tourism as an ordering: Towards a new ontology of tourism. *Tourist Studies*, *4*(3), 277–301

Giddens, A. (1991). *Modernity and self-identity. Self and society in the late modern age*. Cambridge: Polity.

Greenwood, D. (1978). Culture by the pound: An anthropological perspective on tourism as cultural commodisation. In: V. Smith (Ed.), *Host and guests: An anthropology of tourism* (pp. 86–107). Philadelphia: University of Pennsylvania Press.

Greenwood, D. (1989). Culture by the pound: An anthropological perspective on tourism as cultural commoditization. In: V. L. Smith (Ed.), *Hosts and guests. The anthropology of tourism* (2nd ed., pp. 171–185). Philadelphia, USA: University of Pennsylvania Press.

Huyssen, A. (1990). Mapping the postmodern. In: J. Alexander, & S. Seidman (Eds), *Culture and society contemporary debates* (pp. 355–375). Cambridge: Cambridge University Press.

Lee, M. J. (1992). *Consumer culture reborn: The cultural politics of consumption*. London: Routledge.

Lefebvre, H. (1991). *The production of space*. Oxford: Blackwell.

MacCannell, D. (1992). *Empty meeting grounds: The tourist papers*. London: Routledge.

Ogburn, W., & Nimkoff, M. (1964). *A handbook of sociology*. London: Routledge.

Picard, D. (1995). Cultural heritage and tourist capital: Cultural tourism, in Bali. In: M. -F. Lanfant, J. Wood, & E. Bruner (Eds), *International tourism: Identity and change* (pp. 44–66). London: Sage Studies in International Sociology.

Redfield, R. (1953). *The primitive world and its transformation*. Ithaca, NY: Cornell University Press.

Ritchie, J., & Zins, M. (1978). Culture as determinant of the attractiveness of a tourism region. *Annals of Tourism Research*, *5*(2), 252–267.

Ritzer, G. (1998). *The McDonaldization thesis*. London: Sage.

Said, E. (1978). *Orientalism*. New York: Vintage.

Sarup, M. (1996). *Identity, culture and the postmodern world*. Edinburgh: Edinburgh University Press.

Scruton, R. (2002). *The West and the Rest: Globalization and the terrorist threat*. Wilmington: ISI.

Shields, R. (1992). *Lifestyle shopping: The subject of consumption*. London: Routledge.

Sutton, P., & House, J. *The new age of tourism: Postmodern tourism for postmodern people?* http://www.arasite.org/pspage2.htm#_ftn1

Tajfel, H., & Turner, J. C. (1986). The social identity theory of inter-group behavior. In: S. Worchel, & L. W. Austin (Eds), *Psychology of intergroup relations* (pp. 7–24). Chicago: Nelson-Hall.

Turner, L., & Ash, J. (1975). *The golden hordes: International tourism and the pleasure periphery*. London: Routledge.

Wood, R. (1993). Tourism, culture, and the sociology of development. In: M. Hitchcock, V. T. King, & M. J. G. Parnwell (Eds), *Tourism in Southeast Asia* (pp. 48–70). London: Routledge.

Wyllie, R. (2000). *Tourism and society: A guide to problems and issues*. Pennsylvania: Ventura.

Chapter 1

Social Identities and the Cultural Politics of Tourism

Peter M. Burns

Introduction

The potent mix of politics, culture and questions of social identity raises important issues for tourism, which can be seen as a set of cultural, economic and political phenomena, with meanings and applications loaded with ambiguities and uncertainties (Franklin & Crang, 2001). Its rapid growth has subjected host communities to a bewildering array of changes, actor networks and, as Franklin (2004) would have it, a constant re-ordering of society.

It would be a caricature to imagine place and space being occupied only by passive consumers in the role of tourists and a congenial, compliant local population. Tourism is simply too important and valuable to be so dismissed. As a multi-layered, complex global phenomenon, tourism deserves a more nuanced analysis than what the familiar binary divisions ('left–right', 'good–bad', 'right–wrong', and indeed 'hosts–guests') can provide. Regarding the critical issues of tourism, it can reasonably be assumed that the industry is well aware of the environmental impacts and many companies are taking serious steps, in cooperation with international institutions such as the United Nations Environmental Program (UNEP) and United Nations World Tourism Organization (UNWTO), to address issues of physical sustainability: environmental awareness is clearly on the tourism business agenda. However, while a plethora of social scientists have spent decades dealing with social issues of tourism, there is very little evidence to suggest that cultural sustainability in the form of harmonious relationships between host communities, especially in poorer parts of the world, tourists, and the supplying tourism business sectors has gained the same level of importance as the physical environment, or indeed the same level of support as animal protection. Within this context, underpinned by the fact that globalization does not simply 'impact' upon ossified local cultures but interweaves them into the changing global situation, the following four themes emerge

Tourism and Social Identities: Global Frameworks and Local Realities
Copyright © 2006 by Elsevier Ltd.
All rights of reproduction in any form reserved.
ISBN: 0-08-045074-1

for framing the discussion on the critical issues of tourism and identity, which will help structure the present chapter:

- *Cultural politics*: where culture becomes political as increased competition among travel firms forces them to seek further for more undiscovered destinations, or to reinvent existing destinations (Hall, 1998) and their populations according to the latest market intelligence reports on consumer trends.
- *Social identities*: perceptions of race, nation and ethnicity can engender a simplistic view of Other (Said, 1978), creating a global problem of new forms of discrimination, racism and exclusion when juxtaposed with (a) the commercially constructed identities used in the travel industry, and (b) the social realities of local peoples at the destination.
- *Contested culture*: as the private and local, backstage space sought after by tourists in their search for the authentic is violated by their presence (Boissevain, 1996). Additionally, contested in the sense that local people may comprise groups or minorities who disagree with tourism or feel excluded from the identity on display (Richter, 2001).
- *Mediated culture*: culture becomes mediated as locals, academics, planners and managers seek solutions to some of these problems, especially in the context of transforming political economies and post-modern and post-colonial conditions cultures (Higgins-Desbiolles, 2003).

These four aspects (which will be explored further below), together with a final reflexive section to bring the threads together into some cohesive conclusions, form the chapter that commences with a brief contextualization of tourism and globalization.

The Context: A Globalization Continuum?

Mainstream discussions on globalization often miss out the idea of exclusion, not so much about who is 'in' the global village but who is irrelevant. The excluded comprises regions and nations that do not fit the profile of potential consumers or producers, such as large parts of Africa which, after the cold war implosion, no longer hold the attention of the superpowers (or the one remaining superpower) as their capacity for being objects in cold war surrogacy disappears along with the dismantling of political systems of opposition that characterized the global situation between the early 1950s and mid-1990s. On the other hand, the right-wing writers John Micklethwait and Adrian Wooldridge in defending their book on '*The Hidden Promise of Globalization*' in which they praise George W. Bush's grasp of globalization and dismiss concerns over Disneyfication, McWorld and Cocacolonization as being feared only 'wherever Chablis is drunk' said quite specifically that "Globalization does not involve the triumph of any particular culture at the expense of another" (Micklethwait & Wooldridge, 2000). It opens people's minds to an unprecedented range of ideas and influences. Also, it encourages cultural mixing on an unprecedented and thoroughly admirable scale". Monica Amor's (1998) essay on the kind of 'in-between' or 'liminal' worlds inhabited by the self- or socially excluded provides another position bringing together a number of conflicting perceptions on globalization "In the twenty years since Edward Said, in his landmark study *Orientalism*, framed debates about cultural identity and the construct of the Other, there have been extraordinary worldwide political, economic, and social realignments; massive migrations and displacements of peoples; and the development of a seemingly borderless electronic communications network. At the same time, there have been intense and often violent, reassertions of the particularities of cultural, ethnic, and religious identification." While Amor's discussion is about art, her references to 'cultural nomads' and cultural resistance in the face of homogeneity hold resonance for students of tourism.

These three sets of values veer, just like the variety of definitions of globalization, between triumphalism and cynicism. The two ends of this continuum on globalization are captured in the political commentator Thomas Friedman's phrase '*The Lexus and the Olive Tree*'. In his view on the politics of progress, half the world is 'dedicated to modernizing, streamlining and privatizing their economies in order to thrive' (Friedman, 2000, p. 31). The other half hug the olive tree as a dichotomous symbol of traditional values (and local, anchored identities) which effectively impede progress by reifying and idealizing an imagined past (where things were more connected and doors never locked) to the extent that progress is seen as a threat to social identity. Journalistic reflections such as Friedman's may not pass the 'scientific' test, but they provide helpful insight and capture the Zeitgeist that underpins the more theoretical perspectives such as are to be found in the early work of Roland Robertson (1992).

It is they who have access to the electronic superhighway and who communicate with each other across the globe surrounded by seas of poverty that are inhabited by those who do not communicate outside their own reference groups. Even with the electronic revolution, there are still parts of the globe that remain 'uninformed and lacking in 'adequate' and 'accurate' knowledge of the world at large and of societies other than their own (indeed of their own societies)' (Robertson, 1992, p. 184).

Cultural Politics: Framing the Narratives

Cultural politics happen at the intersection between culture and power, the space where civil society meets the body politic; culture, power and politics are not simply inseparable, but are elements of the same amorphous whole that form societies and identities. For complex societies, especially those with contested or multiple identities, cultural politics will also refer to the ways in which power relations and systems of production frame and maintain the various layers of culture.

The relationship between tourism and the cultural politics at a destination is a complex one. It involves the way in which appropriated local cultures are represented in brochures and other media (Dann, 1988, 1996). Oftentimes, it means creating a 'cutesy' non-threatening native backdrop to the leisure-holiday experience: a constructed identity within the global culture of international tourism (Franklin, 2003). In accepting this premise, we also have to accept the dichotomous and yet synchronous processes of localization and globalization as being inseparable (Turner, 1994).

This approach suggests that it is possible to examine tourism not as a true 'object' that science progressively uncovers, but as an historically produced discourse (Torgovnick, 1990) present as the global meshes with and locks into the local, the local–global nexus as

Burns (2001), among others, has termed it. Cultural politics are then affected by both internal and external factors. In other words, culture would change anyway. In this context, Wood (1993) is right in asserting that there is no such thing as a 'pristine culture' waiting to be smashed. Aspects of culture (including material culture in the form of souvenirs) are brought into the tourism system through spatial, temporal and above all, political arrangements. For this reason a clear understanding of the cultural politics of tourism is essential in discussing tourism, globalization and identity.

However, the narratives arising out of the tourism, culture and politics nexus present something of a conundrum. Each of the positions, in their own way, starts from the somewhat simplistic premise that culture is somehow tangible. But, where a plural society collides with tourism even the 'ownership' of culture might be in dispute. An alternative reading might question, in the way that Wood (1993) seems to, the absoluteness of 'Other' cultures. It might be that globalization has created such ambivalent, yet powerful modes of production (especially in the case of tourism) that the idea of an independent culture existing outside the framework of globalizing cultural politics becomes a contradiction. When travel firms use the notion of 'unique culture' in their advertising media for exotic destinations, they are promoting a constructed culture that exists for the brochure, which is linked to the international tour company that in turn is linked to global networks of workers (Sassen, 1998), suppliers and tourists. The local people may cooperate in this enterprise because it might be in their best economic interests to do so (Enloe, 1989). The point also needs to be made that anthropology and mass tourism, just like mechanical image-making and photography, share a common spatial and temporal background from the late nineteenth-century technology and colonialism to the present time. During this period anthropologists and tourists alike discovered the 'pristine' cultures ironically noted by Wood (1993) and, in a sense, turned them into MacCannell's (1992) 'ex-primitives'.

This section has discussed the multiplicity of linkages and interconnections among states, societies and economic enterprises that make up the post-modern and post-colonial world (Narotzky, 1997). The process by which events, decisions and activities in one part of the world can come to have significant consequences for individuals and communities in quite distant parts of the globe (Gardner & Lewis, 1996), especially where their identities have been framed and put up for show by tourist companies following a commercial activity. The following section takes these arguments to their next logical step by framing them more clearly against the notion of social identity.

Social Identities: Moments of Tourism

As Marie-Françoise Lanfant asserted so eloquently in the introduction to the edited book on tourism and identity, the idea of building a social identity in a post-modern world of instant communication and travel without 'abutting it against the identity of others' (Lanfant, Allcock, & Bruner, 1995, p. 7) is an impossibility. Issues of representation and commoditization create fundamental problems for tourism. Representation (in a metaphoric sense) without consultation is a phrase normally associated with politics, but for tourism there are an unimaginable number of cases where representation (in the literal, visual sense) of Other, for example, in tribal dress, in markets, as servants, as harmless, decorative background material to visual travelogues or advertisements for travel (Dann, 1988) can take place as a sort of cultural appropriation without reciprocal benefit or under-standing (Crick, 1996; Franklin, 2003). The argument here is that while more developed nations have cultural stereotypes (such as the various countries of Europe, Northern vs. Southern states in the US, etc.) that are constructed through jokes or history or simply fiction, these are not the only ways in which such advanced places are known. Lesser developed countries have neither the political nor economic clout that allows them to nego-tiate beyond the exploitation of culture as a tourism resource. Neocolonial analysts (Bianchi, 2002) would point towards the power of language (Pidginization or Creolization) while anti-globalists cite the dominance of global brands and 'celebrity culture'.

The role of commoditization and social identity in tourism has been extensively dis-cussed (Franklin, 2003; Greenwood, 1989) and many commentators agree that cultural reproduction at a local level for global markets emphasizes shallow and fleeting 'moments of tourism', where exchange is based on money for vulgarized culture. However, as with most things touristic, the solution (or even the description of the problem) is not so sim-ple. Such negative interpretations have to be balanced against the possibility for the nexus of culture and tourism as a form of identity boosterism that can play a pivotal role in lead-ing people to rediscover or reinforce their identity through traditional dance, crafts and arts (Stanton, 1989; Bricker 2001). For example, since the collapse of the Soviet Union, where unique, ethnic, tribal or national identities were subsumed into the notion that all citizens were 'Soviets', traditional forms of dress, dancing and other folkloric customs have com-bined with tourism to boost (along with a resurgence in national languages) pride in the newly emerging independence and freedom (Burns, 1998).

Meaghan Morris captures the dichotomous essence of these arguments very well: "Wherever tourism is an economic strategy as well as a money-making activity, and wher-ever it is a policy of state, a process of social and *cultural* change is initiated which involves transforming not only the 'physical' (in other words the *lived*) environment of 'toured' com-munities and the intimate practice of everyday life, but also the series of relations by which cultural identity (and therefore difference) is constituted for both the tourist and the toured in any given context" (Morris, 1995, pp. 180–181, italics and parentheses in original). However, the other side to the cultural coin is that identity is being changed 'at home' for tourists from the post-industrialized world (Lanfant et al., 1995) as work becomes displaced from the centre stage of modern social structures (economy, technology, occupational sys-tems) with egocentricity in the form of increased concern for self-actualization and a gen-eralized diffusion of the leisured class coming to dominate the socio-cultural milieu (Selwyn, 1996a). These moments of tourism (epitomized in Europe by the hastily snatched city break from the likes of Lastminute.com or Travelocity.com) do serve MacCannell's (contested) thesis on the tourist that "somewhere, ... in another country, in another lifestyle, in another social class, perhaps, there is a genuine society" (MacCannell, 1976, p. 155).

Having discussed the roles played out in tourism that help construct some aspects of social identities, it can be seen that the commercial nature of these constructions means that while cultural encounters might be synchronous, tourism in its globalized form also comprises a series of encounters that are (in effect) 'moments of tourism' and reflect frag-menting societies that somehow lack a unifying ethic framed by the type of contested cul-ture described in the next section.

Contested Cultures: Collision, Collusion and the Fusing of Histories

If it is argued that culture (and nostalgia) can be appropriated as a resource by the tourism sector, tourism needs to be understood in terms of contested cultures, created by (a) the collision of local realities and globally driven commercialism, and (b) the collusion between state and the tourism sector to construct social identities and to fuse (and perhaps, muddle) histories. For a prime example of this we need look no further than Jerusalem where culture has been contested by three major religions (Christian, Jewish and Islam) that have engaged in violent resistance and contestation for the past millennia. This example is not so extreme as might at first be thought. In modern times, each of the faiths has blurred the distinction between religious pilgrim and secular tourist to create a tourist infrastructure that, in effect, seeks to legitimate their respective moral authority over the Holy city. Tourists become pawns in a cultural–political chess game (Aziz, 1995; Wahab, 1996).

The idea of contested culture as a type of discourse has its roots in Marxist and post-colonial studies which acknowledge that societies are unequally divided along class, gender and generational lines and that the struggle to resist or resolve these issues is bound by varying interpretations of culture and lingering colonial power relationships (the colonization might be metaphorical rather than literal). Resistance in all forms ranging from passive to violent exists because the people of the destinations are drawn into the confluences of multiple relations: between governmental institutions and civil society; tour operators, tourists and local populations; and more directly between visitors and visited. This milieu provides the backdrop against which the relations become discursive and fragmented causing local relationships with the global to reconfigure. These reconfigurations will affect both modes of production and representation.

At least two central questions arising from the constantly reconfiguration of tourism, culture, resistance and globalization remain unanswered: "How do minority groups 'read' tourism?" and "What cultural identities are included and excluded from particular constructions of tourism?" The answers are unlikely to be found in the formulaic responses to tourism by governments and market-makers or reductionist approaches to tourism's analysis such as to be found in Graburn's simplistic (and somewhat elitist) assertions that 'secular ritual' provides a general theory for all forms of tourism (Graburn, 2001, p. 42). Such interpretations of tourism are one-sided and do not allow for its complexities. For example, culture in tourism can be contested, such as when a national government uses assumed postures on racial harmony or multiculturalism or simply by excluding reference to certain groups to promote a constructed worldview. For example, before the political turmoil of the 1988 military coups in Fiji, ethnic Indians (making up some 47% of the population) were virtually excluded from brochures that featured smiling native Fijians. Morris refers to this as 'manufacturing traditions for tourism' (Morris, 1995, p. 181) and goes on to describe how the Singapore tourist authority regularly emphasizes the country's "diverse ethnic traditions [...] in ways that change how actual cultures of ethnicity are henceforth to be lived. Toured communities are increasingly required by the state to live out their (manufactured) ethnicity for the gaze of the others" (italics in original). Morris also reminds us that "it is misleading to assume that the toured [hosts at a destination] may be treated as victims of a process beyond their control" (Morris, 1995, p. 181). From the foregoing, it can be seen that the discussion about culture, globalisation and tourism is important because of what the 'collision, collusion and fusing of histories' that tourism development eventually produces (taking account of the structures that arise from planning: entrepreneurial, social, governmental): a confusing situation in which, as Selwyn (1996a, p. 30) puts it, there is a need to:

> Distinguish between the myths and fantasies of tourists (authentic in some senses as these may be), on the one hand, and politico-economic and socio-cultural processes, on the other, there may in the end, as Baudrillard (1988) has warned, be no way out of the eventual wholesale Disneyfication of one part of the world built on the wasteland of the other

And yet, these nihilistic views towards culture take no account of either the enjoyment taken from tourism or the dynamism added to local cultures as they interact on a bigger stage.

What remains within the contested cultural borders of social identities, which are central to the notion of the cultural politics of tourism, is the question of how local identity is compromised in the face of tourism promotion (whether from inside or outside of national boundaries); a question that leaves us with a major paradox: the assumption that minority (or poor) cultural groups are vulnerable, a generalization that does not always stand up to close examination.

Mediated Culture: The Local–Global Nexus?

Dean MacCannell has argued that the 'empty meeting grounds' of tourism (MacCannell, 1992) have not only supplied new conditions for the appropriation and conversion of tangible objects and intangible elements of culture into commodities, but also that tourism is a post-modern, organic system that provides no alternative to itself, almost a synonym for Fukuyama's 'End of History' (1992) as cultures come together forming a bland, homogenized whole. But in a sense, this does not account for the ways in which culture is mediated in various ways and by diverse agencies including the individual. The resulting mediated culture and meanings inform, but are constantly morphing and reconfiguring. Thus, far from the claims of the end of culture that can be inferred from the writings of Greenwood (1989), MacCannell (1992), and Selwyn (1996b), Wood's (1993) analysis of culture and tourism, which relies on identifying and understanding systems, argues that "The central questions to be asked are about process, and about the complex ways tourism enters and becomes part of an already on-going process of symbolic meaning and appropriation" (Wood, 1993, p. 66).

Such systems and processes will include not only a supply-side point of view framed by the notion of culture-as-attraction but also less-than-passive responses to mediating culture on the part of local peoples and industries. Culture is mediated from both sides of the equation assigning multiple meanings. In the hybrid culture of tourism (that is to say at the local–global nexus) the aim should be for institutions, civil society and (for the purpose of the present chapter) the tourism industry to weave a social fabric that allows culture to be mediated for commercial purposes (thus creating economic opportunities) while at the same time reinforcing mutual respect and mutually beneficial relationships. In recognizing that relationships and social identities across the globe are being changed and hybridized at a rapid pace, Peggy Teo (2002, p. 460) has suggested that tourism research "has neglected to incorporate the discourse surrounding globalization" going on to remark that "Too often, research on sustainable tourism points to a managerial approach" (p. 471).

Having presented the last of the four themes that helped frame the discussion on culture, tourism and globalization, the next section summarizes the key points and raises some critical issues.

Critical Issues: Substantive Implications

The present chapter has attempted to strike a balance between the anti-change perspective and the 'unfettered markets as the viewpoint of salvation'. From the four preceding themes, we can make the following summary (Table 1.1).

The critical issues arising then can all be found in the overarching problem: the approach to research on this topic. There still remains a rift between academics (in the field of social sciences) who still tend to view tourism with suspicion and the industry (and academics in marketing, management and economics) who see tourism either simply as business or as panacea. Both sides, from time to timeare wrong on local cultures, either from a patronizing 'stop the world' perspective or from a simplistic 'markets rule' point of view that fails to allow for the complexities and the need to develop beneficial relationships to underpin social responsible attitudes towards commerce.

Any analysis of tourism must take account the structures that frame the relationships between nation-states and global markets. Susan Strange (1988), in the context of her work on the International Political Economy (IPE), identified these structures as: Security; Production; Finance; and Knowledge. In all of this, the key question is, as Strange asks, *cui bono*? (Who benefits?). Balaam and Veseth (1996) describe why this seemingly simple question is fundamental:

> Asking this question forces us to go beyond description to analysis. To identify not only the structure and how it works, but its relationship to other structures and their role in the international political economy [an understanding which] therefore becomes a matter of holding in your mind a set of complex relationships and considering their collective implications. (p. 101)

The idea of 'collective implications' is one that holds great resonance for tourism and is one to be borne in mind when considering the cultural politics of tourism taking into account tourism's role in development and in fostering the rights and aspirations of the local communities. Tourism has a role in the legitimization and affirmation of cultures through principles of beneficial relationships, autonomy, and self-determination. Tourism strategies can positively contribute to civic pride and positive social identities by helping develop decision-making capacity, creativity, solidarity, pride in their traditions, and rightful attachment to their place, space and identity.

Table 1.1: Critical issues: some substantive implications.

Cultural politics	• Representation of local cultures in a political act • Loccalization and globalization are inseparable • The cultural narratives of destinations are ambivalent and cannot exist without reference to tourism • Multiple relationships mean multiple narratives Inevitably some will be stronger than others
Social identities	• Social identity is a global 'project' that has some parallel to appropriation of Other • Difference is synchronously emphasized (as toured Other) and homogenized (as local culture is drawn into networks of global social behaviors and consumption patters) • Tourism can be expressed as a series of superficial encounters resulting from a desire on the tourists' side for self-actualization and for economic opportunity on the receiving side
Contested cultures	• There is a collision between local realities (expressed through social and economic ambitions) and globally driven capitalism • The collusion between the state and the tourism sector can construct social identities that exclude minorities considered inappropriate to the image of tourism at particular destinations • Histories of sending and receiving populations become inter-twined, fused and muddled
Mediated culture	• The mediation of culture need not necessarily lead to homog-enization (the 'end of history' approach) but rather hybridiza-tion (whereby cultures learn and adapt from each other) • Tourism can be read as a historically produced discourse • The challenge of mediating culture for tourism in a global context, lies in finding appropriate responses to the shift away from state capitalist structures (as found in many developing countries) to the more ambivalent, borderless culture of corporate capitalism

Conclusions: Tourism and the Local–Global Nexus

This chapter has focused on social identities and representation at the local–global nexus and generally concludes that tourism and its alternatives must articulate a vision of both the present and a possible future based on inclusive ('collective' being a little far-fetched) aspirations. If tourism is to have a positive affect on culture it must go well beyond the creation of infrastructure and the improvement of material conditions to strengthen local cultures and languages.

This chapter has argued for a view of tourism as a complex construction constituting a powerful interface between cultures and societies that is organized within a global framework, but which takes place very much at a local level. The fragmented and ephemeral nature of tourism, together with the definitional paradoxes has meant that its growing presence has not generated the same level of social movements in parts of the world where other forms of capitalism (such as GM crops, footwear and clothing manufacturing) have been heavily criticized, even in the form of public demonstrations some of which are organized at a global level. In a sense, this could have more to do with the fragmented nature of the industry at the local level and that vast parts of the operational aspects and indeed staff fall under the tourist gaze, thus creating a level of self-regulation regarding working conditions. Despite their precariousness, the confluences between cultural politics, social identities, contested culture and mediated culture constitute an alternative analytical framework for discussions on the future sustainability of tourism in the broadest context. This framework shows that social life, work, business, nature and culture can be organized differently than the dominant economic models that prevail in many of the tourism debates.

The approach to tourism analysis from the perspective of the cultural construction of the locality can be seen in terms of the defence of local modes of production and tradition as articulated by many social scientists. From the perspective of government institutions, there is room and the need for creative thinking and policy-making alternatives that create frameworks for beneficial interaction with the 'rest of the world'. From the tourism industry perspective, it is time for them to take on the challenge of working with a far greater range of social actors at the destinations they do business with, from social movements to progressive academics and international/local NGOs.

While the gap between academy and industry remains, the spaces of encounter and debate are increasing and as also the ways for academics, business-people, NGOs, local people and their representatives in government to reflect on, and support alternative frameworks for tourism development that are emerging rather than waiting for a universal theoretical solution to the problems arising from the cultural politics of tourism that clearly acknowledge the need to stop thinking about cultures as though they were stuck in time and space.

Acknowledgments

This chapter is reprinted from W. F. Theobald (Ed.) (2005) *Global Tourism* (3rd ed., pp. 391–405), with permission from Elsevier. Thanks are due to Dr Cathy Palmer who encouraged me to write these thoughts out and for her constructive comments on an earlier draft.

References

Amor, M. (1998). Liminalities: Discussions on the global and the local *Art Journal, 57*(4), 28–49.
Aziz, H. (1995). Understanding attacks on tourists in Egypt. *Tourism Management, 16*(2), 91–95.
Balaam, D., & Veseth, M. (1996). *Introduction to the international political economy.* Englewood Cliffs, NJ: Prentice-Hall.

Baudrillard, J. (1988). *Selected writings*. Cambridge: Polity.

Bianchi, R. (2002). Sun, sea and sand: And a sense of spectral danger. *Times Higher Educational Supplement,* July 26, p. 16.

Boissevain, J. (1996). Problems with cultural tourism in Malta. In: C. Fsadni, & T. Selwyn (Eds), *Sustainable tourism in Mediterranean islands and small cities* (pp. 19–35). Valletta: MEDCAM-PUS-EuroMed.

Bricker, K. (2001). Ecotourism development in the rural highlands of Fiji. In: D. Harrison (Ed.), *Tourism and the less developed world: Issues and cases* (pp. 235–250). Walingford: CABI.

Burns, P. (1998). Tourism in Russia: Background and structure. *Tourism Management, 19*(6), 555–565.

Burns, P. (2001). Brief encounters: Culture, tourism and the local–global nexus. In: S. Wahab, & C. Cooper, *Tourism in the age of globalisation* (pp. 290–305). London: Routledge.

Crick, M. (1996). Representations of international tourism in the social sciences: Sun, sex, sights, savings, and servility. In: Y. Apostolopoulos, S. Leivadi, & A. Yiannakis (Eds), *The sociology of tourism: Theoretical and empirical investigations* (pp. 15–50). London: Routledge.

Dann, G. (1996). The people of tourist brochures. In: T. Selwyn (Ed.), *The tourist image, myths and myth making in tourism* (pp. 61–82). Chichester: Wiley.

Dann, G. M. S. (1988). Images of Cyprus projected by tour operators. *Problems of Tourism, 3*(41), 43–70.

Enloe, C. H. (1989). *Bananas, beaches & bases: Making feminist sense of international politics*. London: Pandora.

Franklin, A. (2003). *Tourism: An introduction*. London: Sage.

Franklin, A. (2004). Tourism as an ordering: Towards a new ontology of tourism. *Tourist Studies, 4*(3), 277–301.

Franklin, A., & Crang, M. (2001). The trouble with tourism and travel theory? *Tourist Studies, 1*(1), 5–22.

Friedman, T. (2000). *The lexus and the olive tree*. London: Harper-Collins.

Fukuyama, F. (1992). *The end of history: And the last man*. London: Penguin.

Gardner, K., & Lewis, D. (1996). *Anthropology, development and the post-modern challenge*. London: Pluto.

Graburn, N. (2001). Secular ritual: A general theory of tourism. In: V. Smith, & M. Bryant (Eds), *Hosts and guests revisited: Tourism issues of the 21st century* (pp. 42–50). New York: Cognizant.

Greenwood, D. (1989). Culture by the pound: An anthropological perspective on tourism as cultural commoditization. In: V. Smith (2nd Ed.), Hosts and guests: The anthropology of tourism (pp. 171–185). Philadelphia: Pennsylvania University Press.

Hall, M. (1998). Making the pacific: Globalization, modernity and myth. In: G. Ringer (Ed.), *Destinations: Cultural landscapes of tourism* (pp. 140–153). London: Routledge.

Higgins-Desbiolles, F. (2003). Engagement and resistance through indigenous tourism. Conference paper: *Tourism Identities.* University of Brighton, 10–11 September 2003.

Lanfant, M.-F., Allcock, J., & Bruner, E. (Eds). (1995). *International tourism: Identity and change*. London: Sage.

MacCannell, D. (1976). *The tourist: A new theory of the leisure class*. New York: Shocken Books.

MacCannell, D. (1992). *Empty meeting ground: The tourist papers*. London: Routledge.

Micklethwait, J., & Wooldridge, A. (2000). *A future perfect: The challenge and hidden promise of globalization*. New York: Times Books.

Morris, M. (1995). Life as a tourist object in Australia. In: M.-F. Lanfant, J. Allcock, & E. Bruner (Eds), *International tourism: Identity and change* (pp. 177–191). London: Sage.

Narotzky, S. (1997). *New directions in economic anthropology*. London: Pluto.

Richter, L. (2001). Where Asia wore a smile: Lessons of Philippine tourism development. In: V. Smith, & M. Brent (Eds), *Hosts and guests revisited: Tourism issues in the 21st century* (pp. 283–297). New York: Cognizant.

Robertson, R. (1992). *Globalization: Social theory and global culture*. London: Sage.

Said, E. (1978). *Orientalism: Western concepts of the orient*. London: Routledge and Kegan Paul.

Sassen, S. (1998). *Globalization and its discontents: Essays on the new mobility of people and money*. New York: The New Press.

Selwyn, T. (Ed.). (1996a). *The tourist image: Myths and myth making in tourism*. London: Wiley.

Selwyn, T. (1996b). Tourism, culture and cultural conflict. In: C. Fsadni, & T. Selwyn (Eds), *Sustainable tourism in Mediterranean islands and small cities*. Valletta: Med-Campus.

Stanton, M. (1989). The Polynesian cultural center: A multi-ethnic model of seven pacific cultures. In: V. Smith (Ed.), *Hosts and guests: The anthropology of tourism* (pp. 247–264). Philadelphia, PA: University of Pennsylvania Press.

Strange, S. (1988). *States and markets: An introduction to international political economy*. New York: Basil Blackwell.

Teo, P. (2002). Striking a Balance for sustainable tourism: Implications of the discourse on globalization. *Journal of Sustainable Tourism, 10*(6), 459–474.

Torgovnick, M. (1990). *Gone primitive: Savage intellects, modern lives*. Chicago: University of Chicago Press.

Turner, B. (1994). *Orientalism, postmodernism and globalism*. London: Routledge.

Wahab, S. (1996). Tourism and terrorism: Synthesis of the problem with emphasis on Egypt. In: A. Pizzam, & Y. Mansfeld (Eds), *Tourism, crime and international security* (pp. 175–186). London: Wiley.

Wood, R. (1993). Tourism, culture and the sociology of development. In: M. Hitchcock, V. King, & M. Parnwell (Eds), *Tourism in South East Asia* (pp. 48–70). London: Routledge.

SECTION I:

GLOBAL FRAMEWORKS: THEORETICAL AND COMPARATIVE PERSPECTIVES

Chapter 2

The Politics of Negotiating Culture in Tourism Development

Linda K. Richter

Introduction

Negotiating culture of residents, the objectives of the tourism industry and coordinating compatible development with a variety of other stakeholders is never easy. The current political climate heightens the risks and the stakes for all involved.

The tourism industry has taken the brunt of the pain from the current US foreign policy and the justifiable concerns about global terrorism. But participants in this book are not apologists or uncritical defenders of this important industry. In fact, the decline of international tourism may afford an opportunity to rethink how tourism should regroup, how it can become more resilient, how it can encourage more consideration of various stakeholder groups, and how culture can be used to sustain diversity rather than mask minority viewpoints.

One must not forget that even without the current global struggles, terrorism has been used in destinations as diverse as Hawaii, the Philippines, Fiji, Australia, Jamaica, Egypt, Bali, and Peru over the last 30 years as a weapon against a tourist industry seen as intrusive, culturally insensitive, or in some cases just a tool of a dominant unresponsive government (Richter, 1989; Richter & Waugh, 1991). So, the problems are not new and the struggle to deal with them is not either.

What may be new is that the industry itself, minority cultural groups, and non-governmental organizations (NGOs) may be encouraging, indeed demanding a rethinking of social and political issues that were once simply pushed aside (Richter, 2001). The vulnerability and fragility of tourism are now exposed on a global scale. The ease of sabotage that was highlighted by a few well-placed bombs at a Philippine conference in 1980 and the recent attacks in Egypt and Bali are but a few of the incidents targeting tourists. They illustrate how even the most adept spinmasters cannot sustain tourists unless local people want them (Richter, 1982).

That still leaves the daunting question of how culture gets negotiated? One doesn't start with good faith efforts on all sides. There is a tremendous amount of cultural baggage, to use a tourism metaphor, that is involved. Some groups nearly exterminated like Hawaiians, Native Americans, or Australian aboriginal groups cannot simply be invited to the party or the bargaining table (Altman, 1989).

Even if the dominant groups planning tourism have a political change of heart toward inclusiveness or a renewed sense of vulnerability, those hurt by trading with the "enemy" are not likely to come suddenly ready to deal. Christopher Pforr, a PhD student at the Northern Territories University in Darwin, did an interesting thesis in 2003 on efforts to involve aboriginal and other stakeholders in the development of a strategic plan for the region. No longer was the government going to ride roughshod over the locals. This time it would send invitations to meetings.

As one might suspect the response rate among the aboriginal groups was very low, the meetings rather few, yet the dominant groups were satisfied that at least they had tried and that perhaps the non-attendees did not care (Pforr, 2003). Time, trial and error, plans susceptible to adaptation, and a care to anticipate possible problems are going to be absolutely critical.

Pforr's study reminded this writer of the time when, as the education representative to the now defunct US Travel and Tourism Advisory Board (USTTA), two issues of cultural planning were discussed. The first had to do with who got to come as a tourist to the US. International tourists were sought particularly since 97% of US tourism is domestic and international visitors spend more than Americans. The US lagged Spain, France, and many other destinations in international visitors, but the US government persisted in culturally demeaning assumptions about non-European tourists except for the Japanese. That was the early 1990s. Customs, the Immigration and Naturalization Service, Airline CEOs, destination chiefs like the head of Disney World, struggled to think of ways to boost international arrivals.

At that time there were some 15 million Japanese tourists traveling abroad annually. When this member suggested travel barriers should be made less prohibitive to Indians and other Asians, especially those wanting to visit children studying in the US — that was a non-starter. "They wouldn't go home; they lacked money to travel" were the arguments.

US government statistics showed that there were approximately 100 million Indians out of over 1 billion who had the discretionary economic power to travel internationally, yet the USTTA was chasing the 15 million Japanese! Government stereotypes prevented the US from welcoming more tourists.

The second cultural issue came as plans were developed about how to celebrate the 500th anniversary of Columbus discovering America. One festive idea followed another. Then this author asked, what events in our museums, historical reenactments should deal with those who were already here when Columbus arrived? What do you do about those for whom Columbus' arrival was a cause for remembering the end of one era and the genocide of another — not just in the US but, throughout several North American nations. No one wanted to think about it.

The Gulf War soon turned attention to reviving a suddenly crippled industry rather than a celebration of Columbus' arrival in the New World. But Australia faced a similar challenge in celebrating the anniversary of the arrival of the first batch of British prisoners to Australia. Aboriginal protests were not squashed as savagely as at the centennial but it was still hard for policymakers to appreciate that not everyone in the country sees the nation's history and culture the same way.

Contrast this effort to ignore or gloss over minority cultural perceptions with the deliberate efforts to showcase Robben Island where Nelson Mandela was imprisoned or the places in Africa from which many slave ships departed. Those became tourism attractions based on what A.V. Seaton would call "dark tourism" (Seaton, 1996).

Similarly, the Nazi death camps have become macabre but important tourist sites. The educational value of the experience hopefully transcends those of the mere thrill seeker. More difficult has been the experience of the people in neighboring towns. They benefit from the very tourism that has made their residents pariahs in the eyes of the world. In recent years, towns like Dachau have tried to develop other attractions that might both lengthen the stay of tourists and also alter their tourist perceptions of the residents (Hartmann, 1989).

Unfortunately, there is no template for the stakeholders to put over a cultural issue that allows them to do a certain number of culturally sensitive things, hold a recommended number of meetings and expand tourism at some ideal pace per 1000 residents impacted.

Also unfortunately, riding roughshod over the groups perceived in the way of tourism development has sometimes worked — at least for the short run. Yet, surly survivors may make poor employees or eager saboteurs. So if sensitive and insensitive approaches are not necessarily surefire, what can be done? This chapter suggests policymakers need a repertoire of approaches and responses, including backing off. In other instances, the local people may be enthusiastic about tourism but if it includes pedophilia tours or the hunting of endangered species, then it is important for regional and national policymakers to draw the line for the protection of the larger public interest.

In this chapter, five general approaches will be discussed. This certainly does not exhaust the possibilities, but it is intended to encourage brainstorming about tourism and culture. Moreover, some approaches may be more appropriate for some types of cultural disputes than others. Much ultimately depends on the willingness of policymakers to recognize the need for what has too often been derided as the "politically correct" response. The methodology used throughout has been charitably described as "grounded theory". It essentially involves exploratory open-ended interviews, personal observations, secondary research and over three decades of field research, primarily in South and Southeast Asia on the politics of tourism.

Kansas: Eclectic Inclusiveness

This writer is going to start with her own state. Kansas is larger in land than most European countries but with fewer than four million people. Kansas is not considered a tourist destination by most people but, it too, has had to balance its heritage as a battleground over slavery and segregation with the more positive cultural legacies that might lure domestic and international travelers. Currently, Kansas is broadening its cultural mix and rural lifestyle by developing farm tourism, bird watching trips, and festivals that feature all-Kansas crafts. The festivals were themselves the outgrowth of centennial celebrations that turned out to be so successful that communities decided to continue them and build on their cultural and historic legacies.

In 1954, Kansas became famous when the Supreme Court ordered the desegregation of schools using a Kansas case. Kansas reluctantly dealt with its invisible black minority.

Nicodemus, a totally black town in Western Kansas began to revive the culture that had been built around exclusion. The classic court case, *Brown v. the Board of Education of Topeka, Kansas* is now memorialized in a national monument. Other monuments to black courage and valor have also been erected recently and the story of "Bleeding Kansas" and the battle over slavery are now detailed in brochures and landmarks. Most of these historical markers are less than 15 years old. A certain distance from unsavory situations seems to be a prerequisite for recognizing their importance (Richter, 1999; Horne, 1984).

Other less controversial steps at local cultural identity were the state's many small towns that were pockets of particular European ancestry. Lindsborg, for example is a Swedish town that through architecture, restaurants, crafts and art turned a biennial festival into an 11-month tourist season on their terms. Wilson, a Czech town and several Mennonite towns have also built annual festivals around the dominant culture. In each case, there was little to negotiate culturally, because of the homogeneity of the towns. But lifestyle was an issue. As in New Zealand, small towns have struggled with issues of Sunday closings and the desire to accommodate tourism. How far does one go in preserving one's lifestyle?

Tourism is in many cases a major alternative to the rural decline found elsewhere in the state. Indian remains and mounds dot the Kansas landscape. Many little museums were set up in people's backyards to exhibit these remains and artifacts. That ended in the last 20 years after persistent objections by the Indians and the support of anthropologists. Skeletons were reburied. In one instance, a former Pawnee Indian village had one mound excavated and used for educational purposes under government control, but the other mounds were left undisturbed.

Yet, Native American culture has been slow to develop as a tourist attraction. There are four tribes in the state but except for some reservation gambling in the last 15 years, they are largely invisible. Internationally, the state is known for being part of the Wild West. Dodge City, the cowtowns of Abilene and Wichita put the emphasis on gun battles and cow drives, with occasional Indian battles. Kansas is a land of many military forts and is criss-crossed with famous trails going West. Thus, the heritage featured until the last 25 years has been that of the white pioneer on the prairie or heading West.

It has been easier to add tourist attractions that represent a multi-cultural heritage than to sensitively address long-standing traditions. Sports seems to be the last bastion of culturally insensitive labels. In Kansas, as across the nation, many sports teams are labeled the Redskins, the Indians, the Chiefs. Tomahawk cheers and mock war dances still rankle with many Native Americans. No new schools are adopting such labels, but in the name of tradition many fight to keep these labels.

Macho labels also betray the fact that there are significant gender differences in access and prestige for participants in sports events. In Kansas, for example, the basketball teams at Kansas State University used to be called the Wildcats and the Wildkittens! Now the men's team has stayed the same, but the kittens have become the Lady Cats.

Women have been historically banned from many Olympic events and only included in major marathons after 1969. This situation is ironic because the slowness of the culture to accommodate female sports has occurred despite the fact that a more tolerant attitude would enhance the audience for these tourist-related events (Nelson, 1994; Richter, 1994).

In general, Kansas has had a relatively unhurried but rather diverse experience with cultural tourism. Coming late to tourism development, Kansas has had the space and time to experiment with many types of cultural tourism.

Native American Tourism: From Paternalism to Cultural Autonomy

A second approach to reconciling culture and tourism illustrates how a legacy of oppression and violence has begun to be recast for tourism. In the last two decades Native Americans have begun to control tourism in ways unheard of 40 years ago. They were always an attraction, the exotic "other" — to be featured in Wild West Shows. The women were usually confined to weaving and swaddling babies. Ironically, a few white women were allowed to star in such shows as freak sharpshooters. One, in fact, Annie Oakley, was even praised by Queen Victoria when the show she was in toured England (Savage, 1996). The sorry history of the treatment of Native Americans continues to fester in their living conditions and poor health, but some tribes have seen their plight immortalized in monuments and museums. The "Trail of Tears" museum demonstrates how the more unsavory history of white domination of Native Americans has been documented and unsparingly put forward for all to see and remember. Yet, other models of tourism and native culture demonstrate how the tribes themselves are asserting their own self-determination over tourism.

The reservation system and the de-culturization of the Indian mission boarding schools are now a part of the interpretation of Indian sites. The US Smithsonian Museum of the American Indian opened in 2004 — a rather belated acknowledgment of pre-white culture in North America.

The Bureau of Indian Affairs, which had operated a tight rein on the Indian tribes, has loosened its control in recent years, but not entirely in response to Indian political power. The Indians were driven onto land, which proved in many cases to be rich in oil, fish, forests, or convenient for waste disposal. Allowing them to sell access now was more attractive to policymakers. To do this also allowed greater recognition of tribal law and autonomy.

Indian gaming has now become common in many areas where adjacent non-Indian lands still bar gambling. This is ironic given the government's articulated concern about alcoholism and drug addiction on the reservations. In the name of allowing Indians more self-determination, legislators can permit tobacco and gambling at bargain prices on the reservations while adopting a moralistic posture in the society at large. There is also resistance to tribes buying land outside the reservation for gaming (Alm, 2003, pp. C1 and 8). Unfortunately, bilking and double-crossing Native American tribes has accelerated under the deregulation of tribal interests. Scandals in 2005 have led all the way to US Congressional leadership and the interests who fund their campaigns.

In terms of negotiating culture, however, new authority illustrates some of the variations that exist among tribal groups in terms of what they want from tourism and how they want their culture reflected in it. The old battles with paternalistic government agencies are receding but new disputes within tribes over economic development are now more apparent.

In 1986, this writer traveled the US Southwest studying four tribes. In the process of open-ended interviews with the participants in the growing tourist industry old stereotypes dissolved. There were a variety and complexity of cultural responses to tourism that clearly showed that the old Bureau of Indian Affairs' "one size fits all" approach is clearly inadequate. Similar research in other countries with native peoples developing tourism would probably yield comparable diversity.

The tribes discussed here represent only a snapshot in time, but they illustrate how tribal cultures vary in their response to showcasing their culture through tourism.

The Taos Pueblo in northeast New Mexico lies in the heart of a major tourist region. It has developed its tourism by strictly delineating the sacred from the touristic. Some ceremonies and rituals are strictly off-limits. For everything else there is a price. The Taos are very pragmatic about their approach. They know tourists want to see dancing, eat different but not too different food, and take lots of pictures of Indians. They also need accessible parking and a museum with clean restrooms. The Taos are ready.

The Navaho, the largest tribe in the US has land within four western states. It maintains its own police force, schools, and even time zone! The Navaho also have difficult relations with other tribes like the Hopi whose land they surround. The Navahos approach tourism as useful, a source of employment, and a way of maintaining arts, crafts, and language that might otherwise die out. On the other hand, they resist a museumification of their lifestyle. To the chagrin of the National Park Service, they refuse to keep quaint! Go to one of the towns on Navaho land and the grocery stores and other shops look decidedly ordinary. Despite the mystique about Native American love of the land, litter is a decided problem and disposable diapers sell on reservations every bit as much as on non-reservation land.

At the beautiful Canyon de Chelly the struggle to negotiate culture is real, but not as we might romanticize it. The Bureau of Indian Affairs, the National Park Service, the State of Arizona, and the Navaho Nation are trying to make the park and its surroundings both a tourist attraction and still home to the Navaho. The Navaho want more of the tourism dollars and jobs. Instead, they are allowed to guide the small minority who want to hike the canyon. Meanwhile, the Navaho do not want to live in traditional hogans as the Park Service would like, but in double wide trailers! They also want to have satellite dishes so that they can beam in their favorite television programs. Until recently they wanted to string telephone lines across the canyon, but presumably cell phones have arrived in time to forestall that battle.

Navaho long derided as traditional or primitive are now being criticized for not retaining their ancestral ways — as if the majority has! Thus, the familiar cliché of tourism destroying culture has a new twist: It is the paternalistic government urging the retention of traditional ways, albeit for less than altruistic reasons while most Navahos are intent on a 21st century lifestyle!

The Navaho traditional enemy, the Hopi, are a small tribe now pushed on to three tall mesas, completely surrounded by Navaho land. The Hopi have tried to be "more Indian than thou" and have built their livelihood on tourism. It is their buffer against the Navaho. But unlike the Taos or Navaho, they have approached tourism in a more guarded way.

On the one hand, they operate a conventional motel and restaurant at the top of Second Mesa. They also have a museum. There are a few places where one can buy local pottery. Their ceremonies are open to the public. Yet, they are very strict about no photographs being allowed of the people, the ceremonies and the artifacts in the museum. One can't even take notes on museum items. They have drawn the lines around tourism quite differently than the other two tribes, but they still are proud of and benefiting from tourism. It has kept the last remnants of the Hopi culture alive.

The State of Arizona has done little to preserve Hopi land. The Federal Government has endlessly reviewed Hopi claims but, bowing to the stronger Navaho *de facto* control, has left the Hopi largely alone in their development of tourism as a barricade against Navaho expansion.

Accommodating tourism to tribal objectives is also a goal of the Ute. The Ute are a small tribe in Southwestern Colorado. Their land abuts the Mesa Verde National Park and contains some of the same artifacts and cave dwellings that make the park a tourist magnet.

The Utes took some time to find their niche with respect to tourism. A few turned to guiding groups on day hikes through the Ute territory, but these trips never were as predictable as those organized within the park. They also tried bingo parlors, which were a hit with the Utes, but rarely patronized by tourists.

Ute customs and rituals seem not to be a rallying point for Utes any more than it distinguishes most ethnic groups in the US. Their historic craft tradition was beadwork which most found tedious, poor paying, and in low demand. The Utes got help from the University of Utah anthropologist who helped them to develop their tourist niche. After reviewing their options, the tribe decided pottery would be the best way to break into the tourist market. They didn't remember how to make pottery so they got molds and then painted them. The anthropologist suggested that they paint according to a few patterns and colors so as to be distinctive.

Today, "traditional" Ute pottery is for sale not only in Ute territory but in some of the best catalogs across the country. Few know the "traditional pottery" dates back only to 1985. Is Ute pottery "authentic"? It's theirs and there is nothing like it. The fact that they had a little non-Indian help in its creation may not be mentioned in the souvenir shops, but the fact that they chose this craft in 1985 instead of 1685 doesn't make it any less theirs.

In each of these cases, the tribes have defined their own approach to tourism and in the process have introduced a diversity and complexity to Indian tourism that is too often discussed without differentiation. None of these tribes are wealthy. None have gone the gaming route but they have used tourism to their advantage and in some cases to erect a tradition where none existed before!

Outsiders Develop Cultural Theme Park for Own Agenda

Another approach to sustainable tourism is to co-opt native culture, showcase it, and make the profits from that tourism a joint venture between performers and entrepreneurs. This model, based on the hugely successful Polynesian Cultural Center in Hawaii, has had both its critics and defenders. The Government of Hawaii and the Hawaii Visitors Bureau point out that it is the single most lucrative and visited attraction on Oahu. The Mormon church which owns and runs it cites the impressive number of students who get college educations at their adjacent college even as they work as performers at the center.

The Center features several Polynesian cultures on its extensive grounds. At specific times, there are demonstrations of crafts and dances and songs. Polynesian souvenirs are available and there is an impressive show every evening. The students are recruited from various nations of Polynesia and the state of Hawaii by Mormon missionaries. Once at the

Center they may or may not be asked to perform according to their own cultural heritage. In that sense they are free to consider themselves actors and actresses rather than being on display. A Tongan may be in a Fijian skit, for example (Brameld, 1977).

Critics feel that the students are exploited first by religious proselytizing and then by being used to financially benefit the Mormons. Others contend the attraction is clean, wholesome, culturally empathetic, and allows talented youth an opportunity for a college education. The debate goes on.

The model of the Polynesian Cultural Center insofar as it is an introduction to the ethnic groups of a region has been copied in such attractions as the Philippine government-run Nayong Filipino and Indonesia's Mini-Indonesia. The latter do not have the links to religious conversion and higher education distinctive to the Polynesian Cultural Center.

Showcase One Culture; Ignore Others

Hawaii is not only home to the Polynesian Cultural Center which features the island cultures of the Pacific, but it is also an excellent example of a tourist destination that has been subjected to a variety of cultural approaches over more than 100 years. The United States conquered the Hawaiian islands in the late 1890s, eventually defeating the Hawaiian monarchy. This was during a time when the US was belatedly becoming involved in imperialist conquests in the Philippines, Puerto Rico, and Cuba. It had earlier purchased Alaska and would shortly after the conquest of Hawaii purchase the Virgin Islands. The initial impulse in Hawaii was to protect agricultural corporations like Dole Pineapple and important shipping lines, but the islands became strategically important during World War II.

The Hawaiian people were a fraction of the islanders by this time, having been decimated by disease brought by missionaries and other outsiders. Hawaiian culture is protected more than most of the other ethnic minorities by the fact that land titles were generally leasehold and the monarchy had reserved some money and lands for Hawaiians. Moreover, the legends of Hawaii have been the stuff of tourism advertising and heiaus or Hawaiian temple grounds have been generally respected.

Though radio programs like "Hawaii Calls" and the Kodak Hula Show lured early tourists with a phony Hawaiian culture, their success has in fact paved the way, following statehood in 1959, for a more authentic presentation of the art, music, and culture of the islands. Today, Hawaiian is taught in the schools, a cultural arts director is employed by a five star hotel, and the courts allow "pidgin" — a mixture of Hawaiian and English in court proceedings!

Currently, though the population is a mix that includes Chinese, Japanese, Filipino, Vietnamese, Caucasian, and Hawaiian, it is Hawaiian culture that is accentuated for tourism purposes. Traditional hula is, however, taking the place of ballet for resident youngsters of all races. Hawaiian culture is also gaining some ascendancy in the curriculum at all levels. It has become an important part of distinguishing Hawaii from its island competition in the South Pacific as well as in the Caribbean.

More problematic has been how to present the Japanese-American culture of the islands. The bombing of Pearl Harbor in 1941, which propelled the US into World War II, made Pearl Harbor a major tourist attraction. In the early years following the war, the interpretation of

Pearl Harbor emphasized the sneakiness and warlike nature of the Japanese. But over time the message softened.

The Japanese-Americans living in Hawaii during the war were not rounded up and interned as they were on the US mainland. This reflected their numbers and the lack of centrality of the Hawaiian territory to the US sense of its own geographical heartland. In fact, the Japanese-American units of the American military were sent to the European theaters of war, where they would become the most decorated units of World War II!

As time went on and the numbers of Japanese-Americans in the island assumed more political power and as more Japanese came to visit Hawaii, the touristic interpretation of Pearl Harbor evolved until by the mid-1980s, the bombing had become more of a terrible misunderstanding between two valiant nations. To some that seems like revisionist history, but time and politics may have combined to present a more nuanced but not necessarily inaccurate portrayal of events.

Today, Japanese tourists are a major component of Hawaii tourism, but the promotional emphasis has remained on the exotic Hawaiians (Richter, 1998). For non-Japanese, however, there has been a growing emphasis on Buddhist temples, bon dances, and the festivals of other cultures resident in the islands. Court battles continue to be waged on behalf of Hawaiian property rights, but Hawaiian dependence on tourism has never been successfully challenged since statehood.

Thus, though it was US foreign policy that launched Hawaii on a course that moved from missions to plantations to tourism, today tourism in the islands continues to be largely controlled by state policy and multi-national business. Both are more tolerant of cultural pluralism and vigilant to protect Hawaii's "aloha" brand of friendliness. Those belated concerns have worked to the advantage of those seeking to sustain Hawaiian culture.

National Policies Toward Culture and Tourism

Generally national policies toward tourism reflect economic promotion, target markets, visa, and tax issues, but there are numerous examples of national tourism policies dealing with culture. What follows are some examples.

Small nations face a dilemma when it comes to tourism. The tourist industry can easily overwhelm the local culture. The examples of Bhutan, Jamaica, the Maldives, and Costa Rica are instructive. Not having a national identity enhanced by the trappings of sovereignty including, visas, flag, and tourists can leave a nation exposed to the predatory impulses of other nations.

In 1989, this writer described at length how Bhutan, once a princely state of India, opened itself gradually to tourism and outside contacts, once it saw another princely state, Sikkim, absorbed by India in 1974. In fact, it had avoided a similar fate after the partitioning of India in 1947, chiefly by being remote, on the periphery, and not eagerly sought by Pakistan and India as was Kashmir. It is not that Bhutan wanted tourism. It had been horrified by Nepal's experience where waves of tourists transformed that Himalayan kingdom. But once its very independence was threatened, Bhutan opted for controlled, gradual, upscale tourism which required tourists to spend substantial sums per day to travel along limited itineraries while being carefully monitored (Richter, 1989). Bhutan's experience is in fact somewhat similar to that of the Hopi tribe discussed earlier. Tourism was less a goal than a strategy to protect cultural autonomy.

Jamaica, discovered too late, how difficult it is for a national government to change course with respect to tourism. Cuba did it for more than 40 years, but not without a revolution and 30 years of Soviet subsidies. Jamaican tourism had been based on a servile catering of the black population to the whims of its white North American clientele. When the government of Michael Manley came to power in the late 1970s, the socialist government sought a more dignified and complex image. Its tourism slogan was "Jamaica's more than a beach; it's a Country". The United States, worried that Jamaica might go the way of Cuba or even little Grenada, specifically exempted Jamaica from President Reagan's Caribbean Basin Initiative and discouraged tourism or other investment in Jamaica. The Manley government was defeated and a more pliant government installed. The new tourism slogan said it all: "Jamaica's Jamaica Again" (Richter, 1989).

The Maldive Republic is sufficiently remote from major powers in that it has been able to cater to a specific tourism niche — dive tourism — and being an island group has sought to use enclave tourism as a way to dilute the influence of tourism on the Islamic nation. Whole islands are off-limits to tourists, even as other islands are specifically for tourists and male employees of the tourism industry. This approach protects women and children from tourists, but unfortunately keeps families apart for long periods and assures that development for the industry has little ripple effect to other non-tourist parts of the country (Richter, 1989, 1998).

Malaysia, another Islamic nation, took a different approach. It largely ignored its Muslim heritage in its advertising, because it had already had its share of internal cultural skirmishes in the 1960s. Thus, it promoted its scenic attractions, its golf courses, and its largest casino to the world! The casino is a strange anomaly because gambling is forbidden to Malaysian citizens (Anonymous, 1997).

During this writer's field research in Costa Rica in February and July, 1997, policymakers generously and proudly detailed their newest strategy for supporting sustainable community cultures through careful tourism development. This approach, though only partially implemented, has been sufficiently attractive to encourage all other central American nations to adopt it in principle. In the late 1990s, Costa Rica began an incentive-based effort that was designed to both sustain tourism and improve lives for those impacted by it. The Certificate for Sustainable Tourism (CST) was awarded those establishments — initially hotels — that met certain criteria. Participation in the evaluation was voluntary, but it was encouraged by allowing hotels to note their CST in their advertising and to get discounted advertising space in the national brochures and videos.

The CST was designed to encourage private entrepreneurs to adopt ecologically sustainable practices and good labor policies that took local communities into account in their planning, construction, and hiring. The national government had already set an excellent example by setting aside nearly a quarter of the country into a series of national parks. To assure that the environmental and cultural diversity would not be threatened by the rapid development of tourism outside the parks, this certificate program was embraced as consistent with good development and private enterprise. The early years were encouraging, but in Costa Rica, public policy is often erratic given that the President serves only a single term. Thus, the subsequent development of the CST and its adoption elsewhere is still in the early stages.

Finally, even where national policies and international bodies like the UNESCO and NGOs exist, war and national disasters may make cultural tourism problematic. Sometimes from the ruins, earlier treasures emerge and struggles ensue over which era should be made whole. Dubrovnik, Croatia's experience is illustrative. Though Croatia in general and Dubrovnik in particular suffered horribly during the Serbian attack in the early 1990s, it was in part the incredible heritage of the region that made the Croatian people's plight well-known to the entire world. UNESCO World Heritage Sites dotted the landscape and that body and many NGOs sought to publicize the threat to world treasures and make plans for post-war recovery. Tourism, and with it the re-emergence of the nation's cultural heritage, became a priority for post-war Croatia and its cultural allies around the globe (Richter & Richter, 2001).

Conclusion

> The World is a Book. He who stays at home reads only one page.
>
> St. Augustine

Sometimes St. Augustine's perceptions seem dated. Though culture continues to be the way many nations promote their countries as destinations, the globalization of accommodations, food, touring, and even itinerary formulas has encouraged a mainstream blandness. Culture may too often be confined to the decor, the receptionist at the registration desk, and the evening entertainment. All know people who have collected countries like postage stamps but without much exposure to their distinct cultures.

Still, this chapter has sought to demonstrate how culture can be utilized as a positive and politically helpful element in societies as citizens seek to meld tourism and their own sense of identity. These approaches do not guarantee success, but their examples serve to suggest how culture might be utilized or even ignored so as to develop successful tourism. Of course, the important question is not sustaining tourism for visitors but sustaining citizens through the sharing of their culture and homeland. It is important that we recognize that these are two different questions and the latter ultimately decides the former.

Acknowledgments

The author wishes to thank the Centre for Tourism Policy Studies (CENTOPS) for their wonderful hospitality during the 2003 conference at which an earlier version of this chapter was presented. Kansas State University's Department of Political Science and the Women's Studies Program provided travel support. The American Ethnic Studies Program supported the research on Native American tourism.

References

Alm, R. (2003). Kansas appeals casino ruling. *Kansas City Star*, July 25, C1, 8.

Altman, J. (1989). Tourism dilemmas for aboriginal Australians. *Annals of Tourism Research, 16*(4), 456–476.

Anonymous. (1997). *Driving through Malaysia*. Kuala Lumpur: Government of Malaysia.

Brameld, T. B. (1977). *Tourism as cultural learning*. Washington, DC: University Press of America.

Hartmann, R. (1989). Dachau revisited: Tourism to the memorial site and museum of the former concentration camp. *Tourism, Recreation, Research, 14*(1), 41–47.

Horne, D. (1984). *The great museum: The re-presentation of history*. London: Pluto Press.

Nelson, M. B. (1994). *The stronger women get: The more men love football*. New York: Avon.

Pforr, C. (2003). *Strategic planning for tourism development in the Northern Territory of Australia*. Unpublished doctoral dissertation, University of the Northern Territory, Darwin.

Richter, L. K. (1982). *Land reform and tourism development: Policy-making in the Philippines*. Cambridge, MA: Schenkman Press.

Richter, L. K. (1989). *The politics of tourism in Asia*. Honolulu: University of Hawaii Press.

Richter, L. K. (1994). The political dimensions of tourism. In: J. R. B. Ritchie, & C. R. Goeldner (Eds), *Travel, Tourism and Hospitality Research* (2nd ed.). New York: Wiley.

Richter, L. K. (1998). Exploring the political roles of gender in tourism research. In W. Theobald (Ed.), *Global tourism: The next decade* (2nd ed., pp. 391–404). New York: Butterworth-Heinemann.

Richter, L. K. (1999). The politics of heritage tourism development. In: D. G. Pearce, & R. W. Butler (Eds), *Contemporary issues in tourism development* (pp. 108–126). London, UK: Routledge.

Richter, L. K. (2001). Tourism challenges in developing nations: Continuity and change at the millennium. In: D. Harrison (Ed.), *Tourism and the less developed world: Issues and case studies* (pp. 47–59). Wallingford, UK: CABI.

Richter, L. K., & Richter, W. L. (2001). Back from the edge: Recovering a public heritage. In: S. Nagel (Ed.), *Handbook of global social policy* (pp. 357–372). Basel: Marcel Dekker.

Richter, L. K., & Waugh, W. L., Jr. (1991). Terrorism and tourism as logical companions. In: S. Medlik (Ed.), *Managing tourism* (pp. 318–327). Oxford: Butterworth-Heinemann.

Savage, C. (1996). *Cowgirls*. Berkeley, CA: Ten Speed Press.

Seaton, A. V. (1996). Guided by the dark: From thanatopsis to thanatourism. *International Journal of Heritage Studies, 2*(4), 234–244.

Chapter 3

Sizing up the World: Scale and Belonging in Narratives of Round-the-World Travel

Jennie Germann Molz

Introduction

This chapter is about the 'size of the world' — not in terms of measuring the Earth's equatorial diameter or surface area, but rather in terms of the way travellers perceive and perform the size of the world as they travel around it. Focusing specifically on travellers' use of the Internet and drawing on the websites they publish while travelling around the world and on interviews with travellers, this chapter suggests that round-the-world travellers sense the world as both big *and* small. Furthermore, the way travellers perceive the size of the world is interwoven with the way they imagine their own place in the world. The practice of round-the-world travel is thus bound up in a complex relationship between travel, time and space, scale and belonging.

The stories related in this chapter are drawn from a study of round-the-world travel websites conducted from 2001 to 2005 in which over 200 websites were surveyed and 40 websites were examined in depth through discourse and narrative analysis. For the most part, these websites are personal home pages where independent travellers chronicle the on-going events of their trips. At the heart of these websites are journal entries and photographs detailing the travellers' experiences, but most websites also include general information about the traveller(s) and the trip, including maps and itineraries, travel budgets, packing lists, health advice and links to relevant sites. One of the recurring themes that emerges in the stories these travellers publish online is an ambivalent and changeable orientation toward time, space, and the size of the world that sits uneasily against the discourses of the speed-up of social life, the disappearance of spatial horizons and the onset of 'time–space compression' that comprise recent debates over the implications of globalization and international mobility.

This chapter begins with an investigation of the concept of 'time–space compression' that has emerged alongside theories of globalization. The suggestion that the world is shrinking due to advances in technologies of transportation and communication then leads to questions about scale. How are travellers' movements through time and space constitutive of particular scales? In particular, how do travellers perform the world as both shrinking and expanding? Finally, the chapter discusses the effects of the production of multiple time–space scales of the world on the way travellers perform a sense of belonging in the world as a whole.

Small World, Big World: Travel and Time–Space Compression

Since the late nineteenth century, the modern experience of globalization has been characterized by dramatic new ways of experiencing time and space. The general consensus is that the world is growing smaller and denser, though the precise effects of this transformation have been portrayed in different ways (Kern, 1983; Giddens, 1990; Harvey, 1990, 1996; Lash & Urry, 1994). David Harvey's notion of 'time–space compression' is perhaps the most widely accepted description of the way time and space have been transformed in this way. He writes

> As space appears to shrink to a 'global village' of telecommunications and a 'spaceship earth' of economic and ecological interdependencies … and as time horizons shorten to the point where the present is all there is … so we have to learn how to cope with an overwhelming sense of *compression* of our spatial and temporal worlds. (Harvey, 1990, p. 240; emphasis in original)

The 'shrinking world' is linked to mobility, and in particular to the technologies of transportation and communication that have accelerated the movement of people, objects, capital, information and images around the world (Kern, 1983; Harvey, 1990; Holmes, 2001). Airlines boast of their role in making the world seem smaller. An advertisement for Boeing claims that the company has been "building airplanes that fly faster and farther … connect[ing] continents and cultures around the world.... Which means the distance between any two places in the world has never been shorter". Likewise, the Internet's ability to move data around the world in mere seconds and make instantaneous connections between people on different sides of the world certainly seems to diminish the size of the world. It follows, then that round-the-world travellers — especially those who consistently use the Internet while they are travelling — would experience a sense of time–space compression.

However, the relationship between technologies of travel and communication and time–space compression is a complex and contested one with uneven effects (see Bauman, 1998; Crouch, Aronsson, & Wahlström, 2001). The extent to which Harvey's concept of 'time–space compression' accurately describes the way travellers are experiencing time and space as they move around the world is debatable. Do travellers perceive the world as shrinking, as Harvey's thesis suggests? Or does movement through the world produce other scales as well? And finally, what implications do these multiple and shifting scales have for travellers' identities and for their sense of belonging in a global context?

Geographers Jon May and Nigel Thrift (2001) challenge the historical premise of Harvey's narrative of 'time–space compression' in the nineteenth and early twentieth centuries. They argue that for all of the technologies that *compressed* time–space, there were other technologies that *extended* it. For example, the invention of electric lighting extended the day and opened up new districts at night. From this point of view, May and Thrift maintain that "space is seen to both expand and to contract, time horizons to both foreshorten but also to extend, time itself to both speed up but also slow down and even to move in different directions" (2001, p. 10). Similarly, Glennie and Thrift (1996) argue that time, and we can include space, can be seen as "intrinsically manifold; as multiple and heterogeneous; as a discontinuous process with its own origins and archaeology" (1996, p. 278). This argument for a multiplicity of times and spaces is a more appropriate framework for describing travellers' experiences of time–space. In other words, travellers perceive the world through a multiplicity of scales — as both shrinking and expanding and as both small and big.

To some extent, travellers' stories about flying and using the Internet corroborate Harvey's description of time–space compression in the disorienting sense that the world is collapsing 'inwards upon us' (1990, p. 240). Travellers talk about how small the world is when they use the Internet to link instantly with friends and family on the other side of the world and talk about the disorienting effect of jet travel that seems to dissolve the distance between places. In such cases, travellers get to feel the world as small due to their privileged access to these technologies of corporeal and virtual mobility. However, the experience of time–space compression is by no means consistent or universal in travellers' stories. Alongside such descriptions of time–space compression are descriptions of the way the Internet and technologies of transportation *stretch out* rather than compress time and space.

Kinga and Chopin, two travellers from Poland who hitchhiked overland around the world for five years, describe one of the few flights they took during this time. In this case, unable to book passage on a cargo ship, they flew from Chile to New Zealand. Their comments on the website reveal the ambivalent sense of time and space that resulted from this flight:

> I can't believe we'll be on the other side of the Pacific the day after tomorrow. Just like that …. It's absolutely mindblowing that you can cross half the world in just one flight and find yourself in a totally different world.…
>
> Neverending vastness of the ocean below us, and the sky above us — blending into one infinite darkness, lost in time.… We left Chile on March 6th at night, changed planes in Buenos Aires, flew all night long (really long — 13.5 hours), and woke up in the morning of March 8th New Zealand time. We woke up to a different reality. (*Hitch-hike the World*)

On the one hand Kinga and Chopin express the sense of amazement and disorientation suggested by time–space compression as they consider the way flying will juxtapose otherwise distant cultural and geographical environments. On the other, the actual experience of flying does not necessarily diminish space and time. In contrast, time and space seem to stretch out as Kinga and Chopin describe the 'vastness' of the ocean and the sky, the 'infinite darkness' and the 'really long' duration of the flight. Kinga and Chopin's narrative indicates that something more complex than a straightforward compression of time and space is occurring.

The technologies that travellers engage while travelling around the world do not necessarily accelerate time or diminish space. In contrast, Marie, who travelled overland and alone around the world, notes that travelling can slow time down. She observes that

> [T]ime works differently when you travel. A day is like a week, a week is like a month, and every month feels like a year. By traveling, I can control time and make the years go by slower. (*Marie's World Tour*)

Marie notes that travel seems to extend space as well as slow down time. Elsrud (1998) observes that many female backpackers imagined time as 'pregnant' while they were travelling, a notion that certainly captures the fullness of time that Marie experiences. During her year-long journey overland around the world, Marie endured a month at sea aboard a cargo ship, monotonous bus rides through Australia and a week-long train ride through Siberia. As these journeys extended seemingly forever in time, they also gave her a sense of the vastness of the world. From the ship, the seascape was 'miles and miles of unforgiving ocean' and 'vast mountains of black water'. From the bus, she crossed the expansive Outback, stopping occasionally in 'the middle of nowhere'. And through the window of the Trans-Siberian railway, she contemplated "the flat tree-covered scenery [that] almost never changed" for days on end (*Marie's World Tour*).

Using the Internet can also have the effect of stretching time and space. Despite the connotation of the Internet as 'annihilating space with time', 'time–space compression' is not an inevitable effect of Internet technology. Christine Hine points out that the Internet can have 'multiple temporal and spatial orderings' (2000, p. 11). In addition to describing the Internet as an immediate or instantaneous connection, travellers frequently comment on the 'painfully' and 'excruciatingly' slow Internet connections they find in Internet cafés across the world. So, though the Internet is commonly touted as an emblem of time–space compression, this is not necessarily the most accurate way to describe the way travellers experience or enact time and space on the Internet. A wide range of time–space experiences accumulates on the websites: the impossibly fast movement of data from travellers to their audiences as well as painfully slow Internet connections; or travellers' narratives that express the impossibly slow monotony of travelling on long-haul trains as well as the sense of speed experienced in jet travel. Depending on which technologies of mobility they are using and where, contemporary round-the-world travellers constantly shift back and forth between experiencing time as speeding by and experiencing it as slowing down, and between experiencing the world as small and experiencing it as big. This poses a crucial question in the light of Harvey's notion of time–space compression: is the world really shrinking? Or is it getting bigger?

According to travellers' stories, the world is *both* small *and* big. For example, even as Kinga and Chopin are awed by the way air travel diminishes distance, they are also cognisant of a sense of the length and the vastness that travel brings to both time and space. In other words, they experience the world as both shrinking and expanding as they travel around it, a notion they make explicit in this journal entry posted to their website on the third anniversary of their departure. They write

> Yes, it's three years today since we landed in New York. Neither of us thought then, that the journey would take us such a long time and that after three years we would only be more or less half way through.... We discovered that while it's a 'small world' we're travelling in, at the same time it's too huge to see it all in a year. Or two .... At least not the way we're doing it. Anyway, we still have lots more to go. (*Hitch-hike the World*)

The ambivalence in this particular posting is typical of most travellers' shifting notions of the size of the world and is tied to specific conditions. So when do travellers experience the world as small and when do they experience it as big?

For Kinga and Chopin, the world is big because of the 'way' they are doing it — hitchhiking mainly overland, going 'off the beaten track' to remote areas and stopping for long periods to work. However, as they describe on their website, it is a small world because of the many coincidences they experience (such as being recognised from their website by someone who offered them a ride in Australia) and because they are tied into an international network of hitchhikers and travellers. As members of Servas, an international hosting organization, they already have contacts in many of the places they visit. As this example suggests, the size of the world depends on different factors, two of which are *speed* and *connections*. First, the size of the world is contingent on the mode and speed (or pace) of travel. Second, the size of the world is contingent on connections, including the social networks and 'coincidences' that Kinga and Chopin describe on their website.

Speed and Scale

Harvey's formulation of time–space compression relies heavily on the equation of speed with shrinking. In other words, it is the increasingly *fast* movement of people, goods, capital and information around the world that brings about a sense that the world is shrinking. On travellers' websites, as well, fast speed (such as air travel) is generally linked to the sense that distances are shrinking, while slow speed (on local buses, trains or walking) is linked to the sense that time and space are both expanding. This equation translates to the use of the Internet as well, with high-speed Internet access and a sense of being 'plugged in' to a tight global web contrasted against 'excruciatingly slow' access and a literal and figurative sense of remoteness.

If rapid air travel makes the world seem small, then travelling slowly on the earth's surface can make space seem to stretch out. Areas that seem small on a map extend once the traveller has to cover them by surface travel. To demonstrate this, Bjorn, a Norwegian traveller, posts a map of Nepal on his website and tells his readers

> So, this basically is what Nepal looks like from above.... I've traced my journey in the country with a red line. It doesn't look very far on the map ... but it felt like a veeeeery large country during the bus journeys and the long trek I did. (*Bjorn's Enduring Travels*)

Bjorn moves through scales, using the map to demonstrate how small and manageable the space is and comparing that scale to his own experiences of travelling *through* it. Once travellers actually start moving across the distances that they had previously only consumed as representations or stories, they begin to physically sense the world as a huge entity.

The speed of travel produces different kinds of scale, but the apparent correlation between fast and small, slow and big does not always hold. In fact, the technologies that make the world seem big to contemporary travellers — trains and ships, in particular — are the very technologies that made the world seem exceptionally small in the nineteenth century. As May and Thrift argue, the speed of air travel has the unlikely effect of making the world seem bigger by rendering "other forms of transportation seem much slower than they had once appeared" (2001, p. 19). Multiple speeds produce multiple perceptions of the size of the world, and often in unpredictable ways. The correlation between speed and scale is, however, largely implicit in travellers' stories. The instances in which travellers explicitly refer to the world as 'small' or as 'big' are less about speed and more about connection.

Connections and Scale

The examples discussed so far suggest that scale and differences in scale are not given, but rather are produced, contingent and relative. In addition to speed, the perception of scale is also contingent on connections. As Michel Callon and John Law argue, "size is not a matter of scale but connection" (2004, p. 4). The more connected a certain point in a network is to other points, the more it is "able to 'localise' those others" (Callon & Law, 2004, p. 4). Differences in size, then, are produced when networks are more or less densely connected. Ostensibly, a small world is a tightly connected world. However, the *kind* of connections made between points is as crucial as the number of connections made. Certain kinds of connections make the world feel small, while others make it seem big.

The 'small world' is a social world. In this case, the 'small world' is stitched together by a series of social connections — chains of acquaintances that arguably link all of us within six degrees of separation (see Watts, 1999; Urry, 2003). While round-the-world travellers often arrange to meet up in person with friends or people they have met online, what makes the world seem *small* to them are not these coordinated face-to-face social encounters, but rather unpredictable, coincidental meetings. These coincidental meetings cause travellers to declare that it is not just a small world, but, as one traveller put it, a 'tiny tiny world' after all. In story after story of 'small world' encounters, travellers describe unexpectedly running into people they know or meeting people with whom they share mutual social acquaintances. These stories take on several variations. The most common instances are when travellers run into other travellers whom they have met previously (which suggests that the traveller circuit itself constitutes a small world.) Another form of 'small world' story occurs when travellers run into someone they know in another context, or someone who shares a mutual acquaintance. Suzanne, a traveller from Scotland, recalls a 'small world' encounter in Fiji when she met a girl who was not only also from Scotland, but turned out to be Suzanne's boyfriend's friend's cousin's best friend! For Suzanne this encounter, which certainly calls to mind the 'six-degrees of separation' adage, proved that it is a 'small world' (*Suzanne's World Travel Pages*).

For Sarah, a traveller from the United States, the sense of a small world comes not just from running into people she already knows in other contexts, but also from meeting new people and becoming integrated into their social networks. In an interview, she states

> And that's the small part, is that the network of good people that you find everywhere makes [the world] small in the sense that you are comfortable everywhere that you meet people. I mean, a trip like this isn't about going to the cathedrals and the art museums, it's about meeting people on the third class bus. Because that's what's important. And so that gets small. But the world itself is HUGE.

As Sarah's comments suggest, personal interactions rather than sightseeing trips allow for a feeling of belonging to a tightly-knit global community in contrast to the physical enormity of the world. In these instances, the world is made small by social connections. If social connections make the world feel small, then what kinds of connections make it feel huge? In one sense, the world is made big by the opposite of connection: disconnection. For example, slow or nonexistent Internet connections can make travellers feel physically and figuratively remote. Places that are serviced by infrequent or unreliable transportation networks feel similarly remote in an enormous world. This sense of remoteness is not necessarily unpleasant. In fact, for some travellers, disconnection from social obligations allows them to connect with nature or with the world as a physical entity. In other words, travellers desire to *feel* the hugeness of the world.

For some travellers, a sense of the world's vastness can be found in particular landscapes or environments. In *The Art of Travel*, Alain de Botton writes of finding pleasure in feeling dwarfed. He goes to the desert, he says, "in order to be made to feel small" (de Botton, 2002, p. 159). In a similar way, certain destinations, such as Siberia, the Australian Outback or the Himalayan mountain range, make travellers *feel* the vastness of space. Visiting ancient landscapes or monuments has a similar effect of expanding time–space. These special places overwhelm the traveller with history. Travellers describe standing in awe of huge and ancient structures such as the temple of Borobudur in Indonesia or the great pyramids in Egypt. Travelling around the world and visiting ancient and remote places makes the temporal and spatial enormity of the world *tangible*. Gabriel Josipovici (1996) notes that the purpose of pilgrimages is precisely 'to make distance palpable' and argues that this desire continues to characterise travel today:

> Is not the secular visitor to Rome or Los Angeles, who touches the age-old stones or the ocean, instinctively repeating that ancient gesture and, by so doing, not so much bridging the distance between himself and these repositories of power as acknowledging their otherness and the awe he feels in their presence? (Josipovici 1996, p. 169)

In this sense, connection is not about closeness or tightening of social ties, but rather it is about distance and going to places where the size of the world — in terms of both geographical and historical scales — can be felt.

For some travellers, it is the very act of travelling around the world that provides a sense of the world's immensity. Gerard, a traveller from the United States, comments in an interview that the world seems small until you start travelling:

> [W]hen you get out there and start traveling the world, it is amazing how big it is. It's bigger than I expected, and I've traveled before, and I've traveled extensively. It's a big world we live on.

Once he 'gets out there' and starts moving across the earth's surface, Gerard comes to realise the enormity of the world as an object. Thus, mobility is one form of connecting to the world in a way that makes it seem huge. As Jeff Greenwald (1995) contemplates in his novel, *The Size of the World*, what has been lost in a shrinking world of telecommunications and jet travel is a sense of enormity, which to him also connotes continuity and connectedness:

> The moment one climbs onto an airplane, I realized, one enters into a Faustian bargain. Comfort, convenience and the ability to buy duty-free perfume in any nation on Earth are ours. In return we need only utter, in our heads and our hearts, the mantra of the modern age: *"The world is getting smaller."* ... The Earth was no longer an enormous, mysterious and infinitely varied globe .... An essential quality of travel had been lost. If I had to define it, I'd use the word *continuity*: the sense that the sidewalk in front of one's house is connected, physically, with every other spot on Earth. I wanted to reclaim that feeling. (Greenwald, 1995, p. 5)

The size of the world also expands when travellers consider the vast array of differences they have encountered (or hope to encounter) while travelling around the world. In an interview, Tom states that while the world is small in a spiritual sense, "it's huge when it comes to perspectives and people's outlook on things". Amidst an array of differences — including not only the differences between places and landscapes, but also in the way people view the world — the traveller again feels small or insignificant. This sense of insignificance is, some would argue, an important part of gaining a more cosmopolitan perspective on the world. As travellers begin to realise and experience how many different cultures and world-views there are, they come to recognise the constructedness of their own worldview and become capable of reflecting on their own culture from a more ironic stance.

Conclusion: Implications for Global Belonging

Returning to Harvey's notion of time–space compression, we can see that this perception of the world is relative. Looking at the way travellers describe their own experiences and perceptions of the size of the world shows that scale is complex and contingent, best described in terms of multiplicity. Speed of travel and the kinds of connections travellers forge while travelling influence travellers' perception and performance of the size of the world and their own place in it. The way travellers perceive the size of the world shifts as they move through it and enact different kinds of connection. But what does the size of the world mean for the way travellers perform belonging to the world as a whole?

As travellers alternate between different scales (from small world to big world and back again), they engage different practices of belonging. In the small world of social connection, travellers locate themselves within a social constellation. Their sense of belonging is defined through their place in the social web of the world and their identity is mapped out through social and familial relations. The small world is performed at a human scale, made tighter or looser not in terms of geographic distance, but in terms of human interconnection. Belonging to this small social world involves not only being mobile, but also being connected through social networks and interpersonal encounters.

In a big world, a sense of belonging is derived from being made to feel small. If a small world is produced through social connections, then a big world might be said to emerge through travellers' spiritual connections with a landscape, a historical landmark or indeed the world itself. As travellers move around the world, its massive size as a geological entity becomes tangible. For many travellers, this involves a sense of spiritual connection to something larger than themselves. Feeling overwhelmed by the vast geography and ancient history of the world may make the traveller feel small or insignificant, but this sense of feeling diminished also allows travellers to gain a wider perspective on their place in the world. Furthermore, round-the-world travellers' constant movement juxtaposes different places and cultures and foregrounds for travellers the huge diversity of cultures and environments that co-exist on the planet. Their mobility through the world allows them to locate themselves and their worldview within a much larger physical and cultural context. This ironic perspective on the world "requires a certain distance from one's own culture" (Turner, 2002, p. 55) that allows for both an appreciation of other cultures and a recognition of one's own relative position in the wider world. Belonging to a world made huge by cultural difference requires an ironic distance or even detachment from one's own culture. Sizing up the world thus requires travellers to negotiate between various forms of connection and disconnection, attachment and detachment as they move through and forge a sense of belonging to a simultaneously shrinking and expanding world.

Acknowledgments

Many thanks to Anne-Marie Fortier and Mimi Sheller for their insightful comments on various drafts of this chapter and to the participants of the Global Frameworks and Local Realities conference for their generous and helpful questions.

References

Bauman, Z. (1998). *Globalization*. Cambridge: Polity.
Bjorn's Enduring Travels. Retrieved July 12, 2005, from http://www.pvv.org/%7Ebct/backpack/index.html
Callon, M., & Law, J. (2004). Introduction: Absence-presence, circulation and encountering in complex space. *Environment and Planning D: Society and Space*, 22(1), 3–11.

Crouch, D., Aronsson, L., & Wahlström, L. (2001). 'Tourist encounters'. *Tourist Studies*, *1*(3), 253–270.

de Botton, A. (2002). *The art of travel*. London: Hamish Hamilton.

Elsrud, T. (1998). Time creation in travelling: The taking and making of time among women back-packers. *Time & Society*, *7*(2), 309–304.

Giddens, A. (1990). *The consequences of modernity*. Cambridge: Polity Press.

Glennie, P., & Thrift, N. (1996). Reworking E. P. Thompson's 'Time, work discipline and industrial capitalism'. *Time and Society*, *5*(3), 275–299.

Greenwald, J. (1995). *The size of the world: Once around without leaving the ground*. New York: Ballantine.

Harvey, D. (1990). *The condition of postmodernity*. Cambridge, MA: Blackwell.

Harvey, D. (1996). *Justice, nature and the geography of difference*. Oxford: Blackwell.

Hine, C. (2000). *Virtual ethnography*. London: Sage.

Hitch-hike the World. Retrieved July 13, 2005, from http://www.geocities.com/kingachopin/main_eng

Holmes, D. (Ed.) (2001). *Virtual globalization: Virtual spaces/tourist spaces*. London: Routledge.

Josipovici, G. (1996). *Touch*. New Haven and London: Yale University Press.

Kern, S. (1983). *The culture of time and space: 1880–1918*. Cambridge, MA: Harvard University Press.

Lash, S., & Urry, J. (1994). *Economies of signs and space*. London: Sage.

Marie's World Tour. Retrieved July 11, 2005, from http://www.mariesworldtour.com

May, J., & Thrift, N. (2001). Introduction. In: J. May, & N. Thrift (Eds), *Timespace: Geographies of temporality*. London: Routledge.

Suzanne's World Travel Pages. Retrieved July 13, 2005, from http://www.geocities.com/TheTropics/Paradise/7014/journal.html

Turner, B. S. (2002). Cosmopolitan virtue, globalization and patriotism. *Theory, Culture & Society*, *19*(1–2), 45–63.

Urry, J. (2003). Social networks, travel and talk. *British Journal of Sociology*, *54*(2), 155–175.

Watts, D. (1999). *Small worlds*. Princeton, NJ: Princeton University Press.

Chapter 4

Close Encounters: The Role of Culinary Tourism and Festivals in Positioning a Region

Gerard van Keken and Frank Go

Introduction

No more than ten years ago, going on holiday or for a short break, the opportunities to gain information on a tourist destination were mainly, tourist brochures, media, such as papers, magazines, radio, and television, and last but not the least, word of mouth information from family members as well as friends. While the vendor was in charge of creating the brochure, ads, commercials, and promotional campaign working on the identity, the consumer had to take action to gain information and form an opinion on the chosen destination. The relation between the vendors and consumers has changed dramatically since the increase in the use of internet. The application of virtual tools has exploded spatial constructs and is redefining the role of geographies in relation to how actors, both consumers and vendors, are constructing, imagining, and experiencing identities.

In this context the key question is how an identity can be constructed in the virtual sense and met in the physical space. If a virtual encounter has occurred and the guest is drawn to the tourist destination due to the presented virtual images and scripts, it creates expectations and another issue, namely: How can the tourist destination live up to tourists' expectations by providing experiential reality during (physical) visits so as to avoid disappointment? The host–guest encounters in tourism are part of an attraction system that should be concerned with conscious decision making, identifying key decision-making roles in the development and management of time–space relationships that form the foundation of identity construction, imagination, and experience. A part of this attraction system is festivals that Getz (in Derrets, 2004, p. 32) highlights as 'unique leisure and cultural experiences, powerful travel motivators and facilitators of community pride and development'. Festivals and events provide authenticity and uniqueness, especially with events based on inherent indigenous values; convenient hospitality and affordability; theming and symbols for participants and spectators. Derret continues by saying that the more an event is seen by its host community as emerging from within rather than being imposed on them,

Tourism and Social Identities: Global Frameworks and Local Realities
Copyright © 2006 by Elsevier Ltd.
All rights of reproduction in any form reserved.
ISBN: 0-08-045074-1

the greater would be that community's acceptance of the event. There is growing interest in the notion that festivals and events represent the host community's sense of itself and sense of place. This requires a close reading of the host–guest relationship (Derrets, 2004, p. 33). The question in this chapter is to investigate the relation between contact, encounters, relations, and identity. The way tourists experience their holiday or short break, the connection with the identity of a destination, gives insight into the different levels of encounters of the tourist kind.

Culinary tourism in Zeeland is used as an example in this chapter. Zeeland is one of the 12 provinces in the southwest of the Netherlands. The example of culinary tourism is chosen because Zeeland's identity is partly based on its fishery and agriculture from the past and the present and therefore, produces a lot of seafood and regional products from the land. According to several authors (Hjalager & Richards, 2002; Hall, Sharples, Mitchell, Macionis, & Cambourne, 2003; WTO, 2003), there is a very close relation between gastronomy and local, regional, and national identities. This part of Zeeland's identity, and the tourist product development based on it, is the outcome of a photo survey (de Kam & Lieberom, 2003), and two extensive surveys on Zeeland's identity and image by the Tourist Office Zeeland (van Keken 2004, 2005) which were carried out in the quest for Zeeland's identity.

The building of a gastronomous community, a culinary festival 'The Taste of Zeeland (in Dutch 'de Smaek van Zeêland'),' a culinary guide and a marketing campaign around it, together with the policy of the province of Zeeland on fishery, agriculture, and tourism, proves how the identity of a region can be constructed. The goal of this identity construction is to create unique experiences for both hosts and guests in terms of virtual and physical contact and encounters, and hopefully, good relations between the community of Zeeland and tourists.

Globalization, Localization and Food

Contemporary globalization 'refers both to the compression of the world and to the intensification of the consciousness of the world as a whole' (Robertson, 1992, in Hall & Mitchell, 2002). Place and distance do not matter anymore (Knoke, 1997); almost everything is available everywhere for nearly everybody (at least from a Western point of view). Virtually every nation and the lives of billions of people throughout the world are being transformed, often quite dramatically, by globalization (Ritzer, 2004).

Economic globalization draws most of the attention, but the social and cultural aspects of globalization have a great impact as well. A consequence of globalization is the increase in human interaction worldwide. People meet each other more and more by traveling all over the world, as also virtually. But this human interaction changes in character. Castells (2000) remarks that globalization leads to increasing social fragmentation and differentiation. People live more next to each other than with each other. Everybody creates his own life, there are endless choices to be made. It all leads to extreme individualization, loneliness, social differentiation; family life and club life are under pressure. As Putnam (de Waal, 2002) says in an interview: we rather look at the TV program 'Friends' than actually making friends. Like Giddens (1990) and Baumann (1997, in

Richards, 2002) argue that the modern condition is characterized by an increasing level of social and personal insecurity. With the disintegration of established structures of meaning, people are searching for new sources of identity that provide some security in an increasingly turbulent world.

These are altogether rather pessimistic statements and conclusions. And yes, of course the nature of contact has changed drastically. Roughly speaking, from the Middle Ages till the seventies of the 20th century in our Western world people used to meet in the market-place, streets, pubs, churches, and clubs. People still do, but the character of the contact has changed. Another example of these modern times explains it as well: road infrastructure is not constructed on connecting cities and the communities that live there. They are constructed for traveling, for the transfer, not for meetings (Rademaker, 2003).

Individualization did and does change a lot. But the inclination to meet each other is of all times. Especially ICT and internet have changed the way it happened, happens and will happen drastically. Nowadays we can speak of virtual encounters or relations. The question is: what could be the role of tourism in this respect? From both the perspectives of post-modern societal and contemporary tourism, Urry advocates that tourism is no longer a differentiated set of social activities with its own set of rules, times, and spaces... . It has effectively become part of a broader 'culture' ... with no clear cut directions (Urry, 1996). So tourism is everywhere, part of our daily lives, it has become an integrated part of our culture, but it is also an area where people can meet and relate. Another aspect that is often closely connected with globalization, and cannot be forgotten because of the culinary example in this paper, is that of the McDonaldization of society. McDonalidization of society 'is the process by which the principles of the fast-food restaurant are coming to dominate more and more sectors of American society as well as those of the rest of the world'. According to Ritzer (1998) five themes have standardizing impacts: efficiency, calculability, predictability, increased control, and the replacement of humans by nonhuman technology. Globalization, homogenization, and standardizing impacts on gastronomy are of course visible in fast-food chains such as McDonalds, Burger King, Kentucky Fried Chicken, Pizza Hut, etc. McDonalds for example has, because of the cultural differences, adapted their products to national traditions and taste, such as the 'McKroket' in Holland, the 'McKebab' Burger in India, and the 'Teriyaki Burger' in Japan (www.mcdonalds.com/countries). It is also visible in standardized national and regional dishes/recipes such as paella, sushi, French fries, Wiener schnitzel, spaghetti, etc., which are available almost worldwide. Originally they come from specific countries or regions, but are no longer strongly connected with the Spanish, Japanese, French, Austrian, or Italian culture, their values and meanings.

The notion of 'fast' in fast food deserves also extra attention in this context because it is often connected with modern (Western) life, that is, young, dynamic. Everything has to happen 'fast'. Although, a reversed trend in this respect can be seen by people who worry about all this speed and ask for reflection, destressing, slowing down. An often-brought-up example is the Slow Food Movement that started in Italy in 1989 that puts taste first, and also has started the movement 'Slow Cities'. Slow food stands for traditional, original, delightful, diversity and quietness and is of course the opposite of the fast world. The goal of the slow food movement is to rediscover the richness and taste of the local kitchen and fight against standardization. According to Carl Honoré (2004) this slow food movement is part of a bigger movement that propagates slowness in all parts of our daily lives. In his book 'In praise of Slow, how a worldwide movement is challenging the Cult of Speed' he describes how in our Western world there is a growing dissatisfaction with our way of life, the 24-hour economy. In his worldwide search for signs of slowness Honoré found a lot of proof of people, organizations and projects where one tries to slow down the speed of life so as to find a balance and enjoyment. Slow food is a counterbalance to what a French sociologist Fischler calls 'gastro anomy' (Beardsworth & Keil, 1997) referring to massiveness of food supplies, the abundance of food and has nothing to do with meat products, technologization of food or the publicity overload for consumers. Food has always been an integral part of tourism but has not received much attention until recently (Hjalager & Richards, 2002; Hall et al., 2003; Quan & Wang, 2004; Cohen & Avieli, 2004). Cohen and Avieli (2004) consider it even curious that the most bodily of the senses, taste, and more specifically eating and drinking, remained virtually unexplored in the sociological and anthropological study of tourism, notwithstanding their obvious centrality in the experience. In 1989 Jacques (in Hall & Mitchel, 2002, p. 82) observed already that there is a new search for identity and difference in the face of impersonal global forces, which is leading to the emergence of new national and ethnic demands. Tourism is a part of the search for identity and a desire for economic positioning in contemporary globalization. Tourism and food provides identity in terms of provision of the 'other' and in terms of self-reference.

Close Encounters of the Tourist Kind

At the end of the movie 'Close encounters of the third kind' (1977), directed by Steven Spielberg, Roy Neary (Richard Dreyfuss), one of the main characters, witnesses with a group of people the landing of huge flying saucer. The spaceship opens and a few people, pilots, who have been missing for years, step down the ramp. A few moments later aliens step down and for the first time in history contact is made between mankind and aliens. A few moments later the aliens invite Roy Neary to go with them on a journey in the spaceship to the final frontier: space. He does so because he is interested in who they are, where they come from, and how they live. The title of the movie 'Close encounter of the third kind' refers to the contact there is between humans and aliens, 'hosts' and 'guests'. Although humans could be seen as the hosts because they receive the spaceship, and the aliens as guests because they visit the earth, the roles of host and guest change when Roy Neary decides to go on a journey and enters the spaceship. He wants to make contact with the unknown, the otherness from outer space, with the aliens. So curiosity, interest in the other, is the motivation for his entering of the ship and leaving everything behind. The contact is therefore mutual. If the third kind refers to contact between humans and aliens, the question remains what close encounters of the first and the second kind stand for. A close encounter of the first kind refers to sighting of an unidentified flying object (UFO) and close encounter of the second kind refers to seeing physical evidence of an alien landing. In this chapter 'Close encounters' we want to make a comparison between this movie and several kinds of tourism and the level of contact between hosts and guests. There is a lot of tourism with encounters of the first and second kind. For instance tourism where people stay mostly in their tourist areas, have a glimpse of their surroundings and its culture, only go sightseeing and see physical evidence of another culture, environment, such as landscapes, forests, monuments, towns, etc. Tourism that most of the time lacks contact between hosts and guests. We can compare this with Cohen's 'environmental bubble', where tourists take shelter, needing a degree of familiarity, although they seem to travel in quest of novelty and strangeness (Cohen & Avieli, 2004). The question with this kind of tourism is whether it is sustainable and pays respect to its habitants, culture, heritage and stories.

Close encounters of the third kind in tourism has obviously more to do with contact between hosts and guests and their mutual interests. And it could go even further, as encounters between hosts and guests could be turned into good relations, so that tourism could become more sustainable and respectful. What are the main differences between encounters and relationships? Relationships occur when a customer has repeated contact with a particular provider. Encounters, in contrast to relationships, typically consist of a single interaction between the customer and the provider, and they are typically fleeting rather than lengthy (Gutek, 1995). According to Gutek the essential differences between encounters and relationships result from three issues: (1) whether or not the provider and customer have developed a shared history of interaction, (2) whether or not the provider and customer anticipate interacting again in the future, and (3) whether or not all providers can be considered functionally equivalent. This distinction is important because:

- it affects the experience of both customers and providers;
- it gives insights into organizations, customer and provider satisfaction, efficiency, and effectiveness;
- encounters appear to be more like market transactions than relationships do; then relationships handle more about caring and loyalty into a transaction (Gutek, 1995).

The point the authors want to make here is that tourist destinations are better off with relationships than with encounters. Tourists who develop relationships with a destination and its service providers, develop a shared history of interaction, so that they may return more often. The possibility for caring, being loyal to a destination, its history, its identity are higher, but very hard to achieve. Therefore, perhaps the best one can hope for in the peripheral regions is a blend of encounters and relations, which through their intensity and sincerity, enable to elicit a sensation of 'a close encounter', which Gutek (1995) refers to as 'pseudo-relationship' and which we call 'close encounters of the third kind'.

The questions put forward in this paper are how contact, encounters, and relations between hosts and guests can be central again and used in the world of material, information, mental, and social space (Go & Fennema, 2003). The identity of a country, region, city, or place can be used to enforce contact, encounters, and relations, because our society has turned into a globalized, uniformed, insecure, and rationalized world. This identity has to be used in positioning the destination in a virtual way, for instance through the internet by giving information (information space see Figure 4.1) so that encounters could be elicited. Connecting people around diverse interests (communities; mental space) like activities such as surfing, nature or heritage can lead to encounters with others. But the purpose is that virtual encounters turn into physical visits to the presented destination (material space). When relations arise (social space) targets have been met. But starting a relation is a first step, maintaining this relation is the second. Marketing and promotion, but especially customer relations marketing, is a very good tool for both Destination

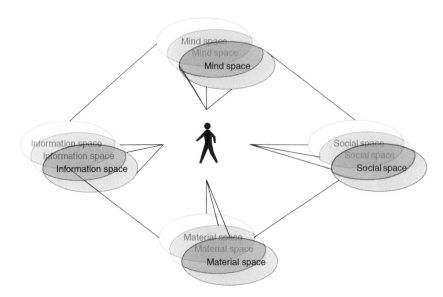

Figure 4.1: Polyinclusion (Go & Fennema, 2003).

Marketing Organizations (DMOs) and tourist companies to bond with their customers and retain them. (Culinary) events are a means of help in this case. Close encounters of the first and second tourist kinds refrain most of the time from contact between host and guest, and shared interaction with the tourist destination and guests are therefore less likely to return, we presume. So the mission could be to develop stimuli in the form of diverse tourist products to make people susceptible for the identity of a region, interaction, and communication so that they might become interested and come back.

The Quest for the Identity of Zeeland

Zeeland (not to be mistaken with New Zealand), one of the 12 Dutch provinces, is known as a holiday province. Originally it was a province of several islands, but nowadays they are connected by the famous Delta works, dikes, bridges, tunnels, and reclaimed land. One third is water and the region would like to be known as the blue-green oasis in the area. Densely populated areas such as the 'Randstad' (Amsterdam, Rotterdam, The Hague), the province Brabant (Breda, Tilburg, Den Bosch, Eindhoven), the German Ruhr area, cities of Belgium such as Antwerp, Gent, Bruges, Ile de France, and London area surround Zeeland as an urbanized circle. With only 370,000 inhabitants it is one of the thinly populated provinces of the Netherlands. In the seventies, eighties, and nineties when competition was not as tough as today, Zeeland was known within Holland and Germany as a sun, sea, and sand destination. But awareness has grown that Zeeland is more than just a coast. Its history for instance is rich, at the end of the Middle Ages, Zeeland, together with Amsterdam, was the center of worldwide trade, referred to as the VOC period. Cities such as Middelburg, Goes,

Zierikzee, Hulst, and Sluis carry the heritage from ancient times with their historical atmosphere of thousands of monuments. Another example is the space, the scenery, the landscapes, and the hinterland, which are pure, authentic, and untouched by urbanization. But tourists do not come as easily as they did in the seventies and the eighties when traffic-jams and rows could be seen near tourist accommodations. Put exaggeratedly: in the early days tourists used to come to Zeeland to stay for two or three weeks for (hopefully) sun, sea, and beach. But the consumer of today has a world of destinations to choose from, prices to compare, not in the least on behalf of internet. The question that was put central in search of Zeeland's tourist future, because there was a mismatch between its identity and image, was 'what is Zeeland's identity and from a tourist point of view what can be done with it?'

Methodology

Identity is a dynamic and if ill-defined, amorphous concept. This assumption formed the foundation for a survey that combined photographs and interviews to gain insight into the identity of Zeeland. Twelve experts, well-known photographers in Zeeland, were asked to look for three photographs of Zeeland. They had to choose photographs out of their collection, which in their opinion rendered Zeeland its distinctive uniqueness. Zeeland is a region made up of peninsulas, as opposed to a contiguous landmass, each with its own characteristic identity. The professional (landscape) photographers from six different islands/areas were asked to identify two distinctive photographs from their collection that best represented their home area and one photograph that captured best the distinctiveness of the Province of Zeeland as a tourist destination. Altogether 36 photographs were collected. These 36 photographs were presented to 90 inhabitants of Zeeland: 30 general entrepreneurs, 30 tourist entrepreneurs, and 30 'ordinary' citizens. This was done because it might appear that one group, because of their daily occupation, would choose different photographs than the others. These 90 respondents were asked to make a top 12 of photographs that they thought were the most distinctive for Zeeland and also to make a top 12 of photographs that were the least distinct. Using the method of multidimensional scaling we found two dimensions by which the inhabitants judged if the photographs were distinctive or not: 'coast versus hinterland and inland water' and 'closeness and cosiness versus looking endlessly'. But this analysis was not enough to discover Zeeland's distinctiveness. The interviews with the residents of Zeeland had to help with that.

A total of 90 interviews led to 26 basic characteristics which were perceptible and material, and classified into two main categories: sea/water and land (Zeeland means SeaLand). The purpose of the interviews was to use photographs of Zeeland as perceptual stimulation and encourage people to interpret and elaborate on the elements in the pictures that made Zeeland distinctive. Upon completion of the research study in all 12 'statements' by respondents were constructed that give an indication of perceived spheres, feelings, and values with regard to Zeeland's identity (de Kam & Lieberom, 2002).

1. The coastal feeling of sea and beach
2. The inspiration of Zeeland's light and skies
3. Battle against the water

4. Small cities and villages at the coast
5. Water(sport) area
6. Fishery and seafood
7. Polder prospects
8. The agrarian hinterland
9. Salt marshes and creeks
10. Folklore and nostalgia
11. The intimacy of the hinterland
12. Monumental Zeeland

Knowing more of Zeeland's identity is not enough for positioning Zeeland as a distinct tourist destination. In the last two years further research has been carried out on both the supply and the demand sides. On the supply side, the host community was put central, because the construction, imagination, and experience of identities have a significant and compelling relationship with tourism decision-making. In May and June 2004, 5162 residents of Zeeland participated in a 25-minute survey on Zeeland's identity. One of the questions was to choose three photographs out of 12, based on the 12 statements, to represent their region. In May 2005, a survey on the demand side was carried out and the same question was asked to 2306 tourists (392 Dutch, 771 Belgians, and 1143 Germans).

The residents of Zeeland ranked 'the coastal feeling of sea and beach' as number one and so did the Dutch, the Belgian, and the German tourists. The residents ranked 'polder prospects' at the second place, 'battle against the water' third, 'the intimacy of the hinterland' fourth, 'the inspiration of Zeeland's light and skies' fifth, and 'fishery and seafood' sixth. Dutch tourists ranked 'battle against the water' at the second place and 'fishery and seafood' third. Belgian and German tourists put 'fishery and seafood' both at the second place. The Belgians put small cities and villages at the coast' on the third place, whereas the Germans put the inspiration of Zeeland's light and skies'. The results show that both from the supply and the demand sides 'fishery and seafood', has a prominent place in either the residents' or the tourists' choice.

The photographs were also used to elicit both the residents' and tourists' feelings when they looked at the photographs. Both the results of the choice for photograph images and spheres, together with the accompanied feelings, will be used in positioning and developing a branding strategy for Zeeland. It is beyond the scope of this chapter to go into further details of this project.

Food and Identity: Culinary Tourism in Zeeland

As global competition between tourist destinations increases the search for distinct products becomes more intense. Gastronomy is seen as an important source of marketable images and experiences for the tourists (Richards, 2002, p. 4). Richards emphasizes that food has become an important factor in the search for identity. Food is one of our basic needs, so it is not surprising that it is also one of the most widespread markers of identity. We are what we eat, not just in a physiological sense, but also in psychological and sociological sense as well. Food has been used as a means of forging and supporting identities, principally because what we eat and the way we eat are such basic aspects of our culture (Richards, 2002,p. 5). Especially when the names of a particular place or region have been put together with the products, eating the products is like experiencing its sense of place, especially when it is done at the tourist destination itself. Experimental marketing in all senses. Zeeland, for example, has mussels from Zeeland, lobster from the Oosterschelde, eel from the Lake of Veere, oysters from Zeeland, black currants from Zuid-Beveland, cheese from Schellach etc. Hughes (1995, in Richards, 2002) points out that there is a notion of a natural relationship between a region's land, its climatic conditions, and the character of food it produces. It is this geographical diversity which provides for the regional distinctiveness in culinary traditions and the evolution of a characteristic heritage. The name of Zeeland comes from two words 'Sea' and 'Land'. The regional produce of Zeeland are seafood and products from the land.

In search for unique experiences for emphasizing Zeeland's identity, the 'Tourist Office Zeeland' organized in the year 2000 (and in 2005 for the sixth time) a culinary festival 'de Smaek van Zeêland' (The Taste of Zeeland). The title was purposely put in Zeeland's dialect. The culinary event was organized in the square of Middelburg's Abbey, which makes it altogether a unique medieval sphere. Culinary events are held these days everywhere in the Netherlands, but culinary events based only on regional products are rare. To make the culinary event more experience-like, cooks prepare the food in an open kitchen while being interviewed by a professional fellow-cook live before an audience. Twenty restaurants participate in the event, almost 20 regional product farmers and sellers and several volunteers. Along with the restaurants where the public can enjoy the regional dishes and regional music, a culinary market with regional products is also organized on the square. Thoughts behind the event are: to enhance regional/local awareness; to create unique Zeeland experiences; to create opportunities for meetings between locals and tourists; to promote Zeeland's gastronomy; to stimulate cooperation and partnership to stimulate innovation.

Marketing the Taste of Zeeland

As years have gone by the marketing of the culinary tourism in Zeeland has proved its success already by the usual marketing tools, like the festival magazine, ads, magazines, tv and radio, press lunches, free publicity and the use of internet. Although one problem is that success is not lasting and is restricted to encounters whereas relations are not created. The success of the festival, which is already there, does not add enough to the (culinary) positioning of Zeeland in the long run. The focus on culinary aspects was enlarged by focusing on cultural aspects as well. The lustrum celebration in 2004 was extraordinary because of a fashion show, where a mix was made with elderly people in their traditional folk costumes and young people showing their designs based on these traditional folk costumes on a catwalk with mussel shells. The mix was also made with a combination of a modern deejay and a choir with old traditional songs about the sea. But for the future new plans have to be made around the identity of Zeeland. An integral marketing and promotion plan has been made. Who are the target groups in the Netherlands, Belgium, and Germany? What are their preferences? How can we 'touch' them with the culinary charm of Zeeland? A more prominent place should be created for the internet. Not brochure-like, which is often still the case in the Tourist Office branch, but as a community site where hosts and guests meet and share their passion and love for Zeeland. The site must be a place to gain information and to get involved in digital stories, to get ideas for visits, stays in restaurants and hotels, ideas to go to culinary events, rural attractions with regional products, stories on cultural heritage, regional cuisine. In short, it should be the possibility of sharing experiences. Thinking has to be done on interactivity, on how relations can be created, getting to know their preferences and interests. How it can be used in for example database marketing? Altogether a culinary community will be built around 'The Taste of Zeeland' as a brand. Ideally, tourism sites should provide an integrated experience: where food is on the main stage heritage should be exploited, and where heritage is the priority, food and culture should be seen as an essential facet (van Westering, Poria, & Liapis, 2000).

Close Encounters of the Tourist Kind

The survey on Zeeland's identity gives a basis for the chosen direction of tourist product development. Two statements put together: 'Fishery and seafood' and 'The agrarian hinterland' give an excellent opportunity for Zeeland's unique and distinct positioning and creating experiences for the inhabitants of Zeeland as well as for the tourists. Touches of other statements such as 'folklore and nostalgia' with people in folk costumes and 'the intimacy of the hinterland' by not attracting mass tourism create altogether a unique event. The taste of Zeeland is a good example where tourists as guests and Zeeland's residents as hosts, do meet Zeeland's culture and each other as well. According to Figure 4.1 this means that 'virtual encounters' should rouse expectations in guests (information, digital stories — the World Wide Web, and mind space — culinary community), so that physical visits are the result and in the end (pseudo-) relations (material space — visits); satisfied guests who love to return to Zeeland for gastronomic experiences (social space — relations) and have a shared history of interaction with their hosts, as meant by Gutek. The experiences at the Abbey have to be unique, nice, personal, and theatrical in various ways like Pine and Gilmore advise in their book 'The experience-economy' (2000) and Wolf in his 'The entertainment economy' (1999). All actors, a network of companies, restaurants and accommodations, organizations, people, volunteers, and important 'software', are crucial in creating the Taste of Zeeland and positioning Zeeland as a gastronomic region. Important in this regard is the possible or experienced hospitality which can be described as a contemporaneous human exchange that is voluntarily entered into and designed to enhance the mutual well-being of the parties concerned through the provision of accommodation, and/or food and drink (Brotherton, 1999, in Santich, 2004).

Two aspects are important here: 'the human exchange' and the 'mutual well-being of the parties'. But a very important aspect, which is missing in this definition, is that the provision is only focusing on material things such as accommodation, food, and drink. Just as important, or even more important than the material things, are the immaterial things, such as the atmosphere, authenticity, constructed identity, surroundings, warmth, love, and the attention that creates well-being and is an integral part of the human exchange. It is this push that enables people to come out of their 'environmental bubble' and opens the possibility of a 'close encounter of the tourist and third kind'. Too often these close encounters of the third kind are missing. Culinary events, where both residents and tourists sit next to each other, create excellent opportunities for (pseudo-)encounters and relations in the long term as also shared experiences.

Here people eat their meals, get to know each other, and their culture and share thoughts. A culinary event like 'The Taste of Zeeland' can be seen as a demonstration of the host community's sense of self and sense of place, providing a unique and authentic experience.

Conclusions

The described research methods to discover step by step what both the residents of Zeeland and the tourists perceive as Zeeland's identity is a good starting point for constructing and deconstructing old and new identities.

As globalization, homogenization, and standardization impacts and fast food continue to conquer the world, another trend is visible in regionalism, uniqueness, authenticity, and slow food. Culinary tourism is strongly connected with a region's identity and is an excellent opportunity to construct these new identities. Zeeland, a peripheral region in the Netherlands, is using culinary tourism in it is destination marketing. Culinary festivals are in the globalized world a good opportunity to construct and enhance a regional identity. Festivals can be used to represent the host community's sense of self and sense of place as Derret (2004) suggested. The festivals can be used to create close encounters of the tourist and third kind, by creating opportunities to meet and have a shared history of interaction as meant by Gutek (1995). Contacts and encounters can be constructed in the information space (internet) where a pretaste might be given, leading to a physical visit with a real taste. The festivals can be used as a tool to get tourists out of their environmental bubble and to get acquainted with the host, their culture, their heritage, their stories, and gastronomy. Sharing these experiences between hosts and guests might lead to a shared passion and love for the tourist destination. This might lead to a culinary and cultural community in the information space and social space, with a mix of encounters and (pseudo-)relations.

References

Beardsworth, A., & Keil, T. (1997). *Sociology on the menu: An invitation to the study of food and society*. London: Routledge.

Castells, M. (2000). *The rise of the network society* (Vol. I). Oxford: Blackwell Publishers.

Cohen, E., & Avieli, N. (2004). Food in tourism, attraction and impediment. *Annals of Tourism Research, 31*(4), 755–778.

Derrets, R. (2004). Festivals, events and the destination. In: I. Yeoman, M. Robertson, J. Ali-Knight, S. Drummond, & U. McMahon-Beattie (Eds), *Festival and events management: An international arts and culture perspective*. Oxford: Elsevier/Butterworth-Heinemann.

Go, F. M., & van Fennema, P. C. (2003). *Moving bodies and connecting minds in space: It is a matter of mind over matter*. Paper EGOS conference, Copenhagen.

Gutek, B. (1995). *The dynamics of service, reflections on the changing nature of customer/provider interactions*. San Francisco: Jossey-Bass Publishers.

Hall, M., & Mitchell, R. (2002). Tourism as a force for gastronomic globalization and localization. In: A. Hjalager, & G. Richards (Eds), *Tourism and gastronomy*. London/New York: Routledge.

Hall, M., Sharples, L., Mitchell, R., Macionis, N., & Cambourne, B. (2003). *Food tourism around the world, development, management and markets*. Oxford: Butterworth-Heinemann.

Hjalager, A., & Richards, G. (2002). *Tourism and gastronomy*. London/New York: Routledge.

Honoré, C. (2004). *In praise of slow, how a worldwide movement is challenging the cult of speed*. London: Orion.

Kam, M. de, & Lieberom, M. (2003). *Op zijn elf en dertigst, een wetenschappelijk Onderzoek naar de (toeristische) Identiteit van Zeeland en de Communicatie van het toerisme in Zeeland, doctoraalscriptie*. Middelburg: Bureau voor Toerisme Zeeland.

Keken, G. van. (2004). *Zeêland om groôs op te wezen en om van te 'ouwen'*. Middelburg: Bureau voor Toerisme Zeeland.

Keken, G. van. (2005). *Het Beeld van Zeeland, een Studie naar het Imago van Zeeland onder Nederlanders, Vlamingen en Duitsers*. Middelburg: Bureau voor Toerisme Zeeland.

Knoke, W. (1997). *Plaatsloze nieuwe Wereld*. Schiedam: Scriptum.

Pine, B. J., & Gilmore, J. H. (2000). *De Beleveniseconomie*. Schoonhoven: Academic Service.

Quan, S., & Wang, N. (2004). Towards a structural model of the tourist experience: An illustration from food experiences in tourism. *Tourism Management, 25*, 297–305.

Rademaker, L. (2003). *Filosofie van de vrije Tijd*. Budel, The Netherlands: Damon.

Richards, G. (2002). Gastronomy: An essential ingredient in tourism production and consumption. In: A. Hjalager, & G. Richards (Eds), *Tourism and gastronomy*. London/New York: Routledge.

Ritzer, G. (1998). *The McDonaldization thesis*. London: Sage Publications.

Ritzer, G. (2004). *The globalization of nothing*. London: Thousand Oaks.

Santich, B. (2004). The study of gastronomy and its relevance to hospitality education and training. *Hospitality Management, 23*, 15–24.

Urry, J. (1996). *Consuming places*. London: Routledge.

Waal, M. de (2002). We kijken liever naar 'friends', dan dat we zelf vrienden maken. In Intermediair, 49, 5 December.

Westering, J., van, Poria, Y., & Liapis, N. (2000). Promoting the links between food and heritage as a resource for tourism: The integration of food and heritage through story telling. In *Local food & tourism, WTO-International Conference*. Cyprus, November 2000.

Wolf, M. (1999). *The entertainment economy. How mega-media forces are transforming our lives*. New York: Random House.

WTO. (2003). Local food and tourism, International Conference, Madrid: WTO. www.mcdonalds/countries

Chapter 5

The Ghost Host Community in the Evolution of Travel Law in World Trade Contexts: A Pragmatic Cosmopolitan Perspective

James Tunney

Context and Approach to the Reflexive Relationship of Law and Tourism

Introduction: The Knowledge Challenge to the Law and Tourism Relationship

The analysis of tourism clearly involves a number of disciplines and is thus likely to involve inter-disciplinary and trans-disciplinary engagement. This engagement occurs at a time of challenge to the construct of knowledge within certain disciplines and associated contexts of meaning. As elsewhere, globalisation creates a sense of dynamism; in general see, for example, Held and McGrew (2003). Such a challenge may both facilitate and distort interaction. Certain disciplines may have key contributions to make. But there is no guarantee that this will transpire. Obviously, law should be one of many parts of tourism discourse. Even if there is awareness of the need to comprehend it, there are still great issues to be addressed. Jurists will approach tourism with the benefits and weaknesses of their disciplinary approach and philosophy. Likewise, other disciplines may have set views of law, which can be mistaken, impaired or out-dated. Accordingly, there should be a necessary awareness of the relationship between law and tourism in the overall unfolding of events and forces. Ultimately the relationship is a complex, reflexive one that is prone to dynamism and where the construct of knowledge is evolving rapidly. The jurist wanting to contribute, communicate and engage in tourism discourse and those coming from other disciplines wishing to engage in such dialogue, need to be aware of both the pitfalls and the possibilities. Epistemological constructs create difficulties. For example, there is evidence that knowledge of law is assumed to be merely knowledge of rules and then an atomistic rather than an holistic approach may be taken, as jurists like Samuel (2003) argue. Many legal academics may be accused of being too insular and ignore the rich philosophical base of their own discipline. Lawyers, who do get involved in travel and tourism contexts, may be self-interested, overcautious and may magnify and exaggerate risk in a negative constraining way. This may have already happened in relation to school trips for example, where the pendulum seemed to shift from ignorance of liability to exaggerated sensitivity and may be moving somewhere in between (especially in view of recent judicial statements about voluntary assumption of risk). Nevertheless, legal awareness is operationally crucial. It is part of a philosophically pragmatic response.

At the same time, at a general level there are benefits of the philosophical approach commonly taken in law, insofar as it may be less hidebound and more open to an explorative freestyle that could cause concern in other disciplines. Ultimately, however, the fact that there are laws, legal systems, legal rules and legal institutions means that such exploration has many restraints that prevent a descent into an unduly post-modernist, and relativist intellectual tailspin. Furthermore, the undercurrents in law and legal development require an awareness of deeper constitutive forces and trends. In particular, the possibility of judicial development of legal doctrine is sometimes ignored by non-legal academics. Lawyers and legal thinkers assist in explaining and predicting (with varying degrees of success depending on the specificity or generality, certainty or uncertainty of issue) what will, may or could happen.

Travel Law?

There is also, however, a degree of flux within law that complicates analysis, prediction and easy extrapolation. For a start, the existence of a body of law called 'travel law' or 'travel and tourism law' may be (and is) contested within law. This is because the nomenclature of law is not as well established as might be supposed and is changing and also that the profession and academy are conservative, as any diachronic study thereof reveals. If the term is accepted, it is easier to accept that international or (perhaps preferably) world travel and/or tourism law exists. Those who are sceptical might reflect on the fact that there are bodies such as the *International Federation of Travel and Tourism Law Advocates,* that international bodies such as the *World Tourism Organization* (now UNWTO/OMC) employ specialists in the domain, international firms engage in it, students are taught it, books and articles are written on the topic and there are journals and refereed journals thereon. In simple terms, travel and tourism law could be used to describe the corpus of legal regulation that focuses on the travel and tourism context and relations and interests therein. In particular, such a definition would suggest the inclusion of the legal regulation of air transport, travel agents, tour operators, tour guides, package holidays, hotel law, national licensing regimes, travel and tourism regulators and the regulation of culture and heritage. Legal regulation of some of these relationships is ancient. Thus, for example, the regulation of innkeepers may be found in many legal systems such as Roman law and in many countries from ancient Greece to ancient Ireland.

But some forces of legal regulation of the relationship are more recent and increasingly significant. The legal regulation of world trade is one such domain. This also creates a challenge of nomenclature in that there are narrow existing descriptions such as 'international economic law', 'international trade law', 'international economic relations' law on the one hand, and arguments in favour of a more comprehensive re-definition along the lines of 'world trade law' perhaps. This is particularly justified when the plurality of legal sites and sources is acknowledged, in conjunction with the increase in global institutions such as the *World Trade Organization*. The nature of international travel (and international and world trade) means that it is one where international regulation is more likely. Indeed, this author argues, but not in this article, that any evolving concept of world trade law properly conceived, would inevitably have to cover any genuine idea of world travel law.

Approach or Method

Both the study of travel and tourism and its law and of the regulation of world trade involve contexts that may be regarded as 'cosmopolitan' in the sense that Beck (2000) and others mention. This means, for example, that the conceptualisation thereof should consider the inherently trans-national dimension of international travel law. Use of the terminology of cosmopolitanism could also be applied to describe a necessary and appropriate disciplinary approach. A consciously cosmopolitan approach may reveal neglected domains. Resort to cosmopolitanism will inevitably involve some reference to some of the literature. Cosmopolitanism is a particularly diverse domain of study as indicated by writers such as Vertovec and Cohen (2002). Thus, the approach taken here is one described as a 'pragmatic cosmopolitan' one, see Tunney (2005a). It can broadly be described as cosmopolitan in both a geographical and where appropriate a disciplinary sense so that a better picture of dynamic domains may be gathered. Such a picture should tend towards a broader sense of the whole, and may help to gain a sense of trend and pattern. While it is cosmopolitan, it is also however here modified by a philosophy that is pragmatic and thus looks to the work of James (1955) and others such as Morales (2004). Adopting such an approach here has led to the argument or hypothesis advanced, namely that there is a danger that the evolution of legal doctrine may be heavily biased towards models of protection of the traveller. It is submitted that a review of the forces of legal regulation of travel and tourism suggest that the local or host community may be neglected as a dominant stakeholder or perhaps paradigm of regulation. It should be noted that the article is not intended to be a comprehensive review of the legal regulation of travel and tourism, as that would require a book on its own, but is rather calculated to be more indicative. The term host (and sometimes local) community will be used to simply indicate the recipient community of tourism. Such simple definitions often invite criticism on the basis of vagueness. History shows that it seems to be easier to identify a community in order to do harm than to do benefit. In recent times, apart from examples of awareness or special provision in relation to certain national parks in the UK and in certain contexts in Costa Rica and elsewhere, the story of local communities and tourism seems to be one of loss and disadvantage, if an inappropriately planned expansion of tourism occurs.

Some Discernible Legal Approaches to Traveller and Tourism

Defining the Contexts

The legal regulation of travel and tourism is clearly based on the central relationship of the individual who is a traveller and/or tourist or a group thereof. When defined in international terms, then the crossing of a border simplifies identification. In addition, there are the providers of tourist services including agents, operators, carriers, entertainment and residential providers. Combinations of these relationships will give rise to a need for regulation in order to avoid and settle disputes. The state of origin and the host state should also be considered and in the host state, the community. While there has been growing awareness of the impact of tourism on the host community, this does not mean that it can easily be translated into legal reality through justiciable concepts that work and operate in legal contexts. Such problems have been seen in relation to the concept of 'sustainability', for example, see Tunney (2004).

There is no real evidence of a single conception of the traveller or tourist in legal discourse, apart from reasonably well-developed domains in relation to refugees or, say, in relation to indigenous people. While it might be supposed to be easy to identify the epistemological and ontological basis, it is not so. It has been indicated that approach taken will partly be a cosmopolitan one. A neglected philosophical context indicated by the discourse on cosmopolitanism itself is that provided by Kant. The Greek and Stoic context of cosmopolitanism heavily influenced Kant, as Nussbaum (1997) and others mention. There seems to be a golden thread that is traceable to the ancient world, which though obscured, indicates continuity in legal regulation of the travel and tourism context. Although some would no doubt argue that it might not be mature law or law at all, apart from special and specific contexts such as the more celebrated Roman Edict. In *Perpetual Peace,* Kant mentions particular features of his idea. It is interesting that it is the domain of hospitality towards strangers that gives rise to the most concrete identification of the concept. He writes in a famous passage that

> In this sense, hospitality means the right of a stranger not to be treated with hostility when he arrives on someone else's territory. He can indeed be turned away, if this can be done without causing his death, but he must not be treated with hostility, so long as he behaves in a peaceable manner in the place he happens to be in. The stranger cannot claim the *right of a guest* to be entertained, for this would require a special friendly agreement whereby he might become a member of the native household for a certain time. He may only claim a *right of resort,* for all man are entitled to present themselves in the society of others by virtue of their right to communal possession of the earth's surface.

And later,

> But this natural right of hospitality, i.e. the right of strangers, does not extend beyond those conditions which make it possible for them to *attempt* to enter into relations with the native inhabitants. In this way, continents distant from each other can enter into peaceful mutual relations which may eventually be regulated by public laws, thus bringing the human race nearer and nearer to its cosmopolitan constitution.

While certain Kantian ideas are seen to have become manifest and concrete and in some way arguably partly attributable to him (such as the League of Nations), his specific elucidation of the concept and context of cosmopolitan right has largely been ignored, despite its ostensible utility. This is not surprising in view of the contestable and in some ways unjustifiably fragile concept or conceptualisation of travel law.

But apart from philosophical approaches, there is revealed purpose behind legal regulation. The most coherent contemporary basis should be the dignity of the individual as mandated by the *United Nations Declaration on Human Rights,* although this may lack sufficient specificity and fail to solve the issue of conflict with the rights of another. That would also provide a basis for protection of the host community. But in reality the plurality of legal systems and regimes means that there are a number of competing rationales that come to mind in variously explicit and implicit modes. Thus there are a number of potential models for the legal promotion and protection of travellers and tourists that emerge nationally, regionally and internationally or at a global and world level. In recent times it is clear that the theoretical or policy basis of protection in law may derive from diverse bases and epistemic communities. Bases mentioned here will include the following (in no particular order):

(a) *The Warsaw Convention.* This part will adumbrate the recent development of protection of the air traveller by briefly indicating the trend of recent cases in relation to Deep Vein Thrombosis (DVT).
(b) *Competition Law/Anti-Trust.* This section will examine briefly the rationale and significance of competition law as a model for indirect protection of the traveller as consumer, with reference to recent developments in the UK.
(c) *Consumer Law.* This section will refer briefly to the protection of the traveller as consumer.
(d) *Free Movement.* This section will refer briefly to the context of free movement.
(e) *Sui Generis Travel Law.* This section will identify the rationale of *sui generis* protection of travellers through particular legislative contexts such as the *Package Travel Directive.*
(f) *Social Tourism.* This section will examine the rationale of 'social tourism' promotion and the efforts to protect the tourist through enabling legislative means.
(g) *World Heritage Law.* This section will mention the context of the legal regulation of world heritage.
(h) *'Soft Law', Codes of Ethics.* This section will assess the rationale of codes and softer law in comparison with other harder legislative or judicial approaches.

The benefit of getting a sense of the whole, however difficult, allows for observation of issues of concern as well as issues that are neglected. This piece will concentrate on what is missing. It will be argued that a review of these arguably most prominent forces in relation to the legal (or hard law) constructs operating in relation to the travel and tourism industry context indicates a general emphasis on a fairly classic notion of the idea of a vulnerable traveller, subject to one or two arguable exceptions.

The Warsaw Convention.   This *Convention* is an example of an international legal instrument. Nevertheless, it falls for local courts to interpret this in the light of other national judgments. There has been much legal debate about the origin, evolution and contemporary development of the *Warsaw Convention*. This is a *sui generis* legal regime that represents an historic compromise governing liability for damage caused to air travellers. One of the main objectives of the *Convention* was to limit liability of air carriers to that coming within the rather artificial definition of an 'accident' in relation to Article 17. While it was argued to be partly advantageous to air travellers, in recent times however, the greatest challenge has come from a number of cases based on potential liability for DVT. Knowledge of the condition is over 60 years old, as indicated by articles such as Simpson (1940). It was first noted in the context of deaths occurring after prolonged sitting in air raid shelters during the Blitz in London. Later it became associated with air travel, see Homans (1954). The 'scientific' link has been contested in some quarters and the evidence is suggested to be principally 'anecdotal'. Airlines and other international agencies are calling for increased scientific study. It is curious as to why there have been so few calls for so long. Although it was perhaps not surprising that such calls paralleled the initiation of legal actions on behalf of people who had suffered or died as a result of DVT. The *Warsaw Convention* is seen to be the protector of the airlines in this context. If this is true, then it is clear that the *Warsaw Convention* has been the cause of inertia and of the persistence (until recently) of a disregard of air-travellers' welfare on behalf of the airlines in the face of emerging evidence.

Unfortunately, some recent cases have justified the airlines inertia. If this situation is correct then it becomes clear that any arguments in favour of the persistence of the *Warsaw Convention* in its present form surely become untenable. However, there remains the possibility of a different direction being taken. In the UK, a recent case has come to a clear decision. The following conclusions indicate the basis of the decision.

> 224. The agreed factual matrix does not disclose an accident under article 17 of the Warsaw Convention. The definition of accident which is to be applied is that set out by the U.S. Supreme Court in Saks, followed here in the Court of Appeal in Morris, in Chaudhari, and approved by the House of Lords in Morris.

> 225. Article 17 does not provide a fault based theory of liability which imposes liability upon the carrier where death or injury is caused by its culpable act or omissions. Nor does a proper construction of the Warsaw Convention lead to the conclusion that it apportioned or reapportioned risks on the basis of a modern risk allocation theory. The balance of risk negotiated by the delegates between the interests of the passengers and the carriers achieves uniformity and certainty. The balance that was struck is set out in the cases of Sidhu and Morris in the House of Lords. The modern risk allocation theory is more suited to ascertaining whether a duty of care in tort exists under domestic law rather than in ascertaining the balance of risk agreed by the delegates at the Warsaw Convention of 1929. Article 17 has remained the same throughout all successive versions of the Convention.

> 226. The tests to be applied is 'a simple criterion of causation by an accident'. That is to be defined as:
> an unexpected or unusual event or happening that is external to the passenger".

227. The agreed factual matrix does not satisfy this definition. It reveals that no event or happening occurred on the flight which was not ordinary and unremarkable and involved no actions of anyone save for the passenger's reaction to that normal and unremarkable flight. There was no unexpected or unusual event or happening. A culpable act or omission by itself which does not amount to an unusual or unexpected event or happening does not come within the definition of accident.

228. The Warsaw Convention provides an exclusive cause of action and sole remedy in respect of claims against a carrier arising out of international carriage by air. The cases of Sidhu, in the House of Lords, and El Al, in the Supreme Court, establish that this is so. The different wording of article 24 in Warsaw-Hague MP4 does not alter the exclusivity of the Convention.

The judgment concluded that neither the Human Rights Act nor the European Convention on Human Rights assisted the claimant's case The House of Lords subsequently agreed on appeal.

This case, in conjunction with Canadian and German decisions, reveals the inadequacy of the *Warsaw Convention* as an effective mode of protection of the traveller and tourist, in this context. Furthermore, it could be argued that there is a causative link between the orthodox interpretation of the *Convention* and the incidence of DVT. While the *Warsaw Convention* purports to protect the air traveller, there is good evidence that the trade-off rather protects the airlines from liability for fault that would otherwise accrue. Nevertheless, pending an authoritative decision at the highest level some other jurisdictions (such as the US) were slightly reluctant to accept that the matter was settled. What a review of such cases does show is how the judiciary will analyse travel contexts and analysis is necessarily stylised and located in the existing framework of legislation, whether that is of international or national origin. However, the Conventions still has a protective sense of the traveller, however flawed it may be.

Competition law/anti-trust. Competition law is regulated at national law in many countries around the world. It is called anti-trust in the US. The EU regulates competition if there is an effect on trade between member states of anti-competitive activity. It should be noted that there is also extra-territorial effect. Thus it is regulated at a national and regional (i.e. regional legal community) level. Although there have been calls for a global or world competition or anti-trust court, it will not happen for years. While the *World Trade Organisation* regime is aimed at state's behaviour, competition law focuses on companies and other undertakings, which are often far more powerful than individual states, in economic terms. Indeed, much international trade is effectively intra-firm trade. Competition law generally covers three or four domains. It usually covers the regulation of monopolies or dominant positions. It also covers agreements, decisions, concerted practices, collusion, conspiracies and communications between undertakings. It covers mergers and permission to proceed. It may also cover state intervention in the market and state monopolies, whether in the public interest or not. The significance of competition law as a strategic force in the shaping of the global environment is probably underestimated. It is crucial in explaining and comprehending the evolution of the international airline industry, in conjunction with the *Warsaw* and *Chicago Conventions*.

Competition law does not purport to directly protect the traveller or tourist. It arguably has not even sought to protect the consumer in a direct fashion. Rather it is indirect and oblique in its approach to the protection of the consumer and as a result the traveller *qua* consumer. Nevertheless, it is a hugely significant, shaping force for protection through its pervasive influence on the entire structure of competition in which undertakings operate. The structure of the airline industry, for example, has been shaped in the EU by competition law. The industry is well aware of the role of competition law (Gregory, 1994). Provisions of EU law such as Article 81 (ex 85) and Article 82 (ex 86) have played a significant role in shaping the industries that are critical in travel and tourism such as travel agents and tour operators. To some extent, EU competition law mirrors US anti-trust law. Nevertheless, although the *Sherman Act 1890* and the *Clayton Act 1914* have close parallels in EU law, there are substantial differences. The 'market integration goal' in EU competition law is not a factor in the US, despite the role of the various states.

In the UK, apart from the context of consideration of EU law, one must also consider the national competition regime. The *Competition Act 1998* transposed substantive EC competition law concepts into national law. The *Enterprise Act 2002* was added to the national law framework. It was notable for a number of reasons. Among those reasons were the imposition of criminal liability for hard-core cartels and the enhancement of processes for the recovery of damages for anti-competitive injury. In addition, it sought to bring competition and consumer law together to a greater extent than had ever happened hitherto. From an examination of the application of EU competition law and (increasingly) national competition law, it is clear that they exert a great influence on the travel and tourism industry. *Ryanair*, for example, benefited from competition law but has been also subject to scrutiny thereby. Nevertheless, competition law systems have been in the past largely confined to mature legal systems in western, liberal democracies. Thus it is clear that the construct of the traveller to be protected is the traveller *qua* consumer, as an economic entity first and foremost. Nevertheless, the attainment of 'allocative efficiency' is the primary objective of competition law. The *Airtours* case was merely one important case, see, for example, Kokkoris (2005). Any coherent study or view of travel and tourism in European contexts should have some sense of the rationale and import of such cases and the many other cases. Such cases involve important judicial decisions that will determine how industries evolve and are thus important in comprehending and predicting. For many this is more important than some academic game whose temporary significance will quickly pass and vanish. Ultimately again, for the purposes of this argument, the individual is seen to be vulnerable to corporate action in this context also.

Consumer law.   Consumer law shares some cross over with competition law, although that cross over is often ignored. Consumer law has generally evolved at national levels but is also protected at EU level. The evolving regime of consumer protection in the context of the EU and beyond necessarily provides benefits for the traveller, also *qua* consumer. The parallel regime of protection of the '*e*-consumer' must also do so to some extent. Evolution of consumer law in the context of the harmonisation of EU law is well documented. The harmonisation process in the EU corresponds with the need to protect the consumer in the *e*-commerce context. The disposition to ensure pro-consumer dimensions of the harmonisation of the regulation of *e*-commerce, such as in relation to *Distance Selling* and *e-Commerce* may have some general, indirect benefits for the traveller as a consumer. In many ways, this is totally independent of the protection in the travel and tourism context, and in some cases explicitly kept separate. Those who argue for a unique context in relation to travel and tourism may argue that any such benefits are accidental, perhaps like the benefits associated with purchase of travel services via credit cards in the UK. This protection of the traveller *qua* consumer is legally mandated on the basis of harmonising the legal regime in EU member states, to attain free movement. Free movement provides a legal basis to achieve harmonisation of laws, to attain a common or single market and to avoid distortion thereof. Legislation in the form of directives or regulation need to have a legal base in the Treaty. The protection of the consumer, however, has been a context where harmonisation has often been 'upwards'. The consumer is generally perceived to be vulnerable and thus in the contexts where the traveller fits into the consumer law construct, it could be seen as a further example of protection of the vulnerable traveller. But there is a problem that has emerged fairly accidentally as a result of the effort to separate package travel regulation and the protection of the consumer. To avoid overlap, the *e*-commerce context and package travel were generally kept separate, with the result that paradoxically, the purchase of element of a holiday on-line may have less protection in certain cases. To follow this argument, see for example Kilbey (2005). However, there is still a sense of a vulnerable consumer, even if that does not always translate into travel law contexts, and indeed there is a case for saying that they are separate.

Free movement.   The essence of the regional legal community that is the European community and EU is based on free movement, notwithstanding the pervasive impact of EU law. For a recent review of case law, see Guyot and Dyson (2004). This has general and specific consequences. It means that shape of the regulatory context becomes clearer, insofar as there are legally enshrined rights, which will guarantee the attainment of free movement so that it is no longer an issue of cultural or political choice. Specific contexts relate to the evolution of rights. For example, in relation to free movement of persons, it has been held that a tourist is entitled to be treated equally in certain circumstances on the basis that they are receiving services which is a corollary of the obligation imposed on states to secure freedom in providing services. This was established in the Cowan case (Case 186/87) in which a tourist in Paris was mugged and initially denied compensation that would have been available were he a French citizen. Again, it is clear that the thrust of such rights is primarily framed in terms of commercial or economic rights (although they mask deeper ones). Furthermore, they establish a mechanism that guarantees non-discrimination on the grounds of nationality. This effectively entrenches the idea of the vulnerable traveller although that was not the chief *raison d'etre* of protection. As with the emphasis of this mosaic of legal contexts, the result has evolved from a range of reasons, without specific deliberation. It is difficult to conceive how study of travel and tourism in the EU would not scrutinise such contexts.

Sui Generis **Package Travel law.**   The regulation of package travel may be a national endeavour, but it has reached its most elaborate level at the EU level. Sometimes the search for the antiquity of travel law may appear as a rosy, historical remembrance. On the other hand, legislative measures such as the EU *Package Travel Directive* and the emerging case law thereon, indicate a relatively clear conceptual basis of protection of the traveller (see Downes, 1993, 1996). The suggestions of the need to move towards a European contract of air passenger's transport might be conceived as another example of *sui generis* regulation, see for example Tonner (2003). However, the protection of the traveller in the latter context might seem to be largely as a function of regulation of the transport market. It must be remembered when considering the legislative rationale of developments in the EU that there may be a range of competing motivations. Different Directorate-Generals have different competences, interests and perspectives, and pursue different policies, see Downes (1997). If travel and tourism are merely conceived as ancillary to some other function of policy, then they are unlikely to obtain the benefits associated with focused response. The contestable origins of travel law from the Middle East onwards was largely concerned with protecting the vulnerable traveller, reflected in the idea of the vulnerable traveller that underpins the *Package Travel Directive*. Its link with other regulation needs to be clarified.

Social tourism.   'Social tourism' has been regulated at national level in some countries and possibly at a regional level (insofar as the former Soviet Union may be considered a regional level of regulation). This almost peripheral force may seem to contradict the dominant paradigm of travel and tourism in some senses. Social tourism is concerned more with the rationale of traveller and tourist promotion rather than with protection. The rationale of the explicit promotion of social tourism and the efforts to protect the tourist through enabling legislative means may have fallen somewhat into disrepute with the fall of the Berlin Wall. Social tourism was often associated with socialism and socialist regimes. Nevertheless, there are many who would seek to celebrate the benefits of social tourism, despite this. Social tourism seeks to promote the social benefits of tourism above or as a complement to the economic benefits thereof. Apart from these examples, there is a long tradition of social tourism in liberal market economies. The facilitation of tourism among socially disadvantaged groups, young people, students, old people and people from polarised communities might be cited. As a rationale for the promotion of travel and tourism, the idea of social tourism is unique in having some coherent conception or construct, calculated to be instrumental in the evolution of law and policy frameworks. Perhaps what might be termed 'neo-social tourism' might reactivate some of the nobler objectives behind such policies by placing them within liberal market economy frameworks.

As a simple starting point it might be stated that (in principle) the idea of social tourism refers to a type of tourism intended to maximise the participation of groups or persons that are disadvantaged, or that would otherwise find it difficult to participate therein. It is clear that social tourism in western, liberal democracies was often philanthropic and voluntary. In turn, the philanthropic origins of social tourism often led to economic development of tourism. The evolution of commercial enterprises associated with Thomas Cook could be seen in this light. Large companies in the UK sought to provide for their workers. Examples of social tourism are cited from the 19th century in France, Austria, Spain, from the start of the 20th century in Portugal and the mid-20th century in Belgium. However, this depends on identification of what constitutes social tourism, and closer inspection of historical evidence reveals plenty more possible examples in those countries and beyond. Particular groups and associations (such as the *Family Holidays Association* in the UK) are central players in social tourism.

In some countries such as Germany, there is evidence that the term 'social tourism' has negative connotations. It is important to emphasise that any situation that involved compulsion in tourism or leisure must be distinguished from any meaningful sense of social tourism, properly understood. Internationally, organisations such as the *International Bureau of Social Tourism* provide international frameworks of support. Notwithstanding the absence of universal models, there are examples, however, of particular laws such as in France and in Belgium. There is also a social tourism tradition in Russia. As France is seen to be one of the most developed, it is unsurprising that there are more legal instruments in the form of decrees and ordinances appertaining to social tourism. In France for example there are decrees on on issues such as holiday villages (Décret, 1968) and social and family tourism organisations, (Décret, 2002) and others on 'holiday checks' and on the conditions of certain tourism activities. The Swiss *Réka Cheque* system is among the most well-known systems of facilitation of social tourism. These are dependent on private and voluntary input. As the history of a celebrated Belgian case makes clear, social tourism laws have been subject to legal challenges as well as having alienated existing tourism providers. If a law that promotes social tourism is framed in an inappropriate way, it may be subject to challenge on the basis that it represents a 'State Aid' and is therefore illegal. Such illegality derives in particular from adherence to regional legal treaties such as the EC Treaty. Nevertheless, social tourism is based on a conception of the traveller and tourist as very vulnerable and indeed so vulnerable that they could not participate in tourism without assistance.

World heritage. The regulation of access to heritage, culture and monuments is inevitably linked to travel and tourism. Travel and tourism has become one of the dominant dimensions of preservation and heritage, culture and monuments. In this context there is national regulation in most countries as well as significant world-level regulation.

World heritage law (another useful description that would be contestable by others) as manifested principally in the *World Heritage Convention*, seems to avoid the focus on the rights of host communities. Indeed, the inherent philosophy is to universalise the heritage. Paradoxically this may effectively transform the outsider, the possibly-perceived vulnerable visitor, into a privileged person at the expense of the resident, albeit as an unintended consequence. Such an approach may seem calculated to exclude the local elements that may have expected the greatest benefit from the exploitation of World Heritage Sites. Some argue that local communities have been uprooted, impoverished and treated as eyesores sometimes in the development of heritage sites. Evolution of restitution principles may re-balance the historical imbalance. Nevertheless, there are many examples of the cultural heritage of the community that owned or created it being enjoyed or exploited by the community that may have been involved in expropriation. The superior claim to retain possession by the expropriating community is merely salt in old wounds. Thus there is evidence of world heritage law favouring the visitor and not the visited. At the same time, there are many examples of national local heritage initiatives. More importantly, *UNESCO* is very involved in the evolution of policy on cultural tourism. Nevertheless, such policy has to feed into the evolution of legal frameworks, otherwise the dominant paradigms may render local community considerations effectively irrelevant.

Soft law/codes of ethics.   Codes of Ethics are sometimes classifiable as 'soft law'. This generally refers to rules that are not actually legally binding, but that may perhaps prefigure how hard law develops. The rationale of codes and softer law in comparison with other harder legislative or judicial approaches has some benefits. The *World Tourism Organization's Global Code of Ethics* has had mixed reviews. While much of it is vague and lacking in specification from a lawyer's perspective, it does have one major benefit. At least it seeks to envisage a *sui generis*, integrated idea of the traveller/tourist construct. While judges will no doubt find it vague in the event of such principles ever being used in a legalistic way, it is remarkable that there are no great codes elsewhere available to turn to. Unlike the *World Tourism Organization*, some Codes and Declarations are of dubious nature. The *WTO Code of Ethics* provides as follows:

Article 7. Right to tourism

> 1. The prospect of direct and personal access to the discovery and enjoyment of the planet's resources constitutes a right equally open to all the world's inhabitants; the increasingly extensive participation in national and international tourism should be regarded as one of the best possible expressions of the sustained growth of free time, and obstacles should not be placed in its way;

> 2. The universal right to tourism must be regarded as the corollary of the right to rest and leisure, including reasonable limitation of working hours and periodic holidays with pay, guaranteed by Article 24 of the Universal Declaration of Human Rights and Article 7.d of the International Covenant on Economic, Social and Cultural Rights;

Although the *World Tourism Organization* has made very clear that it does not want to be prescriptive and legalistic in its approach to such rights, there is no reason why the spirit of the document cannot be reflected in particular laws. The benefit of the *WTO Code of Ethics* (whatever its failings) is that it makes visible in a quasi-regulatory context, the host community. The 'other' appears.

The Context of Invisibility: The Ghost

It may be suggested therefore that the diverse range of sources of travel legislation generally betrays a clear sense of focus on the travel relationship as a commercial one, where the traveller is vulnerable and deserving of protection. This reflects an ancient sense of the vulnerable traveller. Nevertheless, leaving aside historical conquest, invasion and colonisation, the contemporary context of mass tourism as facilitated by technological, economic, political and indeed legal development, requires a consciousness of the impact on local and host communities. There is clear awareness of this impact already, but it is argued here that legal reality may require certain principles to be formulated, if some kind of equilibrium is to be obtained in a proactive rather than a reactive way. Unfortunately however, the most vulnerable hosts are often located in places of poor evolution of the rule of law or severely dysfunctional legal systems, whereas planning law and taxation, for example, may assist communities in developed countries. Thus it is arguably only in contexts of emergent 'soft law', that the vulnerable host appears. Paradoxically, with the predicted growth in Chinese and Indian tourism and with the first Chinese package holidays arriving in the UK, there may be examples of communities in developed countries being punished by their own success, should they have inadequately prepared. This could combine with existing trends towards an almost 'tourists keep out' message as emerged, for example, in some quarters of the Cotswolds in the UK. What would the reaction be if cheap travel from Eastern Europe brings stag parties to rural idylls in the UK, reversing the existing direction? It is surely pragmatic to assess the consequences of such changes on operational and policy grounds.

Thus, from a terminological perspective, if the host community is therefore in some ways invisible, it might be loosely likened to a ghost one. It could be termed a ghost host community insofar as it has 'a faint or false appearance', (Chambers, 2003). In some situations, such as where the local community is actually displaced to build a resort, then the community is a genuine ghost host community in the classic sense of 'a spirit appearing after death', (Chambers, 2003). Or similarly as in the case of tourist honey-pots like Venice, the local or original community may gradually fade away. It is not necessarily argued here that this is inherently negative, although it can be and often is, but rather that there are sound pragmatic reasons at least for avoiding or minimising this Venetian effect. Indeed in one sense, cosmopolitanism may not appear to have undue regard to 'communitarian' or local concerns, although much recent work indicates that it is entirely consistent with such a philosophy. Furthermore, as has been done by some in the International Relations (IR) context, aspects of communitarianism and cosmopolitanism can be reconciled if a pragmatic philosophical approach is taken.

While there is clearly awareness of this phenomenon, there is little evidence of engagement in the reality of the domain where solutions may also need to be constructed, i.e. in the legal domain. Bodies such as *Tourism Concern* have increased awareness of the vulnerable position of the people of the host community. They may not benefit from tourism. They may be marginalised, vilified or humiliated by travel and tourism. They may be the direct object of exploitation. Their homelands may be expropriated, their livelihoods damaged, their environment polluted. They may be threatened by unwelcome cultural practices. Their quality of life may be impaired. The great benefit provided by cheap flights may become a curse. The culture and heritage that is the very subject or object of the travel and tourism may be degraded, diminished or destroyed. Even in the EU, the exceeding of 'carrying capacity', the influx of people and capital may create more direct problems than the counterweight notion of indirect benefits will balance. While a cursory review of legal models of protection in the context of travel and tourism indicates a general focus on the vulnerable tourist, experience points to a vulnerable host community with little sources of emerging protection to draw upon. Judges have liitle occasion to draw upon conceptions of local communities. The nature of the evolution of law through cases also restricts groups rights to some extent. Although the growth of class actions in travel law should be noted. This invisible tendency may be exacerbated by the apparent trajectory of the evolution of world trade. If tourism discourse was channelled more into legal discourse, then the relative invisibility of the vulnerable host community could be avoided, cured or at least conjured. However, there is little evidence of any great degree of cross-fertilisation of studies in travel and tourism and travel law studies. There are recent studies of social adaptation to ecotourism in local communities, such as that by Hernandez Cruz et al. (2005). The role of local communities as stakeholders is being examined in work such as that of Aas, Ladkin, and Fletcher (2005). Models are also developing, such as that of Gursoy and Rutherford (2004). Such studies need to inform the evolution of models, principles and constructs that make visible and enliven the host community and its interests as a counterweight to the clear focus of the vulnerable traveller, principally from developed countries.

World Trade Regulation

Nomenclature Again

At a time of great dynamism in legal thinking, the nomenclature of subjects within law itself is in turmoil. Many would question the accuracy and scope of the term 'world trade law'. A wide definition of 'world trade law' could incorporate some of the domains mentioned above. World trade regulation may be a better one here as those who are sceptical about the very existence, viability or coherence of concepts of travel law may also reject progression to world trade law. In addition, the critics of the *World Trade Organization* are legitimately careful to downplay the possibility of the WTO regime effectively ousting non-trade Conventions and Treaties that achieve broader objectives such as environmental protection, that is seen to be peripheral and marginalised in the trading regime. Presumably the liberal market economy approach to world trade provides a ready-made rationale of traveller and tourist protection. By focusing on the dismantling of trade and tariff barriers and by ensuring market access, the argument would be that the industry and later the traveller and tourist encounters an open market whereby they benefit from enhanced competition. This model is related to the competition/anti-trust model of justification above. It has been argued that regional legal community regulation actually provides for deeper regulation than multilateral liberalising measures, particularly in the environmental context. The fuller range of considerations that may be considered at a regional (i.e. EU) level does not apply at the world trade level. Thus, as mentioned above, there is no multilateral competition framework aimed at corporations. This also allows ostensible immunity or at least perception of immunity from control in relation to international regulatory bodies. Regulatory bodies are subject to national and regional legal regulation, however. In the meantime, the framework of world trade as regulated through the *World Trade Organisation* and associated agreements is of critical importance.

The development of GATS may have profound implications for the traveller and tourist industries. Tricia Paton (2003) in her submission to the IFTTA Conference 2003 argues

> It is submitted that, having a Tourism Annex to the GATS accompanied by a regulatory discipline, a model schedule of commitments and code of best practices would bring legal certainty to the tourism services sector by building on the GATS principles of ensuring trade in services is regulated internationally through multilateral agreements. It would also allow further development of predictable, non-discriminatory and transparent trade in tourism services, as well as laying down rules which are subject to the dispute settlement mechanism of Article XXIII. This is turn would allow international trade in tourism services to increase, thereby stimulating economic growth particularly in developing Member States. At the same time if there is a more transparent and regulated international tourism services market Members will have opportunities to establish themselves directly or through a commercial presence in the territory of other Members. This opens up all markets, both in the developed countries and developing countries, to competition and provides for the development of new ideas.

There is an emerging consciousness of the potential impact of world trade rules, such as GATS on particular contexts such as sustainable tourism. Thus for example it has been argued by Bendell and Font (2004) that

> The elements of sustainable tourism standards most likely to be contentious are those that can be perceived to reduce market access (Article XVI) and not provide national treatment to foreign providers (Article XVII). Carrying capacity limits, demands for local employment and purchase of locally produced goods, and the compatibility of services with local culture — key to sustainability standards — are the most likely to be questioned by liberalization advocates and lobbyists.

The trade liberalisation approach to travel and tourism is not without difficulties. It does not seek to deal with complex and difficult issues. For example, the economic efficiency argument does not cope well with 'cultural' arguments. If the 'neo-liberal' agenda is the sole dictate of development, then it may be imbalanced. Discontent with the evolution of world trade is already deep. Indeed there is an emerging phenomenon described paradoxically as 'anti-globalisation tourism'. Discontent with world trade is widespread. Neo-liberalism and globalisation have generated a growing literature. Arguments abound in academic and popular contexts about threats to democracy from corporate activity. This may be linked to market systems and cultural context. Corporate behaviour is linked to institutions and sometimes the argument is based on the clash between people and corporate power. This democracy–corporate link is in turn linked to global institutions. For some reason, tourism has often escaped the full wrath of the anti-global movement. This is unlikely to remain the case for long. Lawyers have to be careful that the principles they craft are not divorced from *realpolitik*. Travellers and tourists have always been vulnerable. It would be remiss not to see that they may become greater targets in global games. At the same time travellers and tourists inflict social and cultural damage, and the construct of the vulnerable traveller has to be re-aligned somewhat to cater for the vulnerable host. Unlimited access, impelled by free trade principles may backfire.

An holistic approach describes an approach which looks at the 'whole' of a system and not the parts in isolation. It suggests that the system is greater than the sum of its parts. It is a useful philosophical antidote to unduly mechanistic or reductionist approaches. Judicial policy choice, whether in the framework of interpretation of international conventions, principles, regional regulation, national legislation or in the evolution of the common law would benefit from more comprehensive constructs and conceptions.

Conclusion: A Magic Lantern

This paper has argued that law and legal regulation are a crucial part of the construction of the paradigm of tourism and tourism studies. Within legal discourse, there are certain clear constructs or contexts of protection of the traveller and tourist. However, there is a lack of clear conceptual commitment to protect the host community. Law is undergoing transformation, as part of the process of globalisation in which it is reflexively involved. Evolution of world trade regulation represents a significant force in the evolution of tourism. At the same time discontent with the nature of world trade and tourism is manifest. Thus it is argued that a cosmopolitan concept of the travel and tourism continuum and the spectrum of relationships therein could lead to a more comprehensive construct. Such a comprehensive construct should accommodate the idea of the vulnerable host. Like a magic lantern, the academic can project the concept onto the legal stage, so that these important stakeholders become established in the repertory and do not appear merely as occasional stand-ins. As the world trade agenda is not going to disappear, it may be wiser to engage and alter through a positive informing agenda, than sit on the sidelines in the comfortable academic gloom.

References

Aas, C., Ladkin, A., & Fletcher, J. (2005). Stakeholder collaboration and heritage management. *Annals of Tourism Research, 32*(1), 28–48.

Beck, U. (2000). *What is globalization?* Cambridge: Polity Press.

Bendell, J., & Font, X. (2004). Which tourism rules?: Green standards and GATS. *Annals of Tourism Research, 31*(1), 139–156.

The Chambers Dictionary. (2003).

Cowan v. Le Trésor Public, Case 186/87, [1989] ECR 195, [1990] 2 CMLR 613.

Décret (1968) no. 68-476 du 25 Mai 1968. Décret relative aux villages de vacances.

Décret (2002) no 2002-624 du 25 Avril 2002. Décret relatif a l'agrément national délivré à des organismes de tourisme social et familial.

Downes, J. J. (1993). The EC package travel directive, special report for the economist intelligence unit. *Travel and Tourism Analyst*, No 2.

Downes, J. J. (1996). The package travel directive: Implications for organisers and suppliers, special report for the economist intelligence unit. *Travel and Tourism Analyst*, No. 1.

Downes, J. J. (1997). European Union progress on a common tourism sector policy, special report for economist intelligence unit. *Travel and Tourism Analyst*, No. 1.

Gregory, M. (1994). *Dirty tricks: British Airways' secret war against Virgin Atlantic*. Warner: London.

Gursoy, D., & Rutherford, D.G. (2004). Host attitudes toward tourism: An improved structural model. *Annals of Tourism Research*, *31*(3), 495–516.

Guyot, C., & Dyson, H. (2004). Review of European Union case law in the field of tourism. *International Travel Law Journal*, *4*, 199–209.

Held, D., & McGrew, A. (Eds) (2003). *The global transformations reader: An introduction to the globalization debate*. Cambridge: Polity.

Hernandez Cruz, R. E., Baltazar, E. B., Montoya Gomez, G., & Estrada Lugo, E. I (2005). Social adaptation ecotourism in the Lacandon forest. *Annals of Tourism Research*, *32*(3), 610–627.

Homans, J. (1954). Thrombosis of the deep leg veins due to prolonged sitting. *N. Engl. J. Med*, *250*(4), 148–149.

James, W. (1955). *Pragmatism and four essays from the meaning of truth*. New York: Meridian.

Kilbey, I. (2005). Consumer protection evaded via the internet. *European Law Review*, *30*(1), 123–132.

Kokkoris, I. (2005). The reform of the European merger control regulation in the aftermath of the airtours case—The eagerly expected debate SLC v Dominance test. *European Competition Law Review*, *26*(1), 37–47.

Morales, A. (Ed.) (2004). *Renascent pragmatism: Studies in law and social science*. Aldershot: Ashgate.

Nussbaum, M. (1997). *Cultivating humanity: A classical defence of reform in liberal education*. Cambridge: Harvard University Press.

Paton, T. (2003). The impact of the GATS on the provision of international travel and tourism services. Monaco: IFFTA Congress.

Samuel, G. (2003). *Epistemology and method in law*. Aldershot: Ashgate.

Simpson, K. (1940). Shelter deaths from pulmonary embolism. *Lancet 2*, 744.

Tonner, K. (2003). Towards a contract of air passengers transport. *IFTTA Journal of Travel and Tourism Law*, *Summer*, 70–75.

Tunney, J. (2004). The WTO and sustainability after Doha. In: J. Barry, B. Baxter, & R. Dunphy (Eds), *Europe, globalization and sustainable development*. London: Routledge.

Tunney, J. (2005a). A pragmatic cosmopolitan approach to communications technology (CT) in world trade (WT) contexts? *BILETA Annual Conference Proceedings*.

Vertovec, S., & Cohen, R. (2002). Conceiving cosmopolitanism: Theory context and practice. Oxford: Oxford University Press.

Chapter 6

Cultural Identities in a Globalizing World: Conditions for Sustainability of Intercultural Tourism

Johan van Rekom and Frank Go

Introduction

Non-ordinary experiences form the essence of tourism (Jafari & Gardner, 1991). For Western tourists, non-ordinary settings by excellence are provided by cultures, which are markedly different from their own. Traditional Maya farmers in their colourful dresses form an important attraction for visitors to the southern Mexico city of San Cristóbal de las Casas (van den Berghe, 1995). The hill tribes in Northern Thailand attract many foreign tourists to that area (Cohen, 1989). During the 1890s, the traditional dresses of Volendam and Hindelopen, both located in the Netherlands, were successfully exploited by local entrepreneurs (Benjamin, 1992; Koning & Koning, 2002). The effects of these entrepreneurial actions are evident in several other geographical contexts.

On the other hand, streams of tourists, and of foreign entrepreneurs coming with them, do not leave the local culture untouched (Salazar, 2005). More specifically, Western culture, with its urge for efficiency and emphasis on material consumption may influence, humiliate or even absorb the local culture. Social processes can affect the well-being of the locals (Stonich, Sorensen, & Hundt, 1995), and if local identity disappears, the very raison d'être of the tourist stream may vanish in the end. It raises the issue, what responses are available to potentially destructive and unsustainable consumption of peoples, histories and cultures.

Whether globalization will succeed and consequently lead to the disintegration of the local identity of a tourist destination depends on how the local community assesses itself in terms of values. In such assessment community members will typically compare the relative status of their local group identity with status of 'outsiders' who represent the global identity. If within this context the locals perceive themselves as having the highest status, the local identity is likely to resist globalization. This should also be the case, if the social structure prevents members of a low-status local community from switching to a global higher status group or when circumstances arise that allow the local community to detect an opportunity to improve their group status.

Globalization can be defined as "the linking together throughout the world by distance-abolishing technologies of cultural, political and economic events" (Gray, 1998). It creates networks that cut across national boundaries and enable processes in which consumers, firms and governments are increasingly interconnected through a variety of flows, including media, travel, information and communication technology, services and goods, often within 'global market segments that consume global brands'. In contrast, 'localization is about preserving a sense of identity, home, and community' (Arnould, Price, & Zinkhan, 2003, p. 33). Anti-globalists argue that globalization has "de-constructed" both the nation-state and the old metaphysics of presence, thereby creating an altogether new apparatus of (in)security (Featherstone, Lash, & Robertson, 1995). Furthermore, that it leads to cultural homogenization and the prevalence of a global—in practice Western—consumer culture in which 'everything (good, service, image, idea and experience) is evaluated in terms of its market value' (Arnould et al., 2003, p. 102) and ultimately the disintegration of the local culture (Go, Lee, & Russo, 2003).

The development of tourism is not necessarily accompanied by the aforementioned negative consequences. Exactly the confrontation with tourists and awareness of the former's visitation motives, may enhance both the cultural identity and the well-being of members of a local culture (cf., van den Berghe, 1995). Even more so, it can be doubted whether, for instance, the small Dutch town of Volendam would have maintained its own identity so clearly without the tourists streams which remind the inhabitants continuously of their special character. The crucial question, addressed in this paper, is under what conditions the local identity tends to either disintegrate under the pressure of globalization or be sustained by intercultural tourism.

Some basic questions have to be answered before we can address the issue properly. Firstly, clarification of the terminology is required. The word 'identity' is rather a chameleon term used with many different connotations. Secondly, the process by which a more global identity can absorb and "globalize" another identity, needs to be investigated. Such issues will be addressed using the social identity theory. The framework that is developed in this paper helps to predict the proneness of local identity to vanish, at least within the context of selected local cases. Furthermore, it also helps explain why some cultures appear more resistant to globalization than other local cultures that have succumbed to the Western consumer culture. Lastly, a defined local identity can serve as a foundation for establishing a coherent approach to improving a local culture's economy.

Figure 6.1 visualizes the fundamental distinction between the different uses of the concept of 'identity' by Weigert (1986). He starts from the sense of identity expressed in the basic question: "Who am I?" The answer can be given from three fundamentally different perspectives, which Weigert calls the three 'basic modes' of identity. The first answer at hand is the self-awareness that individuals take as the central reality of all that happens to them or that they do. Beginning with self-awareness, Weigert discusses his three basic modes of 'identity'; 'subjective identity' ('I'), 'objective identity' ('Me') and 'intersubjective identity' ('We').

Humans are aware of themselves as agents during their behaviour. Self, as the *subject* of self's knowledge, is the first mode to answer the question: "Who am I?" The person in

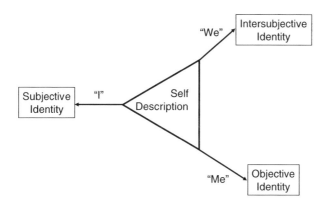

Figure 6.1: Weigert's (1986) basic approaches to identity.

question remembers that it was herself or himself involved in a prior action or event. Nothing more is required for identity over time than the awareness of persistence of the 'self' or 'I'. Weigert (1986) labels this "pure *I* mode" of identity 'subjective identity'. That 'self' is independent of any kind of description. This view on identity of persons is quite different from identity defined in terms of personality traits. If somebody wakes up the next morning as a beetle, like Gregor Samsa, the main character in Kafka's (1960) "Verwandlung", he or she will still have the experience of being the same person—no matter how his or her characteristics have changed. The 'I' mode does not enable me to tell others about *Me*. Vice versa, the *Me* mode of self is irreducible to the *I* mode of self as subject (Weigert, 1986). Weigert calls this mode of identity 'objective identity'. The word 'objective' is used in its grammatical sense; it refers to the object of the identity description. The identity of an object corresponds to its definition. The object's characteristics are its defining features.

Descriptions often serve as a guideline whether individuals do or do not belong to a group. People whose behaviour does not fit in with the way other organization members behave can easily become outsiders. Identities create a sense of belonging. They locate an individual in society (Weigert, 1986). Vice versa, a person's group membership comments on individual features. A member of a very open-hearted and friendly population may be expected to be open-hearted and friendly as well. A person's or an organization's 'objective identity' at any given point in time consists of his or its characteristics. These characteristics form the building blocks for a person's being part of a group, that is his or her 'inter-subjective identity'.

People tend to classify themselves and others into social categories, such as organizational membership, religious affiliation, gender, etc. Categories are defined by prototypical characteristics abstracted from the members. Social classification enables the individual to locate or define him- or herself in the social environment. Self-experience and its definition derive from membership of a group. The *We* mode is grounded in taken-for-granted rules for and assumptions about the group's identity, which can be unpacked by analyzing "the right to say 'We'" (Weigert, 1986). When this paper refers to 'local identity', it implies the mode of identity defining a local group, including the sense of belonging to that local group, in terms of its characteristics, which distinguish the local group from other groups in the known world. In terms of psychological implications we focus on Weigert's *We* mode of identity.

The Dynamics of Social Identity

Even a casual awareness of the world events reveals the power of the 'We' mode of identity in human behaviour. Names such as Tibet, Basques, Kurds, Welsh and Québec represent local identities capable of arousing intense emotional commitment and self-sacrifice on the part of individuals (Brewer, 1991). The social identity theory (Tajfel & Turner, 1979; Ellemers, 1991; Hogg, Terry, & White, 1995) deals with the dynamics of 'intersubjective identity'. Social identity derives from a fundamental tension between human needs for validation and similarity to others and on the other hand a countervailing need for uniqueness and individuation. It mitigates this tension, satisfying the need for assimilation with in-groups while the need for distinctiveness is met through comparisons with other groups. Such group identities allow in-groups to feel the same and different at the same time (Brewer, 1991). This also explains why the strongest in-group identification is shown in high-status minority groups (Ellemers, 1991; Brewer & Weber, 1994). People do actively seek comparisons, and adjust their self-evaluations accordingly. In fact, self-evaluation and self-improvement are the predominant motives for seeking comparative feedback (Collins, 1996). Comparison occurs on dimensions, which are established values among the members of a community. These values, at the same time, guide the group members' action and have the potential to distinguish the in-group from the out-group.

Barth (1970) illustrates how in the Pathan community in Afghanistan the "right to say we" depends upon three central characteristics: *hospitality* — being responsible for a guest's security and providing for his needs, *councils* — group decisions are taken collectively and unanimously, and *isolation of domestic life* from public life. Barth describes how Pathans chose to convert to other tribal identities in circumstances where they are not able to live up to these values. In the extreme north-east of Afghanistan, returns on agriculture are modest. There, Pathans can no longer live up to the value of 'hospitality'. History has shown how Pathan communities changed culture and even language and have become 'Kohistani' (Barth, 1970, p. 131). Barth's example illustrates the link between what a group thinks it is and what its members achieve. It shows how belonging to a certain group implies the urge to realize the values considered to characterize that group. Status, both individual and group status, is defined in terms of these values or characteristics.

Barth researched the fundamental values of the Pathan community, that is those values, which members believe to distinguish them from neighbouring communities. A group's 'distinctive characteristics' are unique from the viewpoint of the insider group; not necessarily from an outsider's perspective. However, the more values the local culture shares with the 'global culture', the less likely it becomes, that its 'distinguishing values' coincide with the fundamental values guiding the community members' behaviour. Only values which are reflected in the community members' concrete behaviour have the potential to distinguish such a community in a meaningful way (van Rekom, 1997).

If the members of a group define themselves as the higher status group, it is likely to strengthen in-group identification, thereby enhancing local identity. Identifying oneself as a member of a group with low status yields an unsatisfactory social identity, which is likely to motivate people to improve it. In-groups may attempt their group affiliation to acquire a more positive social identity by switching over to the higher status group; they are likely to strive for individual mobility (Ellemers, 1991). Higher status may be realized through individual mobility to another group, insofar as individuals have the freedom to switch groups, that is group boundaries are permeable to a certain extent.

Ellemers (1991) identified circumstances under which group identification remains strong even when the group has been assigned a low status. Firstly, if social structure is rigidly stratified group boundaries tend not to be permeable. Any attempts to realize higher status would involve a more fundamental social change, with group members trying to establish a higher status position for their group as a whole. Secondly, in her experiments, people's awareness that their group's status was unstable appeared to elicit a concern with collective status improvement. Thirdly, the conviction that the present status position is lower than deserved may motivate people to redress the injustice done to their group. Liu, Wilson, McClure, and Higgins (1999) show how stories of undergone violence in the past undermine the legitimacy of the low status the New Zealand Maori population has been suffering for a long time. If low status is assigned to a group according to an out-group's values, it enhances, as a counter-reaction, group identification.

In short, group identity in general is enhanced by the relative group status. Under low status circumstances, it is enhanced too if group boundaries are not permeable, and if insider group members perceive group status to be unstable or unfair. The confrontation between a culture, bound to a certain region, and the global culture, which is epitomized by the Western consumption culture, can be reframed in terms of the social identity theory. The local community constitutes a group of insiders. The global culture represents a group of outsiders, which may or may not threaten the local identity. People will compare the relative statuses of the local identity and global identity to establish whether they are better off in the group that they have membership in, at present. If locals, in terms of their own values, conclude that they are better off than outsiders, the local identity will tend to remain stable. However, if — in terms of their own values — locals conclude that they will be better off moving outside the 'global' pressure, it will lead to globalization and the disintegration of the local identity. Such scenario is likely to occur — unless one or more of the exceptional situations identified by Ellemers (1991) apply. Firstly, if the current status of the local group is low, but not unlikely to be improved, local identity will be enhanced. Secondly, local identity will be enhanced, if the pathways to the higher status groups are blocked.

By definition, global culture is open to newcomers. Therefore in the case of globalization, the impermeability of group borders is imposed by circumstances that are external to the direct confrontation of the local and global culture. A third group may be present which controls social interaction. For example, van den Berghe (1995) describes how in southern Mexico, Maya farmers form the lowest class, and social structure is such, that they cannot rise to the higher class of the 'Mestizos' who occupy the more favourable social positions and own the tourist facilities. Here the only way up, for individual Mayas, would be to improve the position of the group collectively.

The development of ethnic tourism is likely to enhance the status of low-ranked groups to some extent, because it reduces the stability of a perceived low status and opens ways to status improvement. The appearance of international tourism creates new circumstances, which may render the old 'status quo' less stable and generate new opportunities for the low-status group. In the same Mexico example, Mestizos realized that the Mayas formed an important asset in attracting foreign tourists (van den Berghe, 1995). Local groups may become more aware, that also externally they are defined as a unique group, and experience certain recognition. In her study on Maya Indians in Belize, for instance, Medina (2003) found that tourists had little interest in mestizo identities and culture. Thereby they inverted the local hierarchy that valued Mestizos over Mayas. The effect of tourism, in this spectrum, might well be one of triggering the local population's idea that their status may not need to be as low as it has been before.

Local identities will always stand out as a relative minority in relation to a more "global culture". As soon as a group perceives itself to be of higher status than the global culture, or moves to a higher status position after emancipation according to one of the two mechanisms mentioned, they are likely to perceive themselves as high-status minorities. Then, cultural identity is likely to be enhanced rather than to disappear. The Mayan Indians of southern Mexico, as well as the island of Bali in Indonesia, are examples of how the local identity has been maintained and cultivated as the consequence of the arrival of tourism. The next section illustrates both cases.

A Booming Recent Destination in Mexico: Mayan Identity in San Cristóbal de las Casas

Mexican Indians, among them the Mayas, are heavily concentrated in the more isolated, high-elevation, agricultural destitute areas, where they were able to retain their culture because their habitat was sufficiently devoid of resources to minimize Spanish, and later mestizo encroachments (Mestizos are the dominant, Spanish-speaking group in Mexico). Indians are culturally marginalized because of their unfamiliarity with Spanish. These Indians constitute a lumpen-peasantry, outside the cultural mainstream of Mexico. It is this extreme marginalization that now makes Indians a prime tourism attraction for Western travellers in search of the primitive, authentic other. Most Mestizos have traditionally looked down on Indians as ignorant, superstitious, backward alcoholic wretches who impede the progress of the country. Only a small minority among the Indians have become successful small- and even medium-sized entrepreneurs (van den Berghe, 1995). Official and private concern for the development of ethnic and cultural tourism has markedly increased in the 1980s and 1990s, particularly in connection with the international project of the Ruta Maya, which involves a joint attempt by Mexico, Guatemala, Belize and Honduras to promote ecotourism and salvage the few remaining patches of the Meso-American tropical rain forests in the Maya cultural area (van den Berghe, 1995). The tourist office in San Cristóbal de las Casas shows among others pictures of living Mayas on the local market. This emphasis on living Indians stems from the early 1990s, however. The first Maya marketer was a Swiss widow, who organized mule-pack expeditions to the Maya ruins in the area of the Lacadones tribe. With their long hair, white cotton gowns and simple subsistence technology, they made picturesque noble savages, with nice aquiline noses that could be convincingly juxtaposed to the bas-reliefs and paintings of the ruins of Palenque and Bonampak (van den Berghe, 1995). It took some time for local Mestizos to realize that foreign tourists had come to see "living Mayas" rather than the colonial town, and to understand why tourists should find Indians interesting. Once local Mestizos started to understand the nature of ethnic tourism, they began to capitalize on it, and to market "their Indians". Interest in things Mayan, both ancient and modern, spread among the local intelligentsia, and the town's intellectual, and cultural life became much more Indian-oriented than it had ever been. Several thousand women began to produce non-traditional weavings for tourists. Many of them started a thriving new craft market. It presented a bustling daily spectacle, a vast street theatre of Maya culture (van den Berghe, 1995). There has been a re-evaluation of the contribution of Indians to the town's life and economy. Previously, Indians in San Cristóbal de las Casas had been seen as a nuisance and an embarrassment; now they were an asset. The city of San Cristóbal de las Casas was "re-Indianized" by consequence of the arrival of tourism. A status improvement has taken place, and along with an important revaluation of local Maya identity.

Southern Mexico is a relatively recent destination. It may be interesting to have a closer look at a destination with a comparable strong local identity, but with a longer history of tourism interest. The Indonesian island of Bali may represent an interesting case.

Indonesia: Bali

In the first half of the 20th century, the Dutch colonial authorities were greatly influenced by an orientalist vision, which regarded the island of Bali as a "living museum" of the Hindu-Javanese civilization, the only surviving heir to the Hindu heritage swept away from Java by the coming of the Islam. In the early 1920s, the Dutch came to regard Bali as the cornerstone of their effort to contain the spread of Islam radicalism and the various nationalist movements that had recently arisen in Java and Sumatra. By looking for the singularity of Bali in its Hindu heritage, and by conceiving of Balinese religious identity as formed though opposition to Islam, the Dutch set the framework within which the Balinese were going to define themselves (Picard, 1997). In the 1920s, Balinese described themselves both as a religious minority, the stronghold of Hinduism threatened by the aggressive expansionism of Islam and Christianity, and as a particular ethnic group, characterized by their customs (Picard, 1997). The Dutch tourist bureau of the East Indies started promoting the island of Bali in 1914. In 1924, a weekly steamship connection was established between Batavia, Makassar and the Balinese city of Denpasar, enabling tourists to visit the island. In 1928 a proper tourist hotel, the Bali Hotel, was built in Denpasar. To entertain their guests, the management of the hotel arranged weekly performances of Balinese dancing, which soon became one of the most popular tourist attractions on the island (Picard, 1997). The performances presented at the Bali Hotel consisted of a series of short dances, strung haphazardly together and suited to the taste and attention span of a foreign audience. The very conception of this tourist program was made possible by the advent of a new style of dance, the Kebyar, which allowed the dance to be detached from both its theatrical content and its ritual context and presented as a form of art in its own right. With Kebyar a dance performance became much more expressive and narrative event, dynamic and linear instead of static and cyclical and hence more likely to be appreciated by

Westerners than traditional styles of music and dance. The favourable image arising was further reinforced by the work and positive writings of foreign artists who had chosen Bali for residence. The first articles written in the 1930s took pride in evoking the artistic reputation of their island (Picard, 1997).

Tourism to Bali was interrupted by the Japanese invasion in 1942. Picard (1993) dates the start of the second wave of tourism to 1 August 1969, the day of the inauguration of the Ngurah Rai International Airport, and the development of luxurious foreign- or Indonesian owned holiday resorts. Since the 1960s a host of institutions have been established to cultivate, develop and preserve the Balinese arts. To a certain extent, these institutions have taken over the patronage formerly exerted by the royal courts: the creation of styles and the establishment of norms. In 1979, the yearly Balinese arts festival in Denpasar was founded. Balinese authorities had little say in the Jakarta government's decision to trade in Bali's charms to refill the coffers of the state, and they were not even consulted about the master plan. In response to the master plan, the Balinese authorities proclaimed in 1971 their own conception of the kind of tourism the deemed most suitable to their island, namely "cultural tourism" (Picard, 1997). Largely unanticipated by planners, there has been a growing share of budget tourists. The Balinese have been prompt to adapt to this unexpected clientele. Most of the owners and employees of the accommodations and services serving this group are Balinese, and, in contrast to the state-initiated luxury projects, links with the local economy are close and numerous (Picard, 1993). Once Balinese culture had become a tourist asset, the Balinese resolved to preserve and promote it, while taking advantage of its prestige abroad and its economic importance at home in order to obtain full recognition of their identity from the state and to improve their position within Indonesia. Given its prestigious reputation, Bali was particularly requested to contribute its "cultural peaks" to represent Indonesian culture in the world (Picard, 1993).

In retrospect, the strong effects on the identity of Bali seem to have taken place at the first wave of tourism. That was the time that Balinese dance was reshaped to maximally please tourists—creating a new form of high art which now is further cultivated in formal institutions. A remarkable side effect of the "staging" (cf., McCannell, 1973) of Balinese culture for tourism was, that Balinese started to adopt the new products, such as a "frog dance" originally designed for tourists, as fully fledged markers of their own identity (Bruner, 1996). The second wave of tourism seems to have capitalized on the identity-strengthening effect of the first surge of tourism to Bali, producing a stable high-status identity for the island.

Implications

In Bali as well as in southern Mexico, we can observe that the distinctive character of the local population triggered a stream of tourists. In both cases, the start of the stream of tourists was triggered by outsiders, in Mexico by the Danish anthropologist, in Bali by the government of the Indonesian archipelago at that point in time. The commercial activities were in hands of the dominant group in the respective countries, and in both locales the local population gradually started to take more and more initiatives, resulting in the long run in a certain degree of emancipation of the local population. The degree of emancipation seems somewhat stronger in Bali: in Mexico, it might still be more difficult to imagine that a Maya rather than a mestizo would become governor of Chapas, whereas a Balinese has become governor of the island. However, we should keep in mind that the development of tourism in Bali started roughly 60 years earlier than Chapas.

Both cases show how "staged authenticity" (McCannell, 1973) may represent an alternative response to potentially destructive and unsustainable consumption of places, histories and cultures. It is a milder strategy that can work, both in publicity campaigns designed to foster identification with a distinct local community and campaigns to promote active citizenship in the classroom. Characteristics of the local community are explicitly set up for tourists. Such staged authenticity confronts tourists with the typical aspects of the local community, but to a similar degree also the locals themselves. For instance, if the owner of a souvenir shop in the Frisian village of Hindelopen had not hired an aged painter to make some new "typical" paintings on wood, the inhabitants of this village by now probably would have forgotten that they had such a local style of decoration. Staged authenticity raises the awareness of members of a local community that their community differs from the "outsiders", or put differently, it represents something special.

A critical aspect of the staging of local identities, however, is whether visitors and locals will accept it as such. This will be critical for the long-run sustainability of these markers, because otherwise those who stage them will not have an incentive to maintain them. Chhabra, Healy, and Sills (2003) found that authenticity need not be a major problem. Bruner (1996) found, that more intellectual tourists, who might resist "unauthenticity" most, can be fairly well satisfied if they are allowed a look, however limited it may be, into the back-stage area. Explanations how local people come up to devise the markers and the shows with the markers of local identity seemed to satisfy his respondents very well. As Bruner's (1996) example of the Balinese frog dance shows, originally "inauthentic" markers, if successful, gradually become to be accepted as more authentic, up to the point where a Balinese couple requested a frog dance for the celebration of their wedding.

Setting a Research Agenda

The discussed cases are suggestive of a positive development of the local identity. However, direct interviews on this issue with members of the local population were lacking. Field research in this area thus far has not been reported, but can be developed using the experience gained in the laboratory experiments in social identity research settings (Ellemers, 1991; Major, Sciacchitano, & Crocker, 1993; Brewer & Weber, 1994). Typically, during such experiments, respondents were given laboratory tasks, which inherently are difficult to generalize to the "real world" outside of the laboratory. More thorough testing of the social identity beyond the laboratory context would be highly desirable, and the development of local identities would provide an ideal area to conduct such tests. One particular insight from both cases is striking: the production and sales of artefacts, as markers of the local identity, seems to be of high significance both to the tourists as well as to the local population. Further in-depth research to the exact meaning of these artefacts, and their precise role in enhancing the local identity, would be highly warranted.

In the situations discussed in this chapter, comparison of the relative statuses is made on three sides: by the local population, by the dominant national population and by the tourists. The locals represent the inside perspective where the results of the comparison are crucial for the continuity of the local identity. If they decide that the local culture is lower in status and neither of the two conditions of impermeable boundaries or unstable group status occurs, the local culture is bound to disintegrate in the long term.

Conclusion

This chapter set out with the question, how local identities can survive in a world of increasing globalization, of which tourism is one of the carriers. Social identity theory stipulates the conditions under which local identities can be strengthened by the arrival of tourists. If for members of a local community access to the higher status national culture is blocked, the locals will strive for collective emancipation of the local culture. In instances when the low status seems unstable and undeserved, an enhancement of the local identity is likely. The discovery of the locale by tourism can be an important trigger to set such processes in motion. The discussed cases of Chapas in Mexico and Bali in Indonesia are highly suggestive of this process taking place. Tourism strengthened in both cases the identity of the local population, and made the nationally dominant groups (Mestizos in Mexico and Javanese in Indonesia) aware of how important the local population of the respective destinations was for attracting tourists to the country.

In the case of Bali, the Indonesian government was highly involved in promoting Bali in all its specificities. The Mexican case shows a more spontaneous development, with hardly any government measures. More conscious policy measures could be thinkable and though. Maintenance of the local community's social identity may be desirable, both from a tourism industry viewpoint, as well as from the viewpoint of local well-being. The staged markers of local identity, as provided by entrepreneurs in tourism can produce an identity-strengthening effect, provided this "staging of authenticity" is executed with sufficient care, both towards the tourists as towards the local population, which still should recognize these markers as their own. In an age, wherein the financing of public goods is increasingly dependent on the private sector, staged authenticity, formulated with care and executed professionally, represents an alternative response to potentially destructive and sustainable consumption of peoples, histories and cultures.

References

Arnould, E., Price, L., & Zinkhan, G. (2003). *Consumers* (2nd ed.). Boston: McGraw-Hill Irwin.

Barth, F. (1970). Pathan identity and its maintenance. In: F. Barth (Ed.), *Ethnic groups and boundaries: The social organization of culture differences* (pp. 117–134). London: Allen & Unwin.

Benjamin, M. (1992). Zuiderzee toen en nu: over zeven kustplaatsen aan de voormalige Zuiderzee, de eigenaardigheden van hun bewoners, de visserij, de dialecten. [The Zuiderzee before and now:

about seven coastal villages on the former Zuiderzee, the inhabitants' characteristics, fishing, the dialects.] *Noordhollands Dagblad*, 27th May 1992.

Brewer, M. B. (1991). The social self: On being the same and different at the same time. *Personality and Social Psychology Bulletin, 17*, 475–482.

Brewer, M. B., & Weber, J. G. (1994). Self evaluation effects of interpersonal versus intergroup social comparison. *Journal of Personality and Social Psychology, 66*, 268–275.

Bruner, E. M. (1996). Tourism in the Balinese border zone. In: S. Lavie, & T. Swedenburg (Eds), *Displacement, diaspora, and geographies of identity* (pp. 157–179). Durham: Duke University Press.

Chhabra, D., Healy, R., & Sills, E. (2003). Staged authenticity and heritage tourism. *Annals of Tourism Research, 30*, 702–719.

Cohen, E. (1989). Primitive and remote. Hill tribe trekking in Thailand. *Annals of Tourism Research, 16*, 30–61.

Collins, R. L. (1996). For better or worse: The impact of upward social comparison on self-evaluations. *Psychological Bulletin, 119*, 51–69.

Ellemers, N. (1991). *Identity management strategies: The influence of social-structural variables on strategies of individual mobility and social change*. Dissertation, Rijksuniversiteit Groningen, 5 September 1991.

Featherstone, M., Lash, S., & Robertson, R. (Eds). (1995). *Global modernities*. London: Sage.

Go, F. M., Lee, R. M., & Russo, A. P. (2003). E-heritage in the globalizing society: Enabling cross-cultural engagement through ICT. *Journal of Information Technology and Tourism, 6*, 55–68.

Gray, J. (1998). *False dawn: The delusions of global capitalism*. New York: The New Press.

Hogg, M. A., Terry, D. J., & White, K. M. (1995). A tale of two theories: A critical comparison of identity theory with social identity theory. *Social Psychological Quarterly, 58*, 255–269.

Jafari, J., & Gardner, R. M. (1991). *Tourism and fiction: Travel as a fiction—fiction as a journey*. Cahiers du Tourisme, Série C, No. 119. Aix-en Provence, France: Centre des Hautes Études Touristiques.

Kafka, F. (1960). *Die verwandlung. In Das Urteil, Das Geheimnis unserer Existenz in dichterischer Deutung* (pp. 23 – 105). Hamburg: Fischer Bücherei. (Original 1935).

Koning, P., & Koning, E. (2002). *Waarheid en Roddel. Volendam, dorp vol luide engelen. 1850-1950. [Truth and gossip. Volendam, village full of noisy angels.]*. Edam: De Stad.

Liu, J. H., Wilson, M. S., McClure, J., & Higgins, T. R. (1999). Social identity and the perception of history: Cultural representations of Aotearoa/New Zealand. *European Journal of Social Psychology, 29*, 1021–1047.

Major, B., Sciacchitano, A. M., & Crocker, J. (1993). In-group versus out-group comparisons and self-esteem. *Personality and Social Psychology Bulletin, 17*, 711–721.

McCannell, D. (1973). Staged authenticity: Arrangements of social space in tourist settings. *American Journal of Sociology, 79*, 589–603.

Medina, L. (2003). Commoditizing culture: Tourism and Maya identity. *Annuals of Tourism Research, 30*, 353–368.

Picard, M. (1993). "Cultural tourism" in Bali: National integration and regional differentiation. In: M. Hitchcock, V. T. King, & M. J. G. Parnwell (Eds), *Tourism in South-East Asia* (pp. 71–98). London: Routledge.

Picard, M. (1997). Cultural tourism, nation-building, and regional culture: The making of a Balinese identity. In: M. Picard, & R. E. Wood (Eds), *Tourism, ethnicity, and the state in Asian and Pacific societies* (pp. 181–214). Honolulu: University of Hawaii Press.

Salazar, N. B. (2005). Tourism and glocalization. *Annals of Tourism Research, 32*, 628–646.

Stonich, S. C., Sorensen, J. H., & Hundt, A. (1995). Ethnicity, class and gender in tourism development: The case of the Bay Islands, Honduras. *Journal of Sustainable Tourism, 3*, 1–28.

Tajfel, H., & Turner, J. C. (1979). An integrative theory of social conflict. In: W. Austin, & S. Worcher (Eds.), *The social psychology of intergroup relations* (pp. 33–47). Monterey, CA: Brooks/Cole.

van den Berghe, P. L. (1995). Marketing Mayas: Ethnic tourism promotion in Mexico. *Annals of Tourism Research, 22,* 568–588.

van Rekom, J. (1997). Deriving an operational measure of corporate identity. *European Journal of Marketing, 31,* 412–424.

Weigert, A. J. (1986). The social production of identity: Metatheoretical foundations. *The Sociological Quarterly, 27,* 165–183.

Chapter 7

Tourist Constructions and Consumptions of Space: Place, Modernity and Meaning

Scott McCabe and Duncan Marson

Introduction

Social life is intrinsically spatially contextualised. Where we live is fundamentally linked to the types of things we do as consumers. What we consume is intricately linked to social identity, 'who we are' (Miller, Jackson, Thrift, Holbrook, & Rowlands, 1998; MacKay, 1997). The spaces and places of home life impact upon the types of places chosen for leisure and tourism and the types of activity we choose to do (Crouch, 2001). In postmodern conceptions of society, space becomes fragmented; boundaries, both physical and symbolic, become blurred; identity is ephemerally linked to place, and not rooted in notions of 'home', 'family' or 'church' (Featherstone, 1991). Mobility and technology gains have brought the far away into the home environment and made home a commoditised, consumer 'good'. Location, location, location are the bywords of fashion, taste, identity and status in the lifestylisation of home, and yet the places of tourist destinations are losing their recognisability as the arbiters of fashion. Cheap flights bring once-exclusive destinations within the reach of budget travellers (Urry, 2002). The places in which we choose to make home are now often determined more by considerations of work, schools or aesthetic sensibilities than by family ties or historical associations. The spatial relations that characterise postmodern societies and their shifting, slipping meanings are as much determined by experiences of tourism places and preferences for particular types of landscape (such as the seaside or mountains) as much as traditional conceptions of home. Tourism places, 'destinations', 'resorts' or 'holiday spots' have become central to modern lives. The collective ability to name places visited as tourism destinations and describe experiences of them are a fundamental part of modern lives as consumers, and help shape identities. Yet individual's engagement in places is changing as societies like the United Kingdom move into the new Century. The fact that tourism is wrapped up with identity in a fairly critical way is not a new concept (cf. Cohen, 1972, 1974; Desforges, 2000; McCabe & Stokoe, 2004). It appears however, that old ideas about the tourist experience as 'fleeting', 'spurious', 'ephemeral'

Tourism and Social Identities: Global Frameworks and Local Realities
Copyright © 2006 by Elsevier Ltd.
All rights of reproduction in any form reserved.
ISBN: 0-08-045074-1

and 'pastiche' are changing as more and more people in society decide to take up semipermanent or permanent residency in another country. There are increasing numbers of people who are willing to give up homes and cultures in exchange for 'a place in the sun'. This raises interesting questions that appear to contradict conventional notions of tourism/place/identity relations. In some spatial contexts it is becoming increasingly difficult to make clear and simple distinctions between tourists, long-term residents and migrants. Similarly in postmodern accounts, the cult of the individual is paramount. In the context of tourism, ordinary people contribute written articles to tourism brochures and feature in the wider media on TV shows dedicated to describing and representing places (destinations), giving accounts of their experiences — the individual it seems is more cogent an arbiter of taste than artists, professionals or conventional celebrities (cf. Dunn's chapter in the present volume). Therefore, modes and types of representations of touristic places are shifting as are touristic experiences themselves.

A more useful theory has been developed within the geography of tourism, cultural studies (e.g. Crouch, 2001), critical sociology of place (e.g. Urry 1994, 1995, 2002) plus a growing literature within environmental and discursive psychology (e.g. Fridgen, 1984; Dixon & Durheim, 2001). Yet despite the recognition that tourism itself and the social construction of place and identity are changing, these links are often made in either a realist/essentialist or overly interpretive/structuralist way which seems to negate the links between the individual and wider social discourses. The purpose of this paper is to argue that individuals make places meaningful. People create links between themselves, places and other people, which involve the construction of lived experiences of places and identity in a simultaneous, mutually inclusive process. The paper argues for a reassessment of the socially constructed nature of consumption of tourism space, using a re-interpretation of Lefebvre's (1991) description of the processes of social construction of space.

In discussing tourist spaces, we provide illustrations of the variety of typological experiences available to tourists from 'day visits', package holidays and long-haul travel as the temporal construction of tourist space is fundamental to the social construction of space. We also argue that the tourist, in socially constructing tourist space, goes beyond the mere 'gaze', the 'fleeting' and the 'momentary glimpse', to reproduce and reify the constructed space or experience in an a posteriori sense. We argue that the tourist not only constructs the space in anticipation of the touristic experience, but also in bringing back the experience into the domestic sphere, which reflects and re-creates the experience and the space. In one sense this is a re-imagined space, but in another it is a more concrete and permanent sense of the space and in that the imagined space then becomes the dominant construct. A collective sense of belonging to or within a place is often contrasted with the postmodern idea of mobility; yet we argue that the tourist constructs a sense of spatial belonging through an agglomeration of spatial experiences and praxes over time. In this sense then belonging is not a fixed construct but one that is an ongoing process.

However, related to the processes through which meaning is given to tourist experience is the moral construction of experience and place. Not all tourism is morally 'good', some forms of tourism are considered to be negative. Mass tourism, sex tourism and socially unacceptable behaviour within destinations (such as 'club culture' in Ibiza, which is widely associated with drug misuse) are positioned by society as negative in terms of the conservation issues associated with mass tourism development; the effect on cultural values of sex tourism; and the wider social problems of unacceptable behaviour, both on the host and the guest cultures. Butcher (2003) has recently argued that tourism experience is connected to moral values, and McCabe and Stokoe (2004) have shown how places and people are constructed in a moral sense in empirically based research in tourists talk about their own and the experiences of others. The last aim of this chapter is to relate those arguments about the moral construction of place to the social construction process.

The Social Construction of Tourist Experience

There is little doubt that space is much more than an empty container in which the more important aspects of social life occur (Dixon, 2001). Space is transformed into places, in a socially constructed and organised way, and therefore this production process is fundamentally political (Lefebvre, 1991). Places are designed and designated for different purposes including tourism, leisure and hospitality most importantly. However the notion of place, and its theoretical construction is a contested area of social science. Theorists who are interested in place and the spatial and temporal aspects of social life come from a variety of disciplinary traditions: geography (e.g. Li, 2000; Mels, 2002), sociology (Cohen, 1979; MacCannell, 1992; Urry, 2002), psychology (Korpela & Hartig, 1996; Fredrickson & Anderson, 1999), as well as broader fields of enquiry such as leisure and tourism studies. Theorists conceive space and place as socially constructed phenomena largely within a postmodern perspective, treating social actors as confronted and overwhelmed by places. Meanings are 'de-contextualised' in that meaning making is taken away from places and history, 'dislocated'. In postmodern accounts there is fragmentation of the proximal and the distant. However, there are opposing schools of thought, treating place and mortal members of societies and their experience within space in a more phenomenological or discursive way (Seamon & Mugeraner, 1985; Tuan, 1980; Li, 2000). Ordinary people whose constructions of space, the meanings attached to places by them are complex and their experiences multiple and similarly contested in theory (Wickens, 2002). People may engage in places in a multitude of different ways, and the negotiations undertaken by them in their encounters are used in identity formations. In other words, ordinary members of society interleave time, space and identity.

In this chapter we propose that space is socially constructed, that is produced by ordinary members of society and that we can better understand the processes of touristic experience through an understanding of the possible ways in which this is achieved. We do this by working through Lefebvre's (1991) insights into the production of space. Lefebvre argued that it is only by developing an understanding of the specialised practices happening within space in its social production can space be disconnected from society and viewed purely on its own terms (Mels, 2002). Mels points out that this is not an uncontested set of ideas; yet in this paper we argue that these specialised practices can be applied to an analysis of the processes undertaken by ordinary actors in experiencing tourist places.

Lefebvre argues that space is treated through political and hegemonic processes, it is ordered, and governed by society, is overlaid with planning and influenced by the processes of capitalism and capital exchange. Throughout the scientification of space, from Aristotelian pure category (along with time), through Cartesian notions of space as an absolute (containing and dominating all the senses), to Kantian conceptions of space as a pure, albeit transcendental category, space is a 'mental thing' (Lefebvre, 1991). It is imperative to think of space in this 'mentalist', philosophical way in order to understand the processes by and through which ordinary people create meaning from experiences within touristic spaces. However, there is a philosophical dualism at the heart of such debates. Theoretical work in understanding space/place/identity and tourism relations appears fixed in a largely interpretative and reductionist way. We argue that people in society formulate relations within space and time, which gives meaning to experiences in particular spaces, which are re-interpreted and represented over time, and are powerful praxes which shape and contribute towards evolving sense of self. This approach is different from Lefebvre (1991) and Augé (1995), who suggest that individuals are limited in their capacities to reflexively construct space with meaning. However powerful the argument that places and time are controlled and ordered at the level of superstructure, in terms of the agency of the ordinary person we suggest there is little evidence which shows that social actors have lost a sense of the temporal rhythm of life, the distinct relationships between work and pleasure (holidays and travel), the feelings and emotions of the seasons, the passing of time through the 'ages of man' etc.

Crucially important, Lefebvre argues for a theoretical dialogue between the 'mental' and the 'social' or the 'philosophical' and the 'lived in practice' space. He makes us think about space in a totally new way. However, he is critical of research and theory development, and was subsequently criticised. He argues that studies describe or inventory space, but these can never give rise to a 'knowledge of space' *per se*. Semiology is criticised by Lefebvre because when codes are worked up from literary texts and applied to spaces, we remain at the descriptive level. Any use of such codes in attempting to decipher social space must reduce that space to the status of message, and any inhabiting of the space as a reading. This remains a problematic feature of texts that take interpretative approaches to meaning making in relation to space and human activity. And this is a continuing problem in the context of touristic representations of space such as the tourism brochure, where theory and empirical work appears incapable of going beyond the descriptive level (cf. Morgan & Pritchard, 1998).

Lefevbre asserted that space is all-pervasive in society and not just an empty container for the important aspects of social life continuing within it. For example, all activity is spoken of in spatial terms; thus we are confronted with a multitude of spaces, each one piled upon the next, which need to be unpacked and the configurations between them worked out, to uncover the 'truth of space'. Lefevbre begins by outlining the fundamental link between spatial relations and political and historical processes of production and capitalism: "Few people today would reject the idea that capital and capitalism 'influence' practical matters relating to space" (1991, p. 9). This is followed by a refute to Kantian conceptions of space: "Could space be nothing more than the passive locus of social relations, the milieu in which their combination takes on body, or the aggregate of the procedures employed in their removal? The answer must be no" (p. 11). Space plays an active role as knowledge in action, for in the existing mode of production there are contradictions. Lefebvre distinguishes between three distinct conceptual groupings or users in the production of space. First is the notion of spatial practice. These are the spaces of the everyday, the ordinary social actor and the routes and networks that connect places of home, work and leisure. This is the space of the everyday, the mortal. The second order is represented spaces, those places appropriated by planners and technocrats who wish to impose meaning upon places and govern the social structure of planning and the use of space. Finally, there are representational spaces. These are spaces of artists and philosophers and can include any other types of spaces but are re-imagined, transformed through the art of pure description into something metaphysical. Most tourism theory focuses on the second level in interpreting the social production of space. Tourism theory argues that the tourism industry represents and misrepresents places of tourism destinations in so much that the industry selectively picks out certain images and characteristics about the physical space of destinations and turns them into 'resorts' — spaces for active and engaged (or partisan) consumption. Places are constructed in such a way so as to alert potential visitors of the types of behaviour which can be expected within them. The representation of space as tourism destination is also intrinsically culturally conceptualised and interlinked. Tourism researchers argue that the representation of place through tourism brochures displays the inherent hegemonic power relations between the centre and the periphery (Tresidder, 1999), the neo-colonial appropriation of the developing world by the developed world (Mowforth & Munt, 1998; Morgan & Pritchard, 1998) or the socio-cultural domination of one group over another (Dann, 1996). These are all good common sense and therefore powerful theoretical observations. Yet we argue that the process of place representation is more complex.

Lefebvre argues in the final category that representational spaces are particularly special. Representational spaces are spaces that are

> ... directly lived through its associated images and symbols, and hence the space of 'inhabitants' and 'users', but also of some artists and perhaps of those, such as a few writers and philosophers, who describe and aspire to do no more than describe. This is the dominated — and hence passively experienced — space, which the imagination seeks to change and appropriate. It overlays physical space, making symbolic use of its objects. Thus representational spaces may be said, though again with certain exceptions, to tend towards more or less coherent systems of non-verbal symbols and signs.(Lefebvre, 1991, p. 39)

We argue here that Lefebvre was fundamentally wrong to suggest that certain types of people in society produce space in a rigid and fixed sense. We propose that if one takes the point of view of the ordinary actor, we can imagine that these three conceptualisations of social–spatial production are possible and practiced by ordinary people in their constructions of experiences and meanings within places. It is possible to conceive and construct a range of experiences and contrast their characteristics to show how encounters with space can be shown to support this notion of space production as fundamental to meaning making for members of society. Each type of experience could be said to lock together in a jigsaw of spatial experience to create a world of contrasting places. The individual may then construct categories of spaces such as, 'home', 'foreign', 'temperate', 'wild', 'comfortable' and 'inhospitable', for example, in a knowing and legitimate way.

For example, on one level there are those brief encounters with space, places that may be passed through or traversed without much immediate and direct contact. Crouch calls these brief encounters 'flirting' with space (Crouch, 2001). Augé (1995) calls these types of places 'non-places'. From two opposing viewpoints we see that space in these small encounters can be perceived totally differently. Augé argues that nonplaces are places where no direct contact amongst people is possible, yet this is clearly not true for everybody. Plane-spotters meet at airports to share in their enthusiasm for their hobby; travellers meet each other to talk about their impending holiday trips, or to share experiences of delays or lost baggage. People enjoy the opportunity to shop and buy things at cheaper prices through 'duty free' so that the experience of nonplaces may not be as bleak and meaningless as Augé suggests. For example, on a train journey, one may pass the time looking out of the window looking at the landscape, and in a reverie, begin to construct the scene as being a place where all sorts of human social activities occur. We may argue that if the train passes through a landscape by a body of water such as a lake or an estuary we may see boats or moorings and harbours. We may imaginatively construct the lives of fishermen and their families, or yachtswomen or pleasure-cruisers and depending on interests or the landscape itself and how it connects with identities, the fleeting journey where mere glimpses of landscape are possible may make a lasting impression on the senses and imagination. It is possible that the masses of people all congregated in airport terminal lounges will perceive the spaces in which they find themselves gazing upon, interacting with or queuing even, differently. The type of trip may be influential — business travellers might perceive the journey in a more passive way than leisure travellers. The temporal context must also be considered, the journey home may be more or less stressful or relaxing. The social construction of space is inextricably tied to the construction of meaning within experience and time.

We need to contrast experiences of 'landscape of place' (as immediate encounter) with 'places' that are constructed in memory over repeated encounters and complex associations. Can places in themselves have identities? What makes places have an identity? Is it possible to have meaningful encounters with local people at destinations? We know that experience of a place is not entirely visual, as Rodaway (1994) points out and later Crouch (1999). Tuan (1974) also refers to the use of music to associate places, such as the use of the accordion to denote France. Certain types of places also evoke different types of experience — the city is contrasted with the countryside, depending upon the spatial context in which we live, the types of feelings, associations and desires of the places of holiday destinations as so shaped.

We often associate the countryside to the place of the natural environment and the former as the exciting places in which to enjoy hedonistic modern pleasures such as shopping, social activity and sexual contact. This is despite the fact that these collective cultural constructions are becoming blurred in the postmodern sense. However, places are not fixed 'containers' of social action and otherwise empty of meaning. Places are fundamentally important and are the subject of complex social construction processes. Places are socially constituted and constitutive of the society (Dixon & Durrheim, 2000). One way in which we can empirically demonstrate this orientation is through the use of language. The following section makes the link between language, identity and space.

The Social Construction of Identity through Talk

Identity theory has recently recognised that identity is more than a purely cognitive process underpinning human action, and can be thought of as a social accomplishment of interaction (Antaki & Widdecombe, 1998; Potter & Wetherell, 1987, 1994). Therefore identity can be studied through language use for the discursive practices in their construction themselves (Edwards & Potter, 1992; Edwards, 1994). The notion of 'identity' being a social, interactional, accomplishment has been conceived in the context of the 'self' for some time (Goffman, 1959). Goffman argued that the contextual nature of social life meant that people create and sustain social roles, or 'identities', in a dramaturgical production of everyday life. This theatre of everyday life was understood to be created for, and directed towards, others in society, which made the direct link between the 'self' and society.

Goffman (1959) argued that roles were played out through personal 'fronts' which are the expressive equipment used to act out performances and these are standardised and fixed. Examples of fronts include sex, age, race, clothes, facial expressions and gestures. Through the performance of a routine using a front, claims are made upon an audience and therefore the performance becomes socialised, modified to fit social expectations of society associated with that role. Performers offer their observers an impression that is idealised in different ways. In the context of performance the "front region" (Goffman, 1959, p. 110) refers to the place where the performance is given. The fixed sign equipment in such a place has been termed the "setting" (p. 110). The front region is the place of the direct encounter. The "backstage" or "back region" (p. 114) is the private place where clothes or equipment can be hidden, scrutinised for flaws or adjusted. The performer can relax here and drop his or her front, forego speaking his or her lines and step out of character. The back region will be adjacent (but concealed from the audience) to the front region. This overtly spatial language in Goffman's theory is crucially important in the social construction of space as the 'site' of the social encounter in which identity is 'worked up' within interaction means that co-participants in a scene engage in co-producing the social world that we know. In other words, social identity is contextually (i.e. spatially contextualised) bound. Thence a moral and social agreement is made between the parties as to how the 'place' should be conceived and constructed. People must decide the appropriate behaviour within the setting. Role theory has been developed and applied eloquently in the context of tourism (cf. Wickens, 2000; Jacobsen, 2001). However, there is a lack of engagement with the language of place construction in tourism research.

The links between the phenomenological thought, the interactional order, the society and the self have been made (Malone, 1997). Malone draws together ideas from Schutz's descriptions of the *Lebenswelt* (Schutz & Luckmann, 1973), to ethnomethodology (cf. Heritage, 1984), Goffman's interaction order (Goffman, 1959) and Sacks who sought to formalise a rigorous method of handling the events of everyday interaction as sociological data (Sacks, 1972). In this way Malone constructs the basis for the identification of the presentation of self in everyday talk through the re-conceptualisation of information, meaning and intention within conversational data (Malone, 1997, p. 144).

> In the interaction order, information, intention, and meaning are dependent on the twin demands of self-presentation and sense-making so there are no simple signs. All information transmission between people must be treated as potentially complex.(Malone, 1997, p. 145)

Self-presentation is understood to be an endless social accomplishment (after Garfinkel, 1967), reflexively created and re-created in the interaction order that prioritises self-presentation and the making of common sense in interaction. In this way, "...meaning is not something that social scientists attribute to interaction. It is the constitutive property of interaction which is necessary for it to continue" (Malone, 1997, p. 147).

In stressing the importance of meaning making within such a phenomenological grounded approach to the concept of 'situated actors', we must also accept the fundamental importance of the spatial situation in which the actors find themselves. Gubrium (1993) argues for a cautious naturalism, in reference to the fact that social constructionism is concerned with the mundane, everyday life and practices that accomplish everyday life for members. Gubrium proposes that we can think of the agent as a practitioner of everyday life and is therein engaged in a production of meaning in the *local setting of activity* (our emphasis) and the overall products of the enterprise. Gubrium refers to this as the *embeddedness* (1993, p. 99) of the social construction process:

> ... stressing the formal and informal organisational parameters of meaning that impinge on the agent or, putting it in reverse order, that provide the agent with interpretive resources. The agent's constructive activity is embedded in a context of interpretation (Gubrium, 1993, p. 99).

It is this ordinary practical quality of constructive agency that allows one to methodologically tolerate the tension between culture and nature, and so features of everyday life are treatable as natural even if they are constructed and members' projects take things for granted and as immutable (1993, p. 100). Place–language is one of those taken-for-granted aspects of social interaction, but which provides such a rich stream of potential empirical data.

In studies of identity this naturalism, or attention to the cultural context of an interaction situation, allows for the analysis of how social actors orient towards and manage performed identities. We argue that the place–identity constructions deployed in everyday discourse can be analysed to demonstrate how they accomplish discursive actions including the justification of certain kinds of person-in-place relations (Schegloff, 1972). Further, such analyses can help understand the political and moral dimension of one's representations of place and of how one locates oneself and others (Dixon & Durrheim, 2000; McCabe & Stokoe, 2004). In this way we may conceive that tourist talk can be used to understand the complex processes by which ordinary actors socially construct places or destinations, and their inhabitants and the other types of users.

In the following section we begin to explore these themes through a discussion of the 'real' and the 'perceived' or the 'imagined' spatial constructions and how these relate to the socially constructed meaning of place and touristic experience.

The Re-Interpretation of 'Real' and 'Imagined' Social Space

Lefevbre concludes with an attempt to steer the theoretical emphasis away from an accent on objects within space, to concentrate more specifically on the idea of space itself (how is the concept of space to be defined and more importantly, what are the social relationships embedded within it). However, the relationship between objects within space and spatial construction processes itself needs to be analysed to fully comprehend the importance of spatiality with regards to the individual or group.

Social space, according to Lefebvre exists due to the interwoven makeup of space and time. Spatial constructions also include within this framework physical objects that participate in a certain social discourse. This 'social discourse' and the idea of space as a container for relationships are interesting in regards to the formation of certain touristic landscapes. Lefebvre suggests that space produces and reproduces society, consequently and consistently creating new meanings and interpretations. This was observable through the discourses of cultural class systems, such as the establishment and the bourgeois culture. This is an interesting point and importantly highlights two critical debates with relation to contemporary touristic space. First, as Hughes (1998, p. 20) suggests, tourism is an important conduit for which meanings of space are organised and categorised. For example, as a destination becomes popular the representation of that particular space is designated a new meaning, one which is potentially deemed to be 'fashionable', depending on a range of different factors. This represented image is embedded within the formation of social spaces by the everyday user of space; the tourist, whose wishes become fulfilled through the use of social group norms and preconceived ideas of motivation. We propose that tourist space is now significantly constructed through the help of certain cultural 'group' intermediaries. For example, people, rather than landscape qualities, or the characteristics of place, become the main focus of choice in determining the type of place being represented or constructed. Through advertising as well as peer groups or others in society, a space becomes signified through its association between and amongst people, including, but not exclusively the indigenous cultural group. Young adds by emphasising that these 'ways of seeing' (1999, p. 388) a particular space, are re-created through social groups, which compete for space by assigning significance to its formation and emphasising its position, as imagined, rather than experienced space.

In relating modes of experience or 'ways of seeing' space in the context of human exploration, Boorstin (1986) illustrates an account of the advent of discovery, which touches upon the same themes. Boorstin draws upon historical discovery to show how, through the geography of the imagination to the widening of community knowledge, space has been constructed in an imagined sense. The many important discoveries throughout human history incorporate the re-interpretation and imagination of space. Christopher Columbus for example, (if one were to over-simplify the emphasis of his own exploration), re-interpreted the landscape of the America's to fit in with his own desires of geographic and cultural assimilation for the advancement of the Spanish monarchy and Catholicism (which created the term 'the New World'). Columbus's subsequent diary (first transcribed by the historian Bartolome De Las Casas) acts as a descriptive representation, which created a spatial formation for which the monarchy could perceive an imagined space. Columbus himself, until witnessing the area with his own eyes on October 14, 1492, relied on perceived spatial constructions from previous travellers, like Marco Polo (Cohen, 1969, p. 72). However, tourism is now an activity of mass participation, and while we could state that Columbus and Polo were founder members of the exploring 'elite', each tourist is in a sense their own explorer, providing friends and family with a significant narrative representation about places, either favourable or negative, and consequently influencing the formulated place-image. This is also now being witnessed in the wider media in the UKcontext through reality TV shows such as 'Place in the sun', which focus much more on people's experiences of places rather than the places in themselves.

These narratives create a distinct sense of power for the individual, and help in re-constructing images of places in which they can locate themselves or alternatively reject the place or culture as one they would visit. In this sense, space becomes almost a secondary consideration to the people with which they become represented and are used for the purpose of social construction, justification and identity ascription. Foucault's work on spatiality and metaphors tends to concur with this notion of justification through re-interpretation. Foucault (in Gordon, 1980, p. 68) states that the geographical metaphor of 'territory' is a concept that transforms the meaning of spatiality from a physical connotation into a polit-ical signifier. 'Territory', in a touristic sense, denotes a shift of power from one designated meaning of space, to another. Columbus's voyage and subsequent exploration constructed his own representation of what he termed as 'the New World', and it would be worthwhile to assess if these 'imagined spaces' change in representation when the contemporary tourist travels to and experiences a foreign landscape.

Jacobsen (2001) recently argues that the tourist, with her or his own individual moti-vations, experiences place in a transient way and can only achieve a fleeting glimpse of the spatial representation. However, even though certain cultural constructions like staged authenticity and hyper-reality make only a fleeting glimpse of cultural reality attainable, it is the individual's own construction of space that designates the most enduring mean-ing. The construction of space through memory, as Lovell (1998) argues, recovers time and space: "In a synchronic gesture, streamlining and unifying some of its diversity and contradictions in order to create viable and cohesive collective images in the present" (1998, p. 12).

This formation, developed through such theoretical ideas as the transient gaze, cultural interaction and social influence creates what is termed as 'imagined space'. The imagined space, while being a formation constructed by the guest, is nevertheless an important source of meaning to the individual who adheres to certain social norms and group behav-iour. Such spatial practices, according to Macnaughten and Urry (1999, p. 172), are over time concretised in the built environment and the enduring character of the landscape, con-sequently proving the importance of the individual in assigning significance to space. In this example, we can again see the shift of power, moving away from the policy makers of tourism destination marketing management, and more towards the tourists who travel to and consequently decipher the space and place. The combination of imagined space and social discourse can create what is described above as a 'touristic territory', highlighting the important features within a particular destination, which appeal on an individual and social level. Territoriality, concludes Soja, refers to the production and reproduction of spa-tial enclosures that not only concentrate interaction but also intensify and enforce its boundaries (1993,150). The mass tourist for example, is one category of activity that changes the meaning of space in a destination, and assigns it a territorial typographical for-mation. The well-researched behavioural characteristics of the young mass tourist (sun, sea, sex, Sangria) could be a result of the need to establish a feeling of territorial belong-ing away from the normality of work and home. This performative process contributes to Lovell's work (adapted from Hirsch & O'Hanlon, 1995), which discusses how landscapes generate actualised 'places' through human action, which in turn invokes a sense of human sociality and identity (1998, p. 6). This collective sociality inadvertently generates the imagined space, acting as a signifier for the individual who wishes to participate in a particular behaviour, which is deemed the social norm. Bird (2002) discusses how local narratives about places are interconnected with the creation — and more specifically the maintenance of — cultural identity constructions. She asks, "how does this construction of place [through cultural narratives] contribute to a sense of cultural identity?" (2002, p. 521). In focusing not on the activities or behaviour of groups of people and how such collective action makes meaning in places or performs a social construction of space, but on narratives, Bird argues that a sense of place is socially achieved. Bird relates how the drawing together of different 'stories', or legends, about Minnesota into a broader set of arguments illustrates how a sense of place is achieved through the narratives. Bird suggests that situated social actors use stories to make sense of their lives within their cultural settings. Place — the physical reality — and the socially constructed reality (Lefebvre, 1991; see also Harvey, 1993) are woven together through the narratives. Bird argues that,

> Through our tales about place, we mark out spatial boundaries, which may extend over a whole town or just over a particular space — a bridge, a hill, a lake. The tale confirms that this piece of space actually means something, and it may also tell us who belongs in that space and who does not.(2002, p. 523)

An interesting issue can be observed from this discussion, the significance of 'tales'. The narrative has 'evolved' into an important conduit for the formulation of space and the subsequent image of place. This can be traced into the contemporary narrative, a tool for assigning spatial representation. Bird concludes that in the context of her study of Minesota, it is unlikely that most people in the community believe these ancient tales. Yet members of the community continue to 're-create and re-create' (2002, p. 542) stories of the past as they relate to 'their' (my emphasis) sense of belonging to the place. We argue that such a process is undertaken when people travel for their holidays. Activities, behaviours, group as well as individuals are woven together in stories and become concretised in the memory and the performed experiences of place are translated into imagined places over time.

The destination formation and spatial construction can influence the behaviour and codes of conduct of the tourist or traveller located within. As Macnaughtan and Urry recount, the spaces of representation not only include the collective experiences of space, but also resistance to dominant spatial practices (1999, p. 172). Indeed, this creation and manipulation of the spatial surroundings does not result in a construction of one specific spatial discourse and meaning. Places can be assigned significance depending on their relevance to the individual, and as Soja (1996, p. 69) expresses further, due to this formation many spatial representations can exist in one single geographical area, as do the spatial practices which accompany them.

The individual significance of spatial construction is of further interest when considering the realm of the modern metropolis, where contrasting space can tangibly exist within the boundaries of a cityscape. San Francisco is one urban example of the multiplicity of spatial constructions possible that generates different meanings for individuals dependent on certain identity traits such as social allegiance. The tourist, through the use of such media amenities as guidebooks and holiday programmes, may conjure up representations of San Francisco based on the touristic symbols of perhaps Fisherman's Wharf and Pier 39. This spatial construction, however, would differ from the gay and lesbian traveller, who may consider the area of Castro Street and the surrounding blocks to be spatially signifi-cant to their travel itinerary because of the relevance this particular space has to their own social identity group. This would again be different for the literary intellectual, who may want to travel to the "City Lights bookstore" (an iconic haunt for the Beat Generation), and then onto the aptly named Kerouac Street. Furthermore, from disseminating all these dif-ferent spatial formations, it is possible to conclude that each of these various constructions of place and space create, manipulate and position San Francisco under one imagined spa-tial representation of 'a cosmopolitan and bohemian city'.

The influencing nature of tourism can project new spatial representations onto destina-tions, where previously place myths would have been minimal and potentially traditional (accentuating the local culture). Cloke and Perkin's (1998) research on the representations of New Zealand for adventure tourism found that Queenstown, located in the southerly area of the South Island, is now considered a 'Mecca' for the adventure tourist who found within the physical landscape an invitation to perform 'dangerous' activities, rather than to merely gaze (1998, p. 208). This contemporary formulation of New Zealand space as being 'an adrenaline junkies paradise' has not only created an important imagined spatial representation for the town and country, but has also provided a particular tourist group with a form of pilgrimage, to indulge and satisfy their own social membership. The spatial re-formulation of the surrounding landscape, coupled with the 'iconic emplacements' (Soja, 1996, p. 249) of such figures as bungee jumping, protagonist A.J. Hackett develops not only an imagined space, where the motivations and fantasies of the individual are constructed, but also a real space, where these fantasies are performed, and identities can be lived out in the company of respected peers.

Spatial Formation and Morality

Shields (1991, p. 90) drawing from the work of Rojek (1995) and Bakhtin (1984) com-ments on touristic features that relate to the topic of evolutionism, morality and power in regards to destination construction. The differing social groups which use surrounding space for a variety of purposes construct not only their own meaning of space, but also consequently judge other users who construct a contrasting or opposing representation of space. Human interaction, as Soja (1993, p. 150) states, is 'stretched' over time and space in a series of unevenly developed and differentiated settings. Hayden (1997, p. 118) elab-orates by stating that just as gender can be mapped as a struggle over social reproduction in various scales of space, the same is true for race and class and many other social issues. Shields refers to the example of the British seaside resort of the Victorian era, where the seaside 'space' was used by the aristocracy and the working classes alike. However, the behaviours of each group (the aristocracy for prospective health benefits of the seawater, but valuable leisure time for the working classes in conjunction with drinking and playing) were constructed by Victorian essayists in a moral sense. The activities of the working classes were believed to be improper and immoral, and thus hotly condemned for their perceived lewd conduct (1992, p. 91). This threat to the social order of classes in shared tourist space, not only distinguishes the issue of social inferiority, but also highlights the inter-relatedness of morality with regards to the social construction of space. It would also be appropriate to state that the working class tourist on holiday in bygone days constructed their imagined space of the seaside through many spheres (perhaps upper class opinion and nature of advertising used by Thomas Cook), as did the upper class tourist through the use of narrative. However, it may be appropriate to suggest that their social status and the influences which constructed and dominated their leisure time influenced their own creation of this imagined space, and consequently influenced the behaviour and activities which they immersed themselves in on holiday. It is these practices, formed out of the social construction of space, which were deemed to be immoral by the upper classes.

This moral dimension is indicative of the increasingly complex relationships between social constructions of space, morality and modernity. In a highly mobile and populated world, the occupation, use and value of space is becoming increasingly contested. What one individual deems to be morally correct may differ greatly from another, depending on the use of the place, the people who inhabit it and the activities which are being performed within. As de Certeau further elaborates, space is a 'practised place' (1988,117), and is assigned spatiality by how society performs within it. This performance not only transforms the existing nature of space into place (as de Certeau suggests), but it also creates a system of signs, that in turn constructs behavioural norms, providing morally 'good' and 'bad' uses of place and constructing place in particularly moral ways simultaneously (McCabe & Stokoe, 2004).

Does the advent of this moralistic 'sign–value' in spatial constructions denote an increasingly blasé attitude to the landscapes themselves? Postmodernism essentially creates what Grossberg describes as 'the aesthetic practice of deconstruction' (1997, p. 480). The production of capitalism has somewhat condensed the commodity into a series of signifiers: a symbolism which has no one true meaning but a variety of different translations and significations. Lash and Urry emphasise the problem this creates by stating that some of these commodities or objects (like that of television, cinema, advertising, etc.) bombard the individual with more signs than they can cope with (1994, p. 3). Could space be perceived within the same theoretical context? Each social group assigns significance to certain destinations based on the imagined space which they construct, and these differing spatial representations will increasingly come into contact and potential conflict with each other. When relating this process to that of the social self, the subcultural boundaries (and consequently the spatial significance generated) becomes blurred and distorted, allowing particular social discourses to interact with one another. This potentially questions the individual's own constructed space, and possibly creates dissonance between representations of why a particular place is important to them. This could explain the need for some social groups to enforce judgement on other subcultures in society in relation to their use of the same space. Kellner (1992) continues this by stating that as modern societies become more complex through the deconstruction of boundaries, identity becomes 'more unstable and increasingly fragile' (1992, p. 143).

Another strand in the moral construction of places is a similar link to temporality. Dixon and Durrheim (2000) discuss the idea of a sense of 'place destruction' (2000, p. 36). They argue that this is 'bound to a nostalgic conception of place-now versus lace-then' (2000, p. 36). We argue that the 'type' of tourist and their socio-cultural background will influence the way in which the history of the place or destination is brought into the totality of the socially constructed touristic experience. For example, a 'cultural tourist' visiting Spain may have a lay geographic knowledge of the cultural history of the place, different from a mass package tourist. Their moral judgements of people, their behaviour and the process of commodification of the destination may be derived from their imagined construction of the destination as well as their own cultural background. Clearly, as this paper has attempted to suggest, the use of space is an important tool for the everyday social actor, as it is not only a way of creating and assigning identity, but also provides a basis for the justification and accountability of identity, through the moral judgement of another.

Final Considerations

In this paper we have attempted to demonstrate how spaces are socially constructed into 'real', meaningful 'places' by ordinary social actors. We deployed Lefebvre's theory that space is socially produced by different user groups and hoped to show that ordinary people construct space in similar ways. We also proposed that through language constructions we can gain access to how place, identity and the political and moral construction of place is 'locally' achieved.

Members create symbolic and imaginary associations through their interactions and their participation in the places of tourism destinations, even though Lefebvre argues that representational spaces are the preserve of artists and philosophers. These are also the spaces of rhetoric and practice — ordinary members can aspire to describe and create meaning within spaces in much the same way, the key question is how society judges us on our use of space. The social construction of place is locally achieved — socially context-bound — it is something that is shared amongst others. The experience of tourism destinations is something that must be legitimised and warranted to others in society as a means of demonstrating that we are 'good' tourists, doing-being-a-proper-member-of-society.

Spatial practice can be informed or made more problematic when we factor in or consider age and experience, the nature of routine or habit and the level of involvement within spaces, either at home or on holiday. Through the process of postmodernism and the fragmentation of space the routine networks that constitute spatial practice are shifting, and therefore there is a possibility that social constructions of places change in their meaning over distance and time, and the possibility of conflicting social constructions could be increased.

In discussing the moral order in which we construct spaces socially, we must consider the locally produced methods through which members of a society position themselves as legitimate users of space. They may position themselves as 'locals' within defined tourism spaces and have different ways and means to construct their own behaviour in distinction to the behaviours of others — both 'real' locals and other tourists. We also argued that cultural knowledge and possibly social background might influence the lay geographical process through which social actors construct places. Yet as the breaking down of class barriers within destinations through low cost airlines providing cheap access for all, moral judgements from different users may provide for contested constructions or sites of resistance.

We argue that place is absolutely crucial to the social construction of self, place and meaning-making in tourist experience. Here we have difficulty in relation to some structuralist, interpretive theoretical assertions. However, we are not arguing for an essentialist typology of tourist. Touristic spaces are sites of consumption and construction, with varying and multiphenomenal experiential contexts. Conventional theory of 'non-places' (Auge, 1995), such as airport lounges, may in fact be sites of pure anticipatory joy, a chance to look forward to the pleasurable experiences to come and to prepare last-minute shopping, enjoy a meal or a drink in a bar. The same place for another traveller may be dull, meaningless and futile, it may be a site of constant use (perhaps for the business traveller or worker) and the experience in this case is tangential, arbitrary, desensitised. However the temporal aspect is crucial. For example, for the leisure traveller if there is a delay, the site of the airport lounge rapidly changes and becomes a site of anxiety and tension, dispute starts between the tourist and the tour operator or airline operator and the time spent in waiting eats into the precious time of the holiday itself — or the joyous return to the home. The space of the lounge is transformed into a negative, claustrophobic and all-consuming environment. The a priori, in situ and a posteriori experience of place is fundamentally significant in the social construction of place and identity.

What are the interactions between Lefebvre's three levels of social construction of space? Particularly considering issues of postmodernity and posttourist, that is does postmodernity mean that we have to make more or better justification for our experiences within space or less? We argue that the 'rootless' nature of postmodernism, with its destructive nature of dismantling boundaries, and emphasis on signs (Norton, 1996), activates a need within the social actor to emphasise place and identity links within interaction. Constructions of space and place attain increasing significance on one level; yet as argued earlier, the relative weight of these interleaved constructions slips and changes between contexts and temporal zones. There is possibly a tension within the individual to lay greater emphasis on constructing and reasserting their identities in spatial representations and constructions, which are peopled by reference groups that support these identity constructions. Could this be an attempt to re-create a distinctive boundary between one designated representation of social space and another? This paper, while theoretical in context, identifies the advantages that empirical analysis would introduce in taking the theoretical work further, and hopes to have opened up for discussion the construction processes of social space and identity.

References

Antaki, C., & Widdicombe, S. (Eds) (1998). *Identities in talk*. London: Sage.

Auge´, M. (1995). *"Non-places": Introduction to an anthropology of supermodernity*. London: Verso.

Bakhtin, M. (1984). *The dialogic imagination: Four essays*. Austin: University of Texas Press.

Bird, S. (2002) "It makes Sense to Us": Cultural identity in local legends of place. *Journal of Contemporary Ethnography, 31*, 519–547.

Boorstin, D. J. (1986). *The discoverers*. Middlesex: Penguin Books Limited.

Butcher, J. (2003). *The moralisation of tourism: Sun, sand ... and saving the world?* London: Routledge.

Cloke, P., & Perkins, H. (1998). "Cracking the Canyon with the Awesome Foursome": Representations of adventure tourism in New Zealand. *Environment and Planning D: Society and Space, 16*, 185–218.

Cohen, A. P. (1969). *The four voyages of Christopher Columbus.* London: Penguin Books Limited.

Cohen, E. (1972). Toward a sociology of international tourism. *Social Research, 39*, 164–189.

Cohen, E. (1974). Who is a tourist? A conceptual review. *Sociological Review, 22*, 27–53.

Cohen, E. (1979). A phenomenology of tourist experiences. *Sociology, 13*, 179–201.

Crouch, D. (2001). Spatialities and feeling of doing. *Social and Cultural Geography, 2*(1), 61–75.

Crouch, D. (Ed.) (1999). *Leisure/Tourism geographies: Practices and geographical knowledge.* London: Routledge.

Dann, G. M. S. (1996). *The language of tourism.* Wallingford: CAB International.

de Boeck, F. (1998). The rootedness of trees: Place as cultural and natural texture in rural South — West Congo. In: N. Lovell (Ed.) *Locality and belonging* (pp. 25–52), London: Routledge.

de Certeau, M. (1984). *The practice of everyday life.* London: University of California Press.

Desforges, L. (2000). Travelling the world: Identity and travel biography. *Annals of Tourism Research, 27*, 929–945.

Dixon, J. (2001). Contact and boundaries: "Locating" the social psychology of intergroup relations. *Theory and Psychology, 11*, 587–608.

Dixon, J., & Durrheim, K. (2000). Displacing place-identity: A discursive approach to locating self & other. *British Journal of Social Psychology, 39*, 27–44.

Edensor, T. (1998). *Tourists at the Taj: Performance and meaning at a symbolic site.* London: Routledge.

Edwards, D., & Potter, J. (1992). *Discursive psychology.* London: Sage.

Edwards, D. (1994). Discursive psychology: Illustrations and some methodological issues. *La psicologia discorsiva: Presentazione ed alaine questioni metodologiche. Rassegna di Psicologia, 11*(3), 9–40.

Featherstone, D. (1991). *Consumer culture and postmodernism.* London: Sage.

Fredrickson, L. M., & Anderson, D. H. (1999). A qualitative exploration of the wilderness experience as a source of spiritual inspiration. *Journal of Environmental Psychology, 19*, 21–39.

Fridgen, J.(1984). Environmental psychology and tourism. *Annals of Tourism Research, 11*, 19–39.

Garfinkel, H. (1967). *Studies in ethnomethodology.* Englewood Cliffs, NJ: Prentice-Hall.

Gordon, C. (Ed.) (1980). *Michel Foucault: Power/knowledge: Selected interviews and other writings 1972–1977 by Michel Foucault.* London: Harvester Wheatsheaf.

Goffman, E. (1959). *The presentation of self in everyday life.* London: Penguin.

Grossberg, L. (1997). Another boring day in paradise: Rock and roll and the empowerment of everyday life. In: K. Gelder, & S. Thornton (Eds) (1997) *The subcultures reader* (pp. 477–493), London: Routledge.

Gubrium, J. F (1993). "For a Cautious Naturalism". In: J. A. Holstein,& G. Miller (Eds), *Reconsidering social constructionism. Debates in social problems theory.* NY: Aldine de Gruyter.

Harvey, D. (1993). From space to place and back again: Reflections on the condition of postmodernity. In: J. Bird, B. Curtis, T. Putnam, G. Robertson, & L. Tickner (Eds), *Mapping the futures: Local cultures, global change* (pp. 3–29). New York: Routledge.

Hayden, D. (1997). Urban Landscape History: The sense of space and the politics of space. In: P. Groth, & T. Bressi (Eds), *Understanding ordinary landscapes* (pp. 111–133). London: Yale.

Heritage, J. (1984). *Garfinkel and ethnomethodology.* Cambridge: Polity Press.

Hirsch, E., & O'Hanlon, N. (Eds) (1995). *Anthropology of landscape: Between place and space.* Oxford: Oxford University Press.

Hughes, F. H. L. (1998). *Ritual, performance and media*. London: Routledge.

Jacobsen, J. K. S. (2001). Nomadic tourism and fleeting place encounters: Exploring different aspects of sightseeing. *Scandinavian Journal of Hospitality and Tourism, 1*(2), 99–112.

Kellner, D. (1992). Popular culture and the construction of postmodern identities. In: S. Lash, & J. Friedman (Eds), *Modernity and identity* (pp. 141–177). Oxford: Blackwell.

Korpela, K., & Hartig, T. (1996). Restorative qualities of favourite places. *Journal of Environmental Psychology, 16*, 221–233.

Lash, S., & Urry, J. (1994). *Economies of signs and space*. London: Sage.

Lefebvre, H. (1991). *The production of space*. Oxford: Blackwell.

Li, Y. (2000). Geographical consciousness and tourism experience. *Annals of Tourism Research, 27*(4), 863–883.

Lovell, N. (1998). *Locality and belonging*. London: Routledge.

MacCannell, D. (1992). *Empty meeting grounds: The tourist papers*. London: Routledge.

MacKay, H. (Ed.) (1997). *Consumption and everyday life: Culture, media and identities*. London: Sage in association with the Open University Press.

Macnaughtan, P., & Urry, J. (1999). *Contested natures*. London: Sage.

Malone, M. J. (1997). *Worlds of talk: The presentation of self in everyday conversation*. Cambridge: Polity Press.

McCabe, S., & Stokoe, E. H. (2004). Place and identity in tourists' accounts. *Annals of Tourism Research, 31*(3), 601–622.

Mels, T. (2002). Nature, home and scenery: The official spatialities of Swedish National Parks. *Society and Space, 20*, 135–154.

Miller, D., Jackson P., Thrift N., Holbrook B., & Rowlands M. (1998). *Shopping, place and identity*. London: Routledge.

Morgan, N., & Pritchard, A. (1998). *Tourism promotion and power: Creating images, creating identities*. Chichester: Wiley.

Mowforth, M., & Munt I. (1998). *Tourism and sustainability: New tourism in the Third World*. London: Routledge.

Norton, A. (1996). Experiencing nature: The reproduction of environmental discourse through safari tourism in East Africa. *Geoforum, 27*(3), 355–373.

Potter, J., & Wetherell, M. (1987). *Discourse and social psychology: Beyond attitudes and behaviour*. London: Sage.

Potter, J., & Wetherell, M. (1994). Analyzing discourse. In: A. Bryman, & R. G. Burgess (Eds), *Analyzing qualitative data* (pp. 47–66). London: Routledge.

Rodaway, P. (1994). *Sensuous geographies: Body, sense and place*. London: Routledge.

Rojek, C. (1995). *Decentring leisure: Rethinking leisure theory*. London: Sage.

Sacks, H. (1972). An initial investigation of the usability of conversational data for doing sociology. In: D. Sudnow (Ed.), *Studies in social interaction*. New York: Free Press.

Schegloff, E. A. (1972). Notes on a conversational practice: Formulating place. In: D. Sudnow (Ed.), *Studies in social interaction* (pp. 75–119). New York: Free Press.

Schutz, A. (1972) [1938]. *The phenomenology of the social world*. London: Heinemann.

Schutz., A., & Luckmann, T. (1973). *The structures of the life-world*. Evanston, IL: Northwestern University Press.

Seamon, D., & Mugeraner, R. (Eds) (1985). *Dwelling, place and environment: Towards a phenomenology of person and world*. Dordrecht: Martinus Nijhoff.

Shields, R. (1991). *Places on the margin: Alternative geographies of modernity*. London: Routledge.

Soja, E. W. (1993). *Postmodern geographies: The reassertion of space in critical social theory* (3rd ed.). London: Verso Publications Limited.

Soja, E. W. (1996). *Thirdspace: Journeys to Los Angeles and other real-and-imagined places.* Oxford: Blackwell.

Thrift, N. (1996). *Spatial formations.* London: Sage.

Tresidder, R. (1999). Tourism and sacred landscapes. In: D. Crouch (Ed.), *Leisure/Tourism geographies: Practices and geographical knowledge* (pp. 137–148). London: Routledge.

Tuan, Y. (1980). Rootedness versus sense of place. *Landscape, 24,* 3–8.

Tuan, Y. (1994). *Topophibia,* New York: Columbia University Press.

Urry, J. (1994). Cultural change and contemporary tourism. *Leisure Studies, 13,* 233–238.

Urry, J. (1995). *Consuming places.* London: Routledge.

Urry, J. (2002). *The tourist gaze, leisure and travel in contemporary societies.* London: Sage.

Wickens, E. (2002). The sacred and the Profane: A tourist typology. *Annals of Tourism Research, 29*(3), 834–851.

Young, M. (1999). The social construction of tourist places. *Australian Geographer, 30*(3), 373–389.

SECTION II:

LOCAL REALITIES: POST-INDUSTRIAL WORLD AND TRANSITIONAL ECONOMIES

Chapter 8

Power, Resources and Identity: The Influence of Tourism on Indigenous Communities

Donald V. L. Macleod

Introduction

This chapter considers the influence of tourism on indigenous communities and their identities through the exercise of power in the form of the utilisation of assets such as land, sea and labour by the industry and tourists, as well as the mixing of tourists with the indigenous population. In its conclusions it summarises the findings and relates them to the processes of making and consuming identity. Throughout the work different forms of power are acknowledged, as represented by politicians, business interests, landowners, the state, and expressed through the local community, groups, families and public initiatives among others. Power is understood as:

> The ability of a person or social unit to influence the conduct and decision-making of another through the control over energetic forms in the latter's environment (in the broadest sense of that term). (Fogelson & Adams, 1977, p. 388)

Considering identity, there are numerous understandings which are relevant to our discussion, including:

- Identity as: 'the identification of the self with a specific social position, cultural tradition or ethnic group; self-conception held in common by a group of people' (Seymour-Smith, 1986).
- Identity as a strategic and positional entity (Hall, 1996).

- Identity as a test to which all human beings are continually subjected (Lanfant, 1995).
- Identity as representative, in terms of folkloric costumes and practices such as music, dance, cuisine, etc., and a way people assert the authority of their knowledge, by claiming their status in terms of identity (Abram & Waldren, 1997).

The contexts of identity that are examined in this chapter include: (1) the stimulation and strengthening of identity through group allegiances and awareness, partly as a result of threats from external forces, and (2) the complexity of identity as manifest through the multiple influences of tourism on people as individuals and as members of groups.

Two very different case studies illustrate these points. (1) Bayahibe in the Dominican Republic: being an example of a country dominated by package tourism based on all-inclusive hotels, where pressure on the local people through competition for resources has promoted their cohesion. (2) La Gomera, The Canary Islands: where the site investigated has been dominated by independent 'alternative' tourists, usually backpacking and staying in rooms and apartments run by local families. The local people have had extensive contact and interaction with the tourists, leading to profound and diverse consequences on identities.

Context and Methodology of this Study

Research for the material on which the case studies are based was undertaken in the traditional social anthropological manner, including participant observation in the field which involves a lengthy period of time spent living amongst the community, observing their practices and occasionally, when possible, participating in activities. The objective is to uncover their ways of thinking, outlooks on the world — the 'emic' experience of the local indigenous population. Occasionally direct interviews were used to elicit specific information, for example local history or family connections. Direct observation of activities and the recording of empirical data such as the volume of tourist activity or the number of active fishermen also served to amass relevant primary research material. Contact with the different destinations has been maintained since 1989 in the case of La Gomera, and 1999 for the Dominican Republic. The process of identity formation and change is ongoing and subject to numerous influences, and it should be emphasised that it is an organic phenomenon, with the consequence that long-term observation is the most appropriate approach to take in order to achieve a deep understanding of the various impacts including tourism.

The two destinations are linked by a common history involving colonisation by Spain. La Gomera is part of the Canary Islands, an autonomous region of Spain, whereas the Dominican Republic (DR) is an independent nation state. Both have Castilian Spanish as their national language, and both officially celebrate their association with Columbus who departed from La Gomera on his explorations across the Atlantic, landing on the island of Hispaniola (which included DR).

In terms of wealth, the two destinations differ markedly, with the DR being regarded as a 'developing' country in terms of its economy (see Howard, 1999, p. 33). They also differ in terms of the type of tourism experienced: the DR hosts package tourists in all-inclusive hotels as a majority of its visitors, whereas La Gomera has a preponderance of independent backpacking tourists staying in private accommodation and, increasingly, apartment complexes. However, the focus of this chapter is on the indigenous communities based in small villages (Bayahibe and Vueltas) whose economies have changed from being based on fishing, to being reliant on the tourism industry. These examples offer us insights into the broad impacts of tourism as an economic framework and cultural interaction process imposed upon (to some extent) and embraced by a destination community. They also illustrate the various influences that tourists have on the local indigenous population and their identities in different forms.

Bayahibe, Dominican Republic

Bayahibe is a village (population 1800 in the year 2001) on the south east coast of the Dominican Republic. It developed around the late 18th century, when, according to the villagers, a Puerto Rican man settled in the area and one of his sons purchased land for his own children. This history, detailed further below, is crucial to an understanding of issues relating to power, resources and identity in this village, which have become intertwined with the tourism industry. It has direct repercussions throughout DR, with a resonance worldwide.

Historically, villagers extracted a near subsistence living and formed part of a peasant economy living from the land and sea, with fishing becoming the dominant mode of livelihood in the 20th century. Bayahibe village was altered by the occupying United States forces in 1916 when they added a metalled road; eventually a church and school were built. But the greatest shift, and it was literally that, came with the purchase of the land on which the village stood, a magnificent beach: an American company, Gulf and Western, had purchased the land in the 1960s and sold it to another company which planned to construct a hotel. In 1973 the village was moved almost half a mile along the coast, with new homes being built to rehouse some of the people. The enforced move incensed many people, some of whom later complained about their poor treatment and the lack of facilities for them. At the time the plan was supported by the autocratic President Balageur, protégé of the dictator Trujillo and favoured by the USA. But more upsetting for the villagers was the belief that the land had been stolen from them by the regional council and was not theirs to sell in the first place. The relocation occurred in 1973 but the struggle to prove ownership of land and gain compensation continues 30 years on.

The reason for this dispute goes back over a century: Juan Brito, the original Puerto Rican settler, arrived in 1798 and his youngest son (one of many children) Juan P. Brito purchased the land from the government for his own children in 1875. The kernel of the argument is that the local council falsely claims that Juan P. Brito eventually sold them the land. The council themselves later sold the land to a private company. A representative for the Britos, who now leads the fight, is pursuing their claim in the courts — as well as writing a history of the village, with a strong emphasis on the Brito family. By the year 2000 there were some 200 descendants hoping for a share of the inheritance. This family claim the equivalent of US$ 16.7 million compensation for the loss of land and rent (compare this to average salaries of less than US$5000/year).

Village Space, Resources and Power

The Brito family and the village had at one time received strong support in their struggle for land from a politician 'Senor Giraldi' during the 1980s, and his portrait is nailed to a tree in the village square, with the words '*Father of the liberation of Bayahibe*' written underneath, next to a painting of the village founder Juan P. Brito. This is an example of how local history, village identity and control over resources are coming together to create a material demonstration of attachment to place and the desire for power over local affairs. Lefebvre (1991) makes the distinction between 'representations of space' and 'representational space': the first — representations — being the space of planners and social engineers, conceptualised in terms of policies in a managerial, bureaucratic manner. The second type — representational — is concerned with users, the inhabitants, and can become a focus of identity: this is what is happening in the 'informal' construction and celebration of local history and heroes in the village centre (cf. Cohen, 1986 on identity and boundaries). These spaces are created through lived experience and become vital elements in the body and soul of the community — the making of identity.

Returning to the disputed beach zone and planning that is 'representations of space': a hotel has since been built on the beach and the sand and sea is cordoned off for the use of customers only — armed guards ensure the boundary is not breached. The hotel management tried recently (1999) to block the entire beach off for private use, and the road leading to it — but the villagers made a rapid early morning protest, blocking the main west-to-east arterial road route and drawing national attention to their plight: the hotel owners retracted. Such an episode has served to consolidate the Brito family in its fight for compensation; it also gives the village a strong sense of unified defiance against encroaching development, and ensured that the villagers pay an interest in local political affairs.

In addition to their impact on land ownership and use, the hotel companies have control over potable water: a subterranean source has been tapped and diverted to supply large hotels either side of the village: of which there were five with around 500 beds each in 2005. The villagers rely on brackish reserves which are becoming increasingly polluted by sewage and sea water — in the year 2000 villagers purchased drinking water from the shop; only the hardiest of old timers drank from the wells, although many continued to bathe themselves and clean their teeth in the outdoor natural rock-pools known as *agua mantiales*. However, the water pipe supplying potable water from the underground supply was finally officially turned on by the President of the country in the summer of 2001: a huge ritual involving dozens of armed guards, helicopters, limousines and the media.

Similarly, electricity supplied by private companies bypassed the village, going directly to the hotels. But by 2001 electricity lines from those companies had reached the village and people could use fridges for the first time (previously they had used ice brought in by lorry) and washing machines. Bayahibe, which had regarded itself (rightfully) as a neglected backwater, underdeveloped compared with many of its neighbours, now had the power, in terms of energy and resources, to help it boost its standing as a village and enhance future development, mostly related to tourism. The Secretary of the Committee for the Development of Bayahibe, Eduardo Brito, felt confident that the village would prosper and build amenities for the current population and immigrants that would support its growing tourist industry.

Major Changes in Identity

Hotel resort tourism dominates the industry in the Dominican Republic; the hotels tend to be all-inclusive, bounded by fences and protected by guards. Very few foreign visitors travel independently — the infrastructure is not prepared — although there are usually rooms for rent in most villages, and on the north coast a few small towns offer apartments and hotels. Bayahibe is surrounded along the coast by large hotels. Apart from the consequences outlined above relating to resource use, they offer direct employment to the villagers, mostly unskilled work, and they have also given the men of Bayahibe a means of indirect employment that has dramatically changed the economic bedrock and to some extent, culture and identity of the village.

Every day, up to a thousand tourists pass through Bayahibe. They disembark at the main beach, simply to take a motor-boat over to the Island of Saona, which is visited by some 100 boats daily, and they remain there for most of the day taking part in beach-based activities: an outing promoted by the hotels as 'the country's number one selling excursion'. The journey to the island lasts around 30 min and is undertaken in fibreglass speed boats driven by the men of Bayahibe. It is estimated that around 100 men from the village work as 'captains' on the boats, most are employed by small companies and a few run their own boats. A French couple initiated the boat-trip business: they took tourists to the island on their yacht in the 1980s. Currently, the boat excursions business based in Bayahibe has an annual turnover worth many millions of dollars. The island itself is part of a national park 'Parque del Este', and the organisation (a quango) that runs it receives around half a million dollars for entrance fees (see Macleod, 2001). Figure 8.1 shows the Dominican Republic and its position within the Caribbean with the island of Saona clearly marked; Bayahibe is situated approximately 15 miles southeast along the coast from La Romana.

In less than 20 years Bayahibe has transformed from being a quiet fishing village where almost all the men went to sea, into a noisy departure point dominated by speed-boats racing to Saona Island and coach-loads of tourists passing through. The tourists do not usually enter the village centre, but are disgorged onto a car park on its edge, and on their return they go straight into their coaches and are shipped back to their hotels. The repercussions of this are many: the men of Bayahibe no longer fish for a living; the fish have moved from this part of the coastline, driven away by noise and pollution; the economy of the village is dependent on the tourist arrivals and is also subject to the changing vicissitudes of businessmen who own boats — new, bigger and more efficient boats mean the smaller boats owned by local men become uncompetitive. As a community the fishermen no longer work together, the skills of fishing are not passed down through the generations; the village seascape itself loses its aesthetic attraction as the few wooden fishing boats are replaced by fibreglass speed-boats. Ironically, the village is increasingly promoted (and consumed by visitors) as a 'fishing village' with a poster image of the gaff-rigged sail boats that once dominated the skyline used to market the village. Only six of these impressive boats remained in 2001 following a devastating

Figure 8.1: Map of the Dominican Republic and the Caribbean.
Source: Columbus World Travel Guide (2004).

hurricane in 1998, and they are increasingly redundant due to the move away from fishing as a career.

In summary, the influences of tourism on identity in the village may be described as follows. There has been a strengthening of kinship grouping for the Britos through their need to cohere and to contest the land claims: this has been a historical process, accelerated in recent times. It might be said that they are developing into an 'aristocratic' lineage in the village and their social identity has become more powerful in tandem with their economic and political influence. Similarly, a bonding of the villagers as a community to contest rights to land and the beach has occurred, and seen physical manifestation in protest activities that generate an awareness of their existence as a relevant political unit.

A more direct impact on the material existence and actual production of the villagers has occurred with the displacement of the labour force through a transformation of the economic base from fishing to a service industry based on tourism. This has changed the type of work associated with the sea — the culture of fishing is being eroded by the alternative opportunities offered by the tourism industry, especially the motor-boat operations. Together with the arrival of day-trippers to Saona Island have come passing trades-people and labourers as well as a few independent tourists wanting rooms for rent. This has led to the development of small-scale accommodation services and increasing interaction with foreign visitors through business transactions and leisure activities: bars, hotel and beach work changing the local domestic identity of parts of the village. A transformation has occurred with the former area of private family homes becoming a place that offers rooms for rent in a zone that also serves visitors through small bars and restaurants.

All this activity and trade has meant an increase in the development of Bayahibe through its growing economy as a tourist destination and nodal point, leading to the raising of its profile nationally and attracting state support and other resources. This has produced a growth in communal self-confidence in the village, which has changed from a peripheral settlement, relatively abandoned by central government, into an important asset and location in need of support and basic amenities, with a heightened sense of political identity and value.

The above examination of Bayahibe has focused on the material impact of the tourism industry on the people, an experience that has influenced their personal lives, family and group community identity through economic and political change. The region supports a type of tourism — hotel dominated mass tourism — in which big business governs the situation. The next example focuses on an area that has experienced low-level numbers of backpacking, independent, alternative tourists. One in which the villagers have had some control over their own economic lives and gained more directly from tourism. Further, and importantly, they have had more direct contact with the tourists, and this has led to tourism having a diverse and complex impact on many aspects of their lives and identities.

Vueltas, La Gomera

Vueltas is a port situated at the mouth of the valley known as Valle Gran Rey (VGR), which is on the southwest coast of La Gomera, a small Canary Island close to Tenerife. Tourism began to increase following the introduction of a ferry service between Tenerife (Los Cristianos) and La Gomera (San Sebastian), in the mid-1970s. It brought over the more adventurous backpackers, who accepted the arduous road journey to the beautiful valley with its unspoilt volcanic sand beaches. These tourists were predominantly Germans, aged between 20 and 45, often well educated, with a desire for a relaxed vacation in an undeveloped region, with sun and an unspoilt natural environment. They usually rented rooms, and later, apartments, built, owned and managed by the indigenous people.

Vueltas was settled at the beginning of the 20th century by fishermen from other parts of the island and Tenerife who knew of the good offshore tuna fishing. They were not made welcome by the largely agriculturally oriented population in the main beach zone and valley, so they built their houses out of stones and also dwelt in the caves on the periphery of the coastal plain. Vueltas became a fishing village with almost every family making a living from the sea. During the 1960s, and 1970s fishing was a very successful industry on the island, however, global trends and changing markets led to its shrinkage. By the early 1980s, a new form of income was arriving in the guise of tourists, and in 1983 an enterprising fisherman invested his savings into converting rooms in his house into an apartment, having seen others on the main beach attract visitors. He later built a set of apartments near the seafront and helped to start an explosion in construction. By the mid-1990s, Vueltas with its population of 350 people had an additional 300 beds for rent (see Macleod, 2004 for a detailed account of the above issues).

From Fishing to Tourism

Between 1990 and 2000, the number of service outlets in Vueltas almost doubled from 33 to 52, and the percentage owned by foreign settlers increased from 27% to 53%. Many tourists decided to stay put and they now operate bars and restaurants, and dominate the boutiques, as well as offering bike-hire, photo shops and dolphin tours. One German settler, known locally as 'Capitano Claudio', has lived in the village for well over a decade and began renting his yacht out to tourists. Eventually he came to own three ex-fishing boats and began to operate several 'dolphin and whale' sightseeing tours on a daily basis. The success of this business helped to attract other tour companies: in 2004 two large (50-seater) boats gave daily tours around much of the coast and advertised themselves using dolphin sighting as a magnet.

This transformation in the economic base of the village, indicative of change in the entire valley, has clear repercussions for identity. The old established profession of fishing has been eclipsed in importance by tourism services; in fact, the leisure-based dolphin tours turn over almost as much money annually as the 50 or so full- and part-time fishermen based at the port. The culture of the fishermen has been quickly transformed by competing employment opportunities and global competition: some older men have been enticed into working on tour boats, others have gone into the supermarket business, whilst the younger men find work in the bars, as labourers on building sites and in white-collar jobs.

Fishing is a complete way of life, with its demands on the fisher's daily timetable, the necessity for knowledge of the sea, the boat and equipment, as well as experience of weather, sea currents, types of fish and so on. Fishermen and their families form a tight community in Vueltas: almost all were linked through kinship (Macleod, 1993, 2004) — fathers would teach sons, and until the 1980s fishermen would hope to marry into another fishing family (Mesa–Moreno, 1982). The sons, wives and daughters of the fishermen had their lives directly influenced by this profession. With the decline in the numbers fishing and the rapid growth of the service sector, some see this demise as a culture on the wane, almost disappearing (Macleod, 2002).

Identity and Its Various Manifestations

Identity is a complex and broad concept, and the fishermen's professional identity is but one facet of their personal and communal selves. On La Gomera, as with many other places, people are strongly associated with the neighbourhood in which they live and/or grew up: there are nicknames for people from specific districts, such as fighters, gossips, pigeons and daredevils. Someone who lived in an adjoining valley would be regarded as an *extranjero* (stranger). Even within VGR there are distinct locales: Vueltas (population 350) is divided into two areas, known as Italia and Abysinnia respectively, split apparently by both physical and political divisions. Vueltas itself is regarded as a peripheral part of VGR and its populace are relative newcomers to the valley. VGR is also regarded as a peripheral and somewhat raffish part of La Gomera, itself peripheral to the larger island of Tenerife, part of the Canary Island archipelago, peripheral to Spain.

However, tourism has changed much of the region's former marginalisation and isolation. Economically, Vueltas finds itself at the centre of a boom on La Gomera, and the municipality has gained wealth from tourism, as well as political standing and funding from the European Union. The indigenous people, who once regarded fellow islanders as strangers, daily come face-to-face with people from other nations or even continents. Their sense of selves as Gomeros and Canary Islanders has been heightened. Following from this has been a gradual realisation that many of their treasured unique arts and crafts, including music, dance and the whistling language 'silbo', are attractive to foreign visitors, who will consume these products of locality and identity in the sense of an experience, as well as purchasing items. One result of this is the increasing investment of money and time into celebrating and learning traditional dance, which visitors find especially enjoyable. This is not strictly a form of cultural involution as McKean (1989) suggested was the case for Bali; rather, the events in La Gomera show a regeneration and a reinforced confidence manifest through increased interest and participation among the younger generation.

The use of the sea and its creatures, once dominated by exploitation for food (as with the land and agriculture) is changing: the value-added activities, the new wealth creators, have become leisure oriented. Dolphin-watching, swimming, leisure-boating, walking in the forest and mountain-biking are all on the ascendant. The 'tourist gaze' (after Urry, 1990) has helped transform the interaction of the population with the natural environment. Equally, ancient crafts such as hand-pottery and the rituals of dance and song have been commodified for aesthetic and entertainment purposes. This transformation has been very rapid, occurring in less than one generation, the past decade of the 1990s being quickest. Some local people complain about the loss of certain (uncommercialised) traditions, the loss of their beach and village to foreign visitors and settlers, and more fundamentally, the loss of the community spirit to a competitive individualism.

Transformations in identities have reached profound levels — into the family lives of the indigenous population, and the personal psyche of individual members of that population. With the arrival of the tourists came an increase in opportunities for meeting people — especially for local men who would pursue the women tourists for sexual opportunities among other reasons. The honour–shame complex of 'Mediterranean' societies (see Goddard, 1987; Gilmore, 1987) was part of the cultural make-up and gender roles well delineated: nudity was frowned upon, men and women bathed at separate ends of the beach until the late 1960s. Women were expected to live sexually modest lives; the permissiveness of Northern Europe had not touched La Gomera. Gradually, with the arrival of tourists who were usually young, single and open-minded, serious relationships developed between local men and tourist women. By 1990 there were over six such couples in Vueltas. Consequently, foreign women were becoming introduced into the kinship network; they brought with them new attitudes towards motherhood, parenting, food, fashion, the behaviour of women and freedom. This has major consequences, not only on the families involved, but also on other observers, neighbours and friends.

Moreover, villagers, particularly young women, were able to see with their own eyes how foreign women behaved; often with far greater freedom and confidence than they themselves possessed. These new tourists gave demonstrable, tangible proof that there are alternative ways of behaving — offering a new definition of womanhood. This 'demonstration effect' might be thought to have influenced local women to reconsider and reconfigure their personal identity, as well as what it means to be a woman. The tourists, and especially the settlers, have participated in the making of new identities on a very personal level.

Power, Resources and Conflict

In terms of power and resources, the foreign tourists and settlers have been able to gain from their economic and cultural capital advantage: most noticeably in the growth of foreign-run business, and recently the purchasing of property where the open market has been operating publicly since the late 1980s. The turn towards a leisure-oriented economy is the prime manifestation of this advantage. It has been strongly supported by the European Union and the Spanish Government funding for the development of the infrastructure including roads, tunnels and an airport: some of this development, however, has not been received warmly by the indigenous residents.

A proposal to transform the seafront into a year-round sandy beach attraction was made by the local council, and was seen as a 'done deal' by some. This would have involved the creation of a concrete promenade and the construction of huge groynes jutting out to sea, which would hinder long-shore drift and trap sand for the entire year — as opposed to the natural system which took the sand away for the winter months. Millions of pesetas had been set aside for the project. However, various people became aware of this major development, and word got around prompting an undercover operation to oppose the project and hence the mayor. It is pertinent to mention that the mayor is in a very powerful position in the municipality and is able to refuse licenses to businesses and influence contract bids. It was generally believed that he favoured his supporters: patronage plays a large part in the political scene.

Eventually a public meeting was held, and two main divisions were apparent: the mayor, his councillors, developers and the right-wing parties were opposed by the left-wing parties, ecologists and a huge throng of local villagers. Both political parties invoked the tourism industry in support of their argument: the mayor saying that it would attract more people to the beach; whereas the opposition believed the unnatural artificial beach would turn the 'green' tourists away. It was apparent at the public meeting that the mayor's project was very unpopular, and it was eventually shelved. This major confrontation over tourism development was a watershed in public affairs and truly established the importance of tourism for the village as well as allowing the people to express their anger about the gradual ruination of the valley and the beach. One newspaper wrote: 'We are able to say that at last democracy has arrived in Valle Gran Rey' (*La Gaceta*, December 1990).

Conclusion

The final example of the protest on La Gomera draws a clear parallel with the experience of the villagers in the Dominican Republic who demonstrated against the hotel's attempts to close off an access road and appropriate the beach. In both cases a section of the indigenous population acted as a group, increasing their sense of solidarity as a unit with similar interests and as a group in opposition to a threat. Both incidents had clear and unambiguous political ramifications with the community acting together to retain control over resources. Tourism and its consequences have been the source of conflict that has indirectly led to the making and consolidation of social identities.

There are many ways in which we can see the people's identity being influenced by tourism on La Gomera, and these are summarised below. The proximity and communication between the indigenous population and the tourists has led to numerous serious partnerships, much general interaction and the introduction of new ideas and ways of behaving, particularly concerning gender roles. There has been a tremendous learning experience, often at a personal level, and new ideas and expectations have been introduced. Added to the sense of increased opportunities, wealth creation due to tourism gives women real chances for independence and enables younger generations of men and women to embrace working lives that do not depend on the traditional primary economy — fishing and agriculture. This influences their 'professional' identity and perceptions of self-reliance and confidence. Furthermore, the repercussions spread, and as a consequence of the increasing possibility of independence for women, gender roles within the family are changing, especially in terms of the wife providing economic support. Additionally, the traditional role of the husband has been challenged.

Due partly to the interest shown by tourists in traditional customs, arts and crafts have experienced a rejuvenation and this leads to a growth of local pride and public display, exemplified by the flourishing of traditional dance groups. In turn, the Gomero's sense of being unique is heightened by constant interaction with foreign nationals: cultural differences become blatant and a daily experience. Interestingly, the indigenous people are themselves becoming consumers of the cultural identities stimulated by the reactions of tourists, and they increasingly enjoy and practice traditional performance arts and purchase or make traditional artefacts.

The transfer of the economic base from fishing to tourism (private accommodation, shops and hotel services) has eroded the fishermen's culture and identity through the diminution of their number and activity, and the gradual loss of knowledge necessary for fishing professionally. A loss of the old ways and sense of community is commonly expressed by the indigenous population. Foreign tourists dominate the public spaces; privacy and tranquillity are being subordinated to tourist activities, construction, traffic and general development. The pace and pressure of life is also helping to reduce family interaction and weaken the kinship dependence: shared meals and the casual visit are falling victim to increased pressure on time and the growth of alternative leisure activities.

Both examples from the Caribbean and the Canary Islands have shown the profound influence of tourism and tourists on the identities of indigenous people and the relevance of power and resources in the process (cf. Britton, 1982). They illustrate how social and cultural identities may be reshaped at a local level by tourism, with new identities being made and older ones, such as 'fishing village' being reconstructed and consumed as a marketed attraction and, paradoxically, consumed to near extinction by the entire process of the growth of the service sector. These case studies draw attention to the importance of appreciating and understanding the diversity of host communities, the complexity of their interaction with tourists and the industry, and the variety of influences and outcomes from the process.

To summarise, we can say that tourism has an impact on a vast array of social identities, and in different contexts it has different degrees of impact, weakening or strengthening, creating or destroying. The case studies have shown tourism to have influenced identities in the following areas: gender (the roles of women and men); work (from fishermen to boat captains and service industry employees); kinship (the strengthening of lineages, and the changing structure of the family unit); politics (the village as a vulnerable group, but also as an assertive unit); ethnicity (the increasing awareness of cultural distinctiveness and heritage). Issues involving power and resources, stimulated by tourism, have influenced change in these social identities, and this is a process that remains ongoing and of increasing relevance to tourists, indigenous people at destination sites and those interested in their future.

Acknowledgments

My thanks, as ever, go to the people of Bayahibe and Vueltas who have helped me with my work, showing patience and offering friendship. Similarly, I am grateful to the Institute of Social and Cultural Anthropology at the University of Oxford, and the University of Glasgow, Crichton Campus for their support over the years.

References

Abram, S., & Waldren, J. (1997). Introduction: Tourists and tourism: Identifying with people and places. In: S. Abram, J. Waldren, & D. V. L. Macleod (Eds), *Tourists and tourism: Identifying with people and places* (pp. 1–12). Oxford: Berg.

Britton, S. (1982). The political economy of tourism in the Third World. *Annals of Tourism Research, 9*, 331–358.

Cohen. A. P. (Ed.). (1986). *Symbolising boundaries: Identity and diversity in British cultures.* Manchester: Manchester University Press.

Columbus World Travel Guide. (2004). *Map of the Dominican Republic and the Caribbean.* www.travel-guide.com/data/dom/dommap.asp

Fogelson, R. D., & Adams, R. N. (Eds). (1977). *The Anthropology of power.* New York: Academic Press.

Gilmore, D. (Ed.). (1987). *Honour and shame and the unity of the Mediterranean* (American Anthropological Association Special Publications. No. 22, pp. 2–21). Washington: American Anthropological Association.

Goddard, V. (1987). Honour and shame: The control of women's sexuality and group identity in Naples. In: P. Caplan, (Ed.). *The cultural construction of sexuality.* London: Routledge.

Hall, S. (1996). Introduction: Who needs identity? In: S. Hall, & P. duGay (Eds), *Questions of cultural identity*. London: Sage.

Howard, D. (1999). *Dominican Republic: A guide to the people, politics and culture*. London: Latin American Bureau.

Lanfant, M. (1995). International tourism, internationalization and the challenge to identity. In: M. Lanfant, J. B. Allcock, & E. M. Bruner (Eds). *International tourism: Identity and change*. London: Sage.

Lefebvre, H. (1991). *The production of space*. Oxford: Blackwell.

Macleod, D. V. L. (1993). *Change in a Canary Island fishing settlement, with reference to the influence of tourism*. Unpublished D. Phil thesis, University of Oxford.

Macleod, D. V. L. (2001). Parks or people? National parks and the case of Del Este, Dominican Republic. *Progress in Development Studies*, *1*(3), 221–235.

Macleod, D. V. L. (2002). Disappearing culture? Globalisation and a Canary Island fishing community. *History and Anthropology*, *13*(1), 53–67.

Macleod, D. V. L. (2004). *Tourism, globalisation and cultural change: An island community perspective*. Cleveland: Channel View Publications.

McKean, P. (1989). Towards a theoretical analysis of tourism: Economic dualism and cultural involution in Bali. In: V. Smith (Ed.). *Hosts and guests: The anthropology of tourism* (2nd ed., pp. 119–138). Philadelphia: University of Pennsylvania Press.

Mesa-Moreno, C.(1982). Antropologica Social de las Communidades Pesqueras en Valle Gran Rey. In: C. Mesa Moreno, J. Pascual–Fernandez, & A. J. Perez Soca (Eds), *La Pesca en Canarias* (pp. 73–115). Tenerife, Spain: CCPC.

Seymour-Smith, C. (1986). *Macmillan dictionary of anthropology*. London: Macmillan Press Ltd.

Urry, J. (1990). *The tourist gaze: Leisure and travel in contemporary societies*. London: Sage.

Chapter 9

The Development of Cultural Iconography in Festival Tourism

Philip Feifan Xie

Introduction

There is considerable interest in touristic iconography (Burstein, 2000; Stampino, 2001; Sternberg, 1997) for travel destinations. The term *iconography* is defined as "the descriptive and classificatory study of images with the aim of understanding the direct or indirect meaning of the subject matter represented" (Bialostocki, 1963, p. 770). Iconography can be viewed as the activity of making products saleable by imbuing them with desirable images (Sternberg, 1997). Tourism scholars have recognized that tourists visit a place because of the image they hold and, moreover, that the touristic destinations themselves are designed to project an appealing image. The images include a series of markers that have been identified, promoted, and marketed to the public. In the field of festivals and special events, cultural markers highlighted by distinctive icons, different languages, dress codes, and religious roots, play a critical role in the success of the events. Although studies of iconography have been widely applied to the tourism experience and destination planning (Gallarza, Saura, & Garcia, 2002), little research has been undertaken in the context of festival tourism. The significance of festival iconography has been neglected in previous research and the marketing value of these markers is yet to be realized.

The focus of this study is on cultural markers, as indicators of festival iconography, in order to understand the significance in a special event. The analysis of cultural markers will provide an important set of approaches to the understanding of iconography. The Canadian American (Can-Am) Festival in Myrtle Beach, South Carolina, was chosen as a case study for the development of festival iconography. The longitudinal nature of the festival and cross-cultural experience offer a primary advantage in studying the evolution of the destination. This chapter introduces the study of touristic iconography through a

Tourism and Social Identities: Global Frameworks and Local Realities
Copyright © 2006 by Elsevier Ltd.
All rights of reproduction in any form reserved.
ISBN: 0-08-045074-1

brief literature review. It examines the changes of cultural markers and their influence upon destination development by using a thematic content analysis and mystery guest methodology. It is suggested that festival iconography, through the use of cultural markers, plays a critical role in event promotion, marketing, and advertising. Three aspects of the research are addressed: (1) the interpretation of current markers and their meaning; (2) the evolution of these markers throughout the years that the special event has occurred; and (3) the significant relationship between cultural iconography and festival tourism.

The Study of Touristic Iconography

The concept of iconography has more in common with semiotics, which is the study of systems of symbols and signs (Hay, 2000). Iconography has long been employed in the field of cultural geography where culture is a text that can be read and interpreted (Geertz, 1973). Traditionally, cultural geographers have concerned with the study of landscape in all of its various forms, from cultural to physical. In particular, the meanings assigned to the urban landscape. Cultural landscape has come to be understood as "a way of life, encompassing ideas, attitudes, languages, practices, institutions and structures of power, and a whole range of cultural practices: artistic forms, texts, canons, architecture, mass-produced commodities and so forth" (Nelson, Treichler, & Grossberg, 1992, p. 5). The underlying assumption of touristic iconography is a destination and should be commodified so that it can be consumed by the tourist. The place of tourist consumption must, therefore, be produced as iconic. The word "iconic" denotes a strong sense of the visual, and means, literally, power-laden image.

Festivals and special events are the most common way to interact with different cultures and customs (Dimanche, 1994; Getz, 1991). Examples such as the Oktoberfest, St. Patrick parade, and Chinese New Year celebrations in Europe and North America provide colorful and entertaining ways of cultural understanding. The cross-cultural distinctiveness forms a variety of images that provide a meaningful experience for tourists. Cultural markers are a primary medium through which people relate to visual images and evoke desire for tourist participation and involvement (Markwell, 1997). The identification and description of these markers became known as iconography (Harbour, 2000). The destination, in order to maintain its attraction for visitors, needs to maintain its appeal through offering icons of what visitors want to experience. Sternberg (1997) suggests that iconography is a process where tourism products are composed to provide visitors with "evocative" images of what they wish to experience about the place they are seeking. The icon, therefore, is produced with images of themes of the destination and its culture. These themes are offered in products such as souvenirs, activities such as tours, and within general establishments such as restaurants and hotels. It is the image of the destination that the tourist consumes, not the reality of day-to-day life of the host destination.

There are two levels of cultural definitions in the context of festival tourism. The first involves the diffusion and institutionalization of the concepts of heritage and culture. The second involves state sanctioning of particular cultural markers and of particular discourses of nationhood (Wood, 1984). A cultural marker such as a national symbol, color, or spatial organization denotes an important source for tourism planning and marketing.

For example, Badre and Allen (1989) identified numerous cultural markers in web sites around the world and proposed the following three stages of using cultural markers: (1) foraging, which involves categorizing cultural markers by country, genre, and language; (2) identifying, which is a detailed inspection of cultural markers listed by country and genre; and (3) patterning, an in-depth analysis of "deep culture" and "shallow culture" and generalization of a consistent pattern for business and marketing. The authors showed that culturability, the merging of cultural markers and usability, has strong implications for business development. Cultural markers can be thought of as something in the mind of the beholder from both producers and consumers as well as something tangible in reality. An example is provided by Moorti (2004) in which the regional Tamil game shows, through cultural markers presented on the mass media, enable audiences to forge complex links between global and national identities, links that confound local/global, tradition/modernity binaries. Through an analysis of touristic iconography in the Tamil game shows, festival tourism plays a key role on a vernacular nationalism and a cosmopolitan sensibility. The commodified culture of the game shows foregrounds a Tamil cultural affiliation that is glossy and depoliticized.

However, cultural iconography is often overlooked in the festival and special event field since it conveys messages and markers, but these are not always clearly expressed. The marketing value of these markers has yet to be realized. Therefore, the analysis of cultural markers provides an important set of approaches to the understanding of iconography. In particular, understanding the evolution of cultural markers in a given festival not only provides a useful tool for promotion and planning, but also reflects a pattern of consumer (tourists) behavior. For example, ancient Hula dance festival in Hawaii originated from historical events, tales, and the accomplishments of the royal rulers. Facial expressions, hand gestures, hip swaying, and dance steps all showcase the ethnic identity of Hawaiian Polynesia. For a long time, the tourism industry in Hawaii heavily promoted the natural features of the islands, not the aboriginal people. However, the figure of the Hula girl first appeared in advertising in 1910, and, by the 1920s, images of Native Hawaiians and specifically Hula iconography had become an integral part of tourism promotions. Gradually, Native Hawaiian culture became commodified and enacted through dance shows as a way of authenticating the destination image (Desmond, 1999). In recent decades, the original meaning of Hula festival has evolved into "ideal" natives who are graciously welcoming to outsiders and who present visitors with alluring encounter with "soft primitivism" (Smith, 1985, p. 5). The choreography of Hula has been influenced by contemporary or modern dance, and, in what Kaeppler (2004, p. 294) calls "recycling tradition", a fusion form of Hula dance was created. Visitors were attracted into a new folk dance — *Hapa Haole* (a performance done by a person of half-white, half-Hawaiian descent). The festival has rejuvenated into a large commercial *luau* show, a smorgasbord consumed by visitors encompassing native food, songs, and a "whitened" Hawaiian.

Canadian American Days Festival

Historically, Canadians have struggled to find their own national identities (Ferguson & Ferguson, 2001). Unlike the United States, Canada has no uncontested defining core heritage into which newly recognized components could be co-opted (Graham, Ashworth, & Tunbridge, 2000). In fact, Canada has existed reactively to Britain and the United States, and has lacked any clear national identity cemented by an unequivocal national heritage. Canada as a country has such a blurred or non-existent image in the United States that there are few, if any, stereotypes that come readily to mind to signal to Americans that someone is Canadian (Simpson, 2000). Canadians are difficult to recognize in the United States because Americans see their northern neighbors as "just like us" with few differences. In addition, Canadians are heavily Americanized before they travel in United States and can easily hide their nationality if they choose. Although it can be argued that wearing a maple leaf on clothing or affixing "eh" to the end of every sentence would show a distinctive culture, Canadian cultural markers have become more and more difficult to identify. Given that situation, a cross-cultural understanding between Americans and Canadians has become expected. Cultural iconography has become major components to identify Canadian customs and heritage. Surprisingly, few cross-cultural festivals in both countries have been promoted thus far. Such festivals generally occur in border cities, as the Friendship Festival held in Niagara Falls. The Can-Am Festival in Myrtle Beach, located 800 miles away from Canada, provides not only a unique opportunity for Americans to understand and appreciate Canadian culture from farther afield, but also an important tourist attraction for Canadian vacationers.

The Can-Am Festival was an outgrowth of Canadians who originally visited the Myrtle Beach area without any special incentives. The success of the event is the result of random chance and the trial-and-error developments over 45 years (1961–present). Repeat visits to the festival are apparently high due to the fact that Canadians can drive to Myrtle Beach in only one day to access good weather instead of taking an extra day to reach Florida. The festival has promoted the development of businesses and enhanced the image of Myrtle Beach. At one time, it was the single event that began the Spring Season. Now the annual events include golfing and auto shows. The Can-Am Festival has had an evolutionary pattern and set the standards and processes by which all events are developed in the Myrtle Beach area. It is one of the most notable international festivals in North America that involves significant tourism development. Patterns can be identified because it has a multiyear lineage (Mayfield & Crompton, 1995; Rose & Kingma, 1989). The festival is held in March and coincides with school spring breaks, especially in the area of origin — Ontario and the Atlantic Provinces in Canada. It is estimated to attract approximately 30,000 tourists annually, including "snowbirds" who are mostly retirees migrating from Canada for the warmer weather during the winter.

Methodology

Two primary methodologies were undertaken in this study: a thematic content analysis and a mystery guest methodology. A thematic content analysis was used to study the adaptation/adjustment issues that influence the strategies (Ramaprasad & Hasegawa, 1992; Turley & Kelley, 1997; Wheelan & Abraham, 1993). The analysis included newspaper articles over 41 years (1961–2002) in order to gather information on the nature of the event and its development. Primary newspaper articles were reviewed as well as editorial pages to gain some insights from a temporal linear perspective. The newspaper reviewed was the Myrtle Beach daily newspaper, *The Sun News*. In addition, tourism brochures and videos about the Myrtle Beach area were collected from the local Chamber of Commerce and historical data was obtained from the city's libraries. The analysis traces an evolutionary nature of the festival that influences the long-term relationships between Canadians and Americans in Myrtle Beach (Butler, 1980; Schultis, Johnston, & Twynam, 1996).

The mystery guest methodology employs observers who attended the event as a "mystery guest", posing as tourists in Myrtle Beach. During the festival, these mystery guests identified cultural markers and asked questions about these markers in relation to the Canadian participants. Mystery guest is a methodology in which a participant is asked to evaluate experiences and identify important factors that influence the nature of the experiences from a guest's viewpoint (Huckstein & Duboff, 1999). The approach has been widely adopted and adapted in consumer reports and the hotel industry (Marvin, 1992; McCarthy, 1998). In fact, mystery guests can be viewed as participant observers to understand more fully the meanings of the event and the contexts of cultural markers. The methodology is very effective because it is a nonintrusive system in which observation is an important element. In addition, the interpretation of the mystery guest and the evaluation of this event were done through identifying the most significant markers during the trip (Withiam, 1995). The authors of the present investigation undertook the roles of "mystery guests" during the festival from 1999 to 2002. A total of 85 participants including information personnel, business proprietors, restaurant personnel, and tourists were interviewed. Field notes were taken to identify the important findings, to help interpret the experience, and to bring a final understanding to the data through a focus group discussion. The focus groups were carried out by experts who had knowledge of the travel industry, particularly in the field of festivals and residency issues (Krueger, 1994). The field notes serves as a memory refresher so that when the focus group interview was held at the end of the trips, the "mystery guests" would have an accurate record to assess the markers and icons they identified on the trip.

Findings of Content Analysis

A thematic content analysis of the newspaper and the symbols were analyzed ranging from 1961 to 2002. The primary purpose of the thematic content analysis was to explore cultural markers and how these markers have been used to develop an atmosphere of welcoming for the Canadians (see Table 9.1). During the 1960s, the festival was in its initial phase of development and there was much enthusiasm among the business community to have additional visitors to Myrtle Beach, especially in the spring when business was very slow. The structure developed for the festival in the first few years included special events, primarily of Canadian interest. There was extensive coverage of Canadian news, and individuals from home communities in Canada were invited to make presentations at local businesses and malls in order to foster an atmosphere of Canadian hospitality (*Sun News*, 1962). Canadian news was viewed as an important marker in this period of time since it opened a window of opportunity for Americans to understand Canada and raised awareness of the country.

Table 9.1: Development of Can-Am Festival in Myrtle beach.

Years	Development of Can-Am Festival	Cultural markers
1960s	Initial phase of the development and enthusiasm from the business community	Canadian news, Canadian individuals
1970s	Heyday of the development and events specifically tailored to Canadian visitors	Advertisements, Canadian flag, the maple leaf, Canadian style breakfast and Mountie
1980s	Expansion and positive reaction from Myrtle Beach communities	Snowbirds, currency exchange rate on par
1990s	Saturation and diversification of the development, business interest in festival waned. The advertisements has down sharply	Golf, Canadian flag
2000 – present	Stagnation and blurring of Canadian distinctiveness	American and Canadian flags (friendship)

The 1970s represented the heyday of the festival in terms of generating interest for Canadians. The business community continued to make the event larger to increase the number of tourists. The planned events were specifically targeted to Canadians. The local newspaper published a special section for the Can-Am Days and provided a detailed schedule of the event. Business participation increased by up to 60% in terms of the number of advertisements placed in the newspaper. An analysis of the advertisements showed the use of symbols, especially the Canadian flag, the maple leaf, and the Canadian Mountie as warm gestures to make Canadians feel welcome. Furthermore, the hotels and restaurants were very eager to attract Canadian customers and held several "Canadian breakfasts" with pancakes and maple syrup.

The 1980s saw the steady growth of Can-Am Festival. To the end, the entire community of Myrtle Beach was involved with the Can-Am Festival week and made Canadians felt welcome through providing a series of incentives, such as having the Canadian visitors' money on a par with US dollar. The festival fostered solidarity among Canadian "snowbirds" (a term describes Canadian seasonal migrants to US for warm weather), tourists and the locals, as they can be viewed as both festival attendees and vacationers. In fact, during 1980s, the "snow birding" became a viable extension of the Can-Am Festival. Satisfied Canadian tourists spread the word in Canada about Myrtle Beach and others came based upon the recommendations from family and friends. A long-term relationship between the festival and local businesses had been formed which benefited both the host and the guests. A total number between 14,000 and 20,000 "snowbirds" can be directly tied to this period. It is estimated that 85% of Canadian visitors were enticed to visit or establish temporary or long-term residence directly because of the Can-Am Festival (Groves & Timothy, 2001). The term "snowbirds" was widely used in advertisements and the signs of flying birds were found in the festival brochures. Myrtle Beach has become one of the favorite destinations for Canadian tourists. The development of the festival appears to be related to familiar markers and symbols that make Canadians feel at home. Eventually, many Canadian vacationers became permanent residents in Myrtle Beach.

Golfing became more popular in Myrtle Beach during the late 1980s and early 1990s. As a result, there was a slow shift from the Can-Am Festival to golfers. The business community used promotions to attract golfers because they were more affluent and golfing had a longer season than the spring break. Fierce competition forced the local businesses to change their marketing strategies by emphasizing golf and other sporting events, rather than the Can-Am Festival. There was a decrease (approximately 10%) in the number of advertisements since 1985. Although the exact number of advertisement revenue decline was unclear, a general phenomenon was the Canadian cultural markers dwindled significantly in the mass media. The critical break years for the festival were in 1997 and 1998 when the number of advertisements from the business community was almost zero. The programs specifically for Canadians became small with the underlying thinking that Canadians were "just another group" that comes to Myrtle Beach. Cultural markers, save maple leaf flags, disappeared from the promotions.

The beginning of a new millennium has witnessed the continuing downward trend for advertisements and incentives that are specifically designed for Canadians. To make matters worse, employees, hosts, and other direct contacts within the community do not know how to respond to Canadians or questions relating to Canadians. Although the Can-Am Festival was still a major event in the hearts of Myrtle Beach business and leadership community, it is in a refractory phase and needs to be restructured to create new cultural markers. In fact, the existing markers can be reflected in a deep-rooted friendship and history between Canada and United States. For example, a common marker seen in 2002 advertisements is two flags crossing each other and special pins for tourists to remember the long-term friendship, especially in the wake of the September 11 terrorist attack. Some advertisements even stated that "We are All Americans" reflecting both solidarity between the two groups and the view by Americans that Canadians are not very different.

Findings of Mystery Guest

Mystery guest methodology was used to identify the cultural markers with regard to the festival from 1999 to 2002. Conversations with Canadian tourists showed that the majority originated from the Province of Ontario traveled through Buffalo, Pittsburgh, West Virginia, Virginia, North Carolina, in order to arrive Myrtle Beach. The primary route for the Atlantic Provinces, such as New Brunswick and Nova Scotia was Interstate 95 along the East Coast. The major cultural marker, along with the route, was the Canadian flag. The Canadian flag was very prominent in most businesses and tourist centers from the Canadian border to the Virginia border. The last tourist information point that used the Canadian flag was the West Virginia Welcome Centre, which is around 500 miles away from Canadian border. Canadian flags were not seen until 25 miles from the Myrtle Beach. In particular, there were very few

Canadian flags in this last 25-mile stretch for Can-Am Festival. The flags were posted in the Myrtle Beach area in about 5% of the business districts. This phenomenon suggests that northern states were aware of Canadians, but Myrtle Beach was an isolated case in the South.

There were welcome signs all along the main streets, especially the business routes in the Myrtle Beach area. The initiation or the first event was a welcome reception showing different kinds of flags and Canadian symbols. The structure of these receptions was that locals made opening ceremony and arranged festive contests from 9 am to 12 pm on the first day of the festival. Specially designed T-shirts were sold from the local stores and sale of these shirts was very brisk; in fact, most venues sold out the T-shirts within the first day. It is not possible to determine the exact number of people attending the festival, as there were about 20,000 Canadian "snowbirds" in the Myrtle Beach area. They used this festival as a focal point for their final activities before returning to Canada for the summer. The local newspaper contained a special section to emphasize each day's events. Pictures of Canadians enjoying themselves were also prominent. Canadian entertainers were invited for special performances throughout the week. Noticeably absent were special signs direct to Canadians. For example, there were only a few signs with the words "Welcome Canadians" at area businesses. Another element observed in mass media was direct advertisements on television and newspaper for Canadian customers. There seemed to be two primary types of business response to Canadians. One was no visible recognition of the Can-Am Days by some businesses. Another response was business sponsorship to promote the festival. Most sponsoring businesses were located in the area malls and provided some type of incentives, such as 50% discounts for Canadian visitors.

Open-ended interviews were conducted by the authors as "mystery guests" during the festival from 1999 to 2002. The primary focus was on three aspects: (1) Have you seen many Canadians that week? (2) Did the business have any special promotions for Canadians? (3) How do you identify a customer or tourist as Canadian? The overwhelming answer for the first question was that there have been many Canadian visitors that week. This response was in a direct opposition to tourist officials and individuals from *Sun News* who reported that the number of Canadian visitors for the week had waned dramatically. The majority of the responses to the second question indicated that most businesses (80%) did not have any special promotion programs, and the personnel who were in the primary contact positions did not even seem to know what Can-Am Days were or how to respond to Canadians on a personal level. The third question about how to recognize Canadians was designed to identify personal cultural markers. Canadians were recognized by their clothes, especially T-shirts, shoes, hats, and each of these items had a distinct symbol that could identify them as Canadian. Other Canadians were recognized in restaurants by asking for specialty items such as vinegar or identifying French fries as chips. The last identifier represents a misconception by the Americans about Canadians' food preferences. Perhaps the closer association of Canadians with Great Britain extends some British cultural markers to Canadians. Some Canadians were identified by their attendance at the reception. Others were identified through their license plates, however, these license plates are not a good indicator because one does not know if they are snowbirds or spring break tourists in town for the festival. The primary difference between the demographics of the snow-birds and the Can-Am visitors was that the former are older and the latter are younger with children.

Conclusions

Festival tourism encompasses an image fabrication of events and places that are ready for tourist consumption. The cultural festivals allow tourists to experience a place of memory through representations of a series of markers. It is argued that festival tourists are not cultural anthropologists seeking authentic experiences. Rather, they are consumers looking for purchasable versions of the culture they seek. Tourism is a commodity to be consumed. To some extent, tourism brings "pseudo-events" (Boorstein, 1992) which are representations of what tourists seek. Images and markers are offered to tourists as objects to consume through souvenirs and activities. The festival destination, in order to maintain its attraction for tourists, needs to maintain its appeal through commercializing the past and offering icons of what tourists want to experience.

The continued evolution of the Can-Am Festival provides the tourism researchers with an important lens through which to explore the iconography at work in shaping the destination. The festival is a special event to celebrate Canadian culture and heritage in the United States. The festival has gone through a series of changes from the original goal of attracting Canadian motorists to the current stage as an integral part of local culture. As a result, the awareness of Canadian culture has been promoted. The American business community seems to have learned the cultural idiosyncrasies of the Canadians and managed to do business with them. The business has gone through a cycle from vigorous promotions to laissez-faire approach. The components that originally attracted Canadians to Myrtle Beach remain, but Canadian visitation patterns have changed substantially and may even be reduced over the coming years. In particular, cultural markers exhibited during the festival have evolved from omnipresent Canadian flags to symbolic friendship pins. There exist misconceptions toward Canadian markers from locals and this can be improved in the future as more and more Canadians participate this festival. Canadian identity is viewed as relative, rather than absolute as reflected in the markers. However, it seems that friendship is the primary root that has given the festival life and has made it endure of this event.

The major issue regarding the event is the loss of community support for this festival from the general public as well as the business community. The decline of the festival's popularity is not of a lack of interest, but of leadership to be able to refocus the festival in order to revive the cultural markers and create new icons for this festival. This research suggests that study of cultural markers, as an indicator of iconography, remains a neglected field for event planning and management. Cultural markers help assess the importance and evolution of a special event. The development of cultural markers in Can-Am Festival shows a strong role in event promotion, marketing, and advertising. Further, the relationships between communities and businesses have been influenced by the gradual changes of these markers. Further research should consider using these markers, as an important marketing tool, to improve the quality of special events.

References

Badre, A., & Allen, J. (1989). Graphic language representation and programming behavior. In: G. Salvendy, & D. Smith (Eds), *Advances in human factors/ergonomics* (pp. 59–65). Amsterdam: Elsevier.

Bialostocki, J. (1963). Iconography and iconology. In: *The encyclopedia of world art* (Vol. 7, p. 770). London: McGraw-Hill.

Boorstein, D. (1992). *The image: A guide to pseudo-events in America*. New York: Vintage.

Burstein, A. (2000). Jefferson and the iconography of Romanticism: Folk, land, culture and the romantic nation. *Journal of the Early Republic, 20*(2), 311–313.

Butler, R. (1980). The concept of a tourist area cycle of evolution: Implications for management of resources. *Canadian Geographer, 24*(1), 5–12.

Desmond, J. (1999). *Staging tourism: Bodies on display from Waikiki to sea world*. Chicago, IL: University of Chicago.

Dimanche, F. (1994). Cross-cultural tourism marketing research: an assessment and recommendations for future studies. *Journal of International Consumer Marketing, 6*(3/4), 123–134.

Ferguson, W., & Ferguson, I. (2001). *How to be a Canadian: Even if you already are one*. Toronto: Douglas & McIntyre.

Gallarza, M., Saura, I., & Garcia, H. (2002). Destination image: Towards a conceptual framework. *Annals of Tourism Research, 29*(1), 56–78.

Geertz, C. (1973). *The interpretation of culture: Selected essays*. New York: Basic Books.

Getz, D. (1991). *Festivals, special events, and tourism*. New York: Van Norstrand Reinhold.

Graham, B., Ashworth, G., & Tunbridge, J. (2000). *A geography of heritage*. New York: Oxford University Press.

Groves, D., & Timothy, D. (2001). Festival, migration, and long-term residency. *Teoros, X, 20*(1), 56–62.

Harbour, C. (2000). Picturing performance: The iconography of performing arts in concept and practice. *Choice, 37*(9), 16–34.

Hay, I. (2000). *Qualitative research methods in human geography*. Oxford, UK: Oxford University Press.

Huckstein, D., & Duboff, R. (1999). Hilton hotels. *Cornell Hotel and Restaurant Administration Quarterly, 40*(4), 28–38.

Kaeppler, A. (2004). Recycling tradition: A Hawaiian case study. *Dance Chronicle, 27*(3), 293–311.

Krueger, R. (1994). *Focus group*. Thousand Oaks, CA: Sage Publications.

Markwell, K. (1997). Dimensions of photography in a nature-based tour. *Annals of Tourism Research, 21*(1), 131–155.

Marvin, B. (1992). Keeping score on service. *Restaurants and Institutions, 102*(22), 128–142.

Mayfield, T., & Crompton, J. (1995). Development of an instrument for identifying community reasons for staging a festival. *Journal of Travel Research, 34*, 37–44.

McCarthy, T. (1998). Make voice mail a friend, not a foe. *Lodging Hospitality, 54*(9), 18.

Moorti, S. (2004). Fashioning a cosmopolitan Tamil identity: Game shows, commodities and cultural identity. Media, Culture & Society, 26(4), 549–567.

Nelson, C., Treichler, P., & Grossberg, L. (1992). Cultural studies: An introduction. In: L. Grossbert, C. Nelson, & P. Treichler (Eds), *Cultural studies* (pp. 1–16). New York: Routledge.

Ramaprasad, J., & Hasegawa, K. (1992). Creative strategies in American and Japanese TV commercials: A comparison. *Journal of Advertising Research, 32*(1), 59–67.

Rose, L., & Kingma, H. (1989). Seasonal migration of retired persons: Estimating its extent and its implication for the State of Florida. *Journal of Economic and Social Measurement, 15*, 91–104.

Schultis, J., Johnston, M., & Twynam, G. (1996). Developing a longitudinal research program to measure impacts of a special event. *Festival Management and Event Tourism, 4*(1/2), 59–66.

Simpson, J. (2000). *Star-spangled Canadians–Canadians living the American dream.* Toronto, Canada: HaperCollins.

Smith, B. (1985). *European vision and the South Pacific.* New Haven: Yale University Press.

Stampino, M. (2001). Picturing performance: The iconography of the performing arts in concept and practice. *Theatre Journal, 53*(1), 173–174.

Sternberg, E. (1997). The iconography of tourism experience. *Annals of Tourism Research, 24*(4), 951–969.

Sun News (1961–2002). Newspaper published in Myrtle Beach, South Carolina.

Turley, L., & Kelley, S. (1997). A comparison of advertising content: Business to business versus consumer services. *Journal of Advertising, 26*(4), 39–48.

Wheelan, S., & Abraham, M. (1993). The concept of intergroup mirroring: Reality or illusion? *Human Relations, 46*(7), 803–825.

Witham, G. (1995). Measuring guest perceptions: Combine measurement tools. *Cornell Hotel and Restaurant Administration Quarterly, 36*(6), 416–424.

Wood, R. (1984). Ethnic tourism, the state, and cultural change in Southeast Asia. *Annals of Tourism Research, 11*, 353–374.

Chapter 10

Reconciliation Tourism: On Crossing Bridges and Funding Ferries

Freya Higgins-Desbiolles

Introduction

The impact of tourism on the economic development of a nation has been a long-standing topic of inquiry within tourism analysis (for example Bull, 1995; Lundberg, 1980; Lundberg, Stavenca, & Krishnamoorthy, 1995; WTO, 1980a). Subsequently attention focused on the impact of tourism on the socio-cultural fabric of communities that are engaged with tourism (Smith, 1989; Lanfant, Allcock, & Bruner, 1995; MacCannell, 1992; Turner & Ash, 1975; for example). This article, however, investigates the possibility of tourism to contribute to the socio-cultural development of a nation and to foster social justice and reconciliation within a divided society. This chapter situates reconciliation tourism as a component of tourism as a force for peace. This discussion begins with a macro view of the international documents and codes agreed for at the international level, which are founded on the premise of tourism fostering peace and understanding; it then surveys examples from the international arena of tours for higher aims and provides a brief overview on the relevant literature to date. The focus then shifts to the Australian context where efforts have been exerted for achieving reconciliation between Indigenous and non-Indigenous Australians since the 1990s. A case study of the Ngarrindjeri community's efforts through their tourism venture of Camp Coorong Race Relations and Cultural Education Centre will be utilised to assess the potential for tourism to contribute to the achievement of reconciliation in Australia as well as some of the obstacles in the path of this endeavour.

Tourism as a Force for Peace and Understanding

One of the many interesting topics in the field of tourism research is that of tourism's potential contribution to global peace and understanding. Many would agree that tourism can contribute to knowledge of other places, empathy with other peoples and tolerance that stems from seeing the place of one's own society in the world. The premise that tourism fosters peace and tolerance is one of the mainstays of important international documents and codes released by bodies like the World Tourism Organization (WTO). Importantly, there are examples from around the globe of tours that are seeking conflict resolution, greater understanding and even movements for global social justice. However, it remains a matter of some dispute among tourism analysts as to whether tourism can help foster peace and secure a more harmonious world.

International Statements, Codes and Institutions

There are many statements, codes and documents that start from the premise that tourism fosters peace and understanding. The pathfinder in this endeavour was the 1980 *Manila Declaration on World Tourism* that described tourism as a "vital force for peace and international understanding" (WTO, 1980b). This was followed by the *Tourism Bill of Rights and Tourist Code* that was adopted at the WTO's General Assembly held in Sofia, Bulgaria in 1985, which cited tourism's contribution to "… to improving mutual understanding, bringing peoples closer together and, consequently, strengthening international cooperation" (WTO, 1985). *The Charter for Sustainable Tourism* drafted by the World Conference on Sustainable Tourism held in the Canary Islands in 1995 recognised in its preamble that "… tourism affords the opportunity to travel and to know other cultures, and that the development of tourism can help promote closer ties and peace among peoples, creating a conscience that is respectful of diversity of culture and lifestyles" (WTO, 1995). *The Global Code of Ethics for Tourism* presented to the WTO's General Assembly meeting in Santiago, Chile in 1999 asserted that

> firmly believing that, through the direct, spontaneous and non-mediatized contacts it engenders between men and women of different cultures and lifestyles, tourism presents a vital force for peace and a factor of friendship and understanding among the peoples of the world.(WTO, 1999)

In addition to these declarations and statements, there is an institutional structure that advocates for tourism as a force for peace known as the International Institute for Peace Through Tourism (IIPT). This nonprofit organisation was founded by Louis D'Amore in 1985, and focuses on

> … fostering and facilitating tourism initiatives which contribute to international understanding and cooperation, an improved quality of environment, the preservation of heritage, and through these initiatives, helping to bring

about a peaceful and sustainable world. It is based on a vision of the world's largest industry, travel and tourism — becoming the world's first global peace industry; and the belief that every traveler is potentially an 'Ambassador for Peace'.(International Institute for Peace through Tourism, n. d.)

This organisation has undertaken a variety of initiatives ranging from global conferences, establishment of peace parks, development of curricula, student and tourism executive ambassador programmes to assist developing countries with tourism, collaborations with other organisations like UNESCO in the *UN Year for the Culture of Peace* in 2000 as well as passing its own declarations such as the *Amman Declaration on Peace through Tourism* (IIPT, n. d.).

Examples of Tourism for Higher Aims

There are many efforts to offer tourism directed to higher aims than recreation and relaxation. Some of the more notable examples include, university study abroad programmes; Earthwatch tours which give conservation skills and experience; community development tours of Oxfam Community Aid Abroad (Oxfam CAA) in Australia;[1] and Habitat for Humanity's 'Global Village' programme in which volunteers use their holidays to help build low-cost, good housing for communities around the world.

There is also tourism that is the antithesis of conventional tourism known as 'reality tours'. These are tours that go to develop communities and endeavour to show what real life is like in that community, including problems of violence, poverty and disempowerment. The aim of these tours is to make tourism contribute to the solutions to these problems by educating the tourists not only to see the problems in the places they visit, but also relate them to their own community and take up action to improve the world in some way as a result. An example of this type of tour is the Oxfam CAA tour to Guatemala that takes people to visit human rights organisations, literacy projects and development projects in a country that has suffered decades of civil war. Oxfam CAA has also created a Community Leadership Programme (CLP) in partnership with the University of Queensland that is focused on teaching about community development through a four-week tour of India. What distinguishes CLP from Oxfam CAA's other tours, is that participants make a twelve-month commitment to volunteer in community development programmes through Oxfam CAA or other organisations in order that their experiences of community development in India are utilised to foster "… an ongoing process of building effective community involvement in Australia around issues of human rights, international justice, sustainable development, North/South partnership and poverty alleviation".[2] There is also the reality tours programme of Global Exchange based in the United States that includes destinations such as South Africa, Northern Ireland, Palestine/Israel, Cuba, the Mexican state of Chiapas, as well as communities closer to home in California and the US–Mexican

---

[1.] See: htpp://www.caa.org.au/travel/"
[2.] See: http://www.caa.org.au/CLP/index.html

border area.[3] Like the CLP of Oxfam CAA, Global Exchange is developing tours that are designed to induce change:

> The idea that travel can be educational and positively influence international affairs motivated the first Reality Tour in 1989. Global Exchange's Reality Tours are not designed to provide immediate solutions or remedies to the world's most intractable problems, nor are they simply a kind of voyeurism. Rather, Reality Tours are meant to educate people about how we, individually and collectively, contribute to global problems, and, then, to suggest ways in which we can contribute to positive change. (See footnote 3)

Research into Tourism as a Force for Peace

Tourism research is responding with more concentrated analysis on this tourism segment and is yielding interesting insights. While the assertion that tourism fosters peace remains contentious (see for example Var, Ap, & Van Doren, 1994; Brown, 1989; Din, 1988), research is yielding insights into the lesser claims that tourism can foster attitudinal change in tourists and promote cross-cultural understanding (Var et al., 1994). Pizam (1996) conducted empirical surveys into tourism contact between citizens of hostile nations and was led to conclude that tourism contact does not automatically result in better relations and that some conditions are more conducive for fostering these outcomes (1996, pp. 210–211). Ryan and Huyton (2000a) in their research into tourism demand for Aboriginal experiences made a passing note that these experiences led some tourists to a new way of seeing natural settings as 'spiritual' places. McGehee and Norman (2002) have examined Earthwatch tours utilising the social–psychological perspective of social movement theory and found that there is evidence that these experiences contribute to consciousness-raising and in particular, lead participants to link the personal and the political. Beaumont's (2001) recent work on ecotourism is also of relevance; starting from the claim that proponents of ecotourism assert that these experiences foster an environmental ethic, she surveyed ecotourists to a Queensland National Park and found that while there is potential for this to occur, much work could be done to enhance this capacity of these experiences. One recent book by Wearing entitled *Volunteer Tourism* (2001) investigates "experiences that make a difference". Wearing provides the first sustained analysis into volunteer tourism as a subset of alternative tourism distinguished by the tourists' motivations to contribute to social and/or environmental benefits in the places they visit. He describes volunteer tourism as "… a direct interactive experience that causes value change and changed consciousness in the individual which will subsequently influence their lifestyle, while providing forms of community development that are required by local communities" (2001, p. x). His examination of such case studies as Youth Challenge International and One World Travel (now Oxfam CAA Travel Group) has yielded valuable insights and illuminated promising avenues for future research into tourism that fosters "genuine exchange"(Wearing, 2001, p. 172).

---

[3]See: http:www.globalexchange.org/tours

This chapter attempts to contribute to this area of research by investigating the capacity of tourism to contribute to reconciliation within Australian society, particularly by demonstrating how one community, the Ngarrindjeri, have utilised the tourism facility of Camp Coorong to work towards reconciliation for the future of their children and the benefit of all Australians. However, first, the context of Indigenous tourism in Australia will be described and the record of achievement on reconciliation will be summarised before the case study is examined.

The Context of Indigenous Tourism in Australia

Indigenous[4] involvement in the Australian tourism industry has been of increasing importance in recent decades. While it has recently been asserted that the volume and the nature of the demand for Indigenous Australian tourism experiences might have been misrepresented previously (Ryan & Huyton, 2000a, 2000b), it remains a significant phenomenon nonetheless. Indigenous tourism products and imagery, in particular, are significant to the Australian tourism industry because marketing Indigenous 'product' helps create 'Brand' Australia and distinguish Australia as a destination in a highly competitive market (see *Selling Australia*, 2001). But the Indigenous communities who would be relied upon to supply this 'product' are facing much bigger issues simultaneously. While tourism from a mainstream perspective appears to be a frivolous activity because it is concerned with fun and enjoyment, from an Indigenous perspective it is a much more serious topic. For as Pilger pointed out in his writing about Australia in the run up to the 2000 Sydney Olympics, the Indigenous peoples who became a focus in the international media spotlight and were the delight of the Opening Ceremonies were suffering Third World levels of poverty, ill-health and premature death rates (Pilger, 2000).

It is useful to place Indigenous involvement in contemporary tourism within the context of Indigenous history and politics from which it developed. It was only as recent as 1967 that Indigenous Australians uniformly received citizenship rights in Australia and which ultimately led to their receiving fair wages for their labour, allowed free movement off missions and halted the forced removal of children. Officially, the suggestion to explore tourism as a promising source for Indigenous community development was articulated in the 1991 *Report of the Inquiry into Aboriginal Deaths in Custody* where it was seen as a promising source of self-esteem and economic opportunity (National Aboriginal and Torres Strait Islander Tourism Industry Strategy, 1997). This was followed by the *National Aboriginal and Torres Strait Islander Tourism Industry Strategy* (NATSITIS) which included "choice for Aboriginal and Torres Strait Islander people about their involvement in the tourism industry" and "a means of economic independence for Aboriginal and Torres Strait Islander participants" as some of the aims for Indigenous tourism policy (NATSITIS, 1997).

---

[4]Indigenous Australia refers to both Aboriginal communities and Torres Strait Islander communities. There are important distinctions to be made between them and their experiences.

From the outline provided above, it is evident that Indigenous Australians' involvement in tourism has a long and important historical context that is distinct from that of mainstream tourism operators and the tourism industry. This context reveals that when Indigenous Australians engage with tourism they may be simultaneously attempting to secure their Native Title rights, to build the self-esteem of their youth through revival of culture and to secure a reconciled community in which their children can grow up in safety and comfort, as well as the obvious economic benefits that tourism can provide.

Crossing Bridges: Reconciliation in Australia

Reconciliation is a defining issue for the Australian nation. As Geoff Clark, former chair of the Aboriginal and Torres Strait Islander Commission (ATSIC), has stated

> The future of Australia is meshed with the future for the First Peoples. We look back, to find a better way forward. Reconciliation is people being different but finding solutions together. It is about Healing, Justice and Truth. For the future, Australia's heritage must embrace all its peoples and cultures. (Council for Aboriginal Reconciliation, 2000)

Reconciliation between Indigenous and non-Indigenous Australians became an official aim of the Australian nation when the Australian Commonwealth parliament established the Council for Aboriginal Reconciliation (CAR) in 1991. It was given a nine-year mandate in which to chart a path to reconciliation through consultations with communities, education campaigns and projects. However, much of its work has been undermined by the policies that the Howard Liberal government has pursued since taking office in 1996; this government has promoted what it calls 'practical reconciliation'[5] in opposition to Indigenous demands for an official apology for past governmental policies and self-determination as seen in the *Treaty* campaign for example. Thus, when the CAR released its *Corroboree 2000 — Towards Reconciliation, Australian Declaration Towards Reconciliation* and *The Roadmap for Reconciliation* documents in 2000, a great rift was evident between the government's vision for reconciliation and that of Indigenous Australians and their supporters.[6] As a result, reconciliation has returned to a people's movement in the absence of federal governmental leadership. This people's movement for reconciliation was potently symbolised by the quarter of a million people who crossed Sydney Harbour Bridge together on 28 May 2000 and who were joined in other bridge

---

[5]Practical reconciliation entails a commitment to improve the physical manifestations of Indigenous disadvantage such as ill-health, pre-mature death rates, poor education levels, substandard housing and substance abuse. The services to be offered through this initiative are services that most in the non-Indigenous Australian community take for granted.
[6]See: http://www.antar.org.au/rec_inquiry_subs.html concerning the inquiry into "… progress towards national reconciliation, including the adequacy and effectiveness of the Commonwealth's response …" which provides many details on these issues.

walks around the nation by many thousands of more Australians. The hard work still continues in communities around the country as they hold reconciliation events, form reconciliation learning circles and undertake projects large and small to build more bridges for understanding. It is in this vein that reconciliation tourism operates at a low-key level, fostered by the daily efforts of people, eventually chipping away at the barriers between Indigenous and non-Indigenous Australians.[7]

Case Study in Reconciliation Tourism: Camp Coorong Race Relations and Cultural Education Centre

Camp Coorong, located two hours southeast of the South Australian capital of Adelaide, is one such facility. Camp Coorong was founded in 1985, originally as a place for Ngarrindjeri youth to return to land and reconnect to culture, but it soon became known as a place for South Australia's school children to come and learn about Ngarrindjeri culture and history with the long-term aim that this experience will contribute to reconciliation between Indigenous and non-Indigenous Australians. Camp Coorong is a community-based education facility and tourism enterprise founded by George Trevorrow and currently managed by Tom and Ellen Trevorrow on behalf of the Ngarrindjeri Lands and Progress Association (NLPA). Its aim as stated by Tom Trevorrow

> We don't put a value on the dollar — we put education and love and understanding first, and I suppose that's what may make us different compared with other businesses.... We're not doing this to get rich - we're doing it to help solve a problem.(A Talent for Tourism, 1996, pp. 7 and 9)

Since becoming involved in tourism in the 1990s, Camp Coorong has been cited as one of five successful Aboriginal tourism ventures (Schmiechen, 1993, p. 3). Its record of achievement is visible through its use as a case study in tourism documents and videos such as: *A Talent for Tourism* (1996), *On Our Own Terms* (1996) and *Strong Business, Strong Culture, Strong Country* (1996). Camp Coorong has also received a number of tourism awards.

Camp Coorong offers a variety of services and experiences. The facility provides, dormitory style accommodation, three family-size cabins with self-catering facilities and ensuite baths; an ablutions block; conference facility; and large kitchen and dining room. The experiences on offer include, a bush tucker and bush medicine walk through Bonney Reserve, a rare part of the Coorong with remnant vegetation; a basket-weaving workshop;

---

[7]Federal Tourism Minister Joe Hockey is quoted on an Australian Aboriginal tour operators' website as claiming "... some ninety percent of metropolitan Australians haven't even met, let alone sat down and had a meaningful conversation with an indigenous person. Without this happening how can we hope to understand and connect with indigenous Australians?" Accessed at: http://www.aboriginaltouroperators.com.au/news/april2003/april2.html on 22 May 2003.

a field trip to the Southern Ocean via Parkna Point where a large midden[8] (holding perhaps millions of mollusc shells and ancient grinding stones) is viewed; and a tour of the Cultural Museum or Keeping Place located at the facility.

Each of the experiences offered contributes to the effort at fostering reconciliation:

- The walking trail demonstrates Ngarrindjeri bush tucker (foods) and bush medicine and is conducted at Bonney Reserve, a site where a fringe camp[9] existed as late as the 1980s. During the walk, tourists are told of how the Ngarrindjeri ancestors once lived, how European invasion has impacted on this lifestyle, how the natural environment has been severely damaged by non-Indigenous water and land use practices (such as unsustainable agricultural production and irrigation) and how the Ngarrindjeri community lives today, retains traditional knowledge and uses the bush tucker and bush medicine available.

- In the basket-weaving workshops offered at the Camp, basket weaving is taught in the context of its place in weaving cultural ties among the Ngarrindjeri community and connecting the people to their environment. The story of how the art of basket weaving was revived and restored to the larger community reveals how the Ngarrindjeri have had to negotiate the demands of contemporary living with maintaining traditions. It also sheds light on how traditions and culture of Aboriginal peoples are held to external yardsticks of authenticity, a situation that played out with tragic consequences in the Hindmarsh Island Bridge controversy (see Higgins-Desbiolles, 2002 for further discussion). During this session, the video made by the South Australian Museum entitled *Ngurunderi: A Ngarrindjeri Dreaming* (1987) is shown, which tells how Ngurunderi's journeys and actions are recounted and remembered through the Ngarrindjeri landscape.

- The visit to the Southern Ocean via Parkna Point provides an opportunity to visit a very large midden that is one of many located in the dunes of the Coorong National Park. A talk was held here explaining how the Ngarrindjeri moved camps methodically through the seasons, how burial grounds were placed adjacent to the campsites (which the middens are the remains of) and how the science of archaeology has supported the information passed down in Ngarrindjeri oral traditions. This is also the place where issues of contemporary import are raised, including, the fear that tourism and recreational users of the National Park will violate these places; and the problematic relationship with the South Australian Museum and other museums around the world who hold Ngarrindjeri

---

[8]The term 'midden' is used by archaeologists worldwide to describe any kind of feature containing waste products relating to day-to-day human life. Where people have repeatedly camped and dumped their refuse, archaeologists find valuable sources of data on societies and peoples. Many Ngarrindjeri middens indicate a long and extensive occupation of their lands, an abundant and well-utilised ecosystem and a sophistication of lifestyle that means that these sites are important markers of native title and sources of Ngarrindjeri pride in their sustainable livelihood.

[9]Fringe camps existed on the outskirts of non-Indigenous settlements and were places where people gathered due to displacement from traditional lands. The fringe camps are important in the argument on native title because they show that the Ngarrindjeri have an unbroken relationship to their lands and waters that can be more difficult for nations which were more comprehensively removed to missions to prove.

remains or artefacts within their collections, which the Ngarrindjeri would like returned for proper burial or keeping.[10]

- The visit to the Camp Coorong Museum or Keeping Place provides an opportunity to learn about the laws that governed Ngarrindjeri lives in the past including Aboriginal exemption papers which made certain Aboriginal people 'honorary members of the White race'; the life on the mission at Raukkan (formerly Point McLeay mission); Ngarrindjeri contributions to Australian society such as serving as soldiers in Australian forces in the Boer War, World Wars I and II; and the injustice that was meted out in return, as happened, for example, when returned Ngarrindjeri servicemen were denied access to services that other war veterans received.

- The four- to five-day tour that covers the entirety of Ngarrindjeri lands provides an opportunity to discuss all of the issues above and a good deal more. On this tour, visitors can realise the breadth of Ngarrindjeri lands, the variety of environments, the diverse group that make up the Ngarrindjeri *lakalinyeri* (or clans), as well as be reminded that Aboriginal Australia is made up of a diversity of peoples, cultures, traditions and societies. It is during this tour that one can learn about the political and social structures that governed the Ngarrindjeri prior to European invasion including the highly democratic, representative governmental structure of the *tendi* that has been revived in recent times to serve contemporary Ngarrindjeri purposes. This tour includes some of the stories from the Dreaming as it stops at sites where the acts of Dreaming ancestors such as Ngurunderi have left their marks upon the land at places like the Bluff at Victor Harbor and the Granites near Kingston. It is also during this tour that the issues concerning the Hindmarsh Island Bridge are sometimes raised if someone inquires and the damage that the conflict has wrought on the Ngarrindjeri community are recounted (more detail on this conflict follows).

Who Comes to Camp Coorong?

Camp Coorong was originally designed to offer Ngarrindjeri youth an opportunity to return to their ancestral lands and engage in cultural learning. However, it was soon catering to South Australian school groups of all ages as an educational facility supporting their curricula in Aboriginal Studies. It has since expanded to serve a variety of clients including, university students in such specialised programmes as medicine, environmental management and cultural studies; environmental groups; reconciliation groups such as Australians for Native Title and Reconciliation; staff and volunteers of nongovernmental organisations concerned with social justice; motoring tourists on the Melbourne to Adelaide route; tour groups on privately run tours such as ecotours and four-wheel drive,

---

[10]A significant precedent for the return of these ancestral remains occurred in April 2003 when Edinburgh University, the Australian Museum and the Royal College of Surgeons in London organised for the return of 300 Ngarrindjeri ancestors to the community at a ceremony held at Camp Coorong (Rehn, 2003, p. 8). This positive event also places a heavy emotional and organisational burden upon Ngarrindjeri elders and the community which are committed to re-burying each individual in their original resting place.

adventure tours; and Indigenous groups. Of the tourists who come, there are many local, state and national visitors who compose the domestic market, as well as international visitors coming from some 45 nations from around the globe.

Perhaps the most exciting tours for the Ngarrindjeri are the visits by Indigenous groups, which include, members of the Ngarrindjeri community who come to re-connect to culture and country; visits by other Aboriginal groups from around South Australia and Australia who come to network and learn from Camp Coorong's experience; and Indigenous people from around the world who come to learn and share their experiences so that global networks are forged. For example, Port Adelaide's Tauondi Aboriginal College's students in the Cultural Tour Guiding programme come frequently to learn about culture and how to deal.

What Visitors Have Said about Their Experiences at Camp Coorong

From a review of the Guest Books placed in the Museum of Camp Coorong between 1990 and 2002, some insight can be gained into how the experiences at Camp Coorong have affected participants. Some of the non-Indigenous visitors have written,

* "Education is the key to reconciliation — may the stories live forever"
* "May this Camp prosper and teach Australia its forgotten history" — 3/2000
* "Reconciliation is a difficult process. Camp Coorong helps to overcome our ignorance"
* "Much to learn, much reconciliation to take place. All the best in getting back your identity and recognition"
* "A wonderful idea that can help make a difference to how we all live together — we hope"
* "It hurts but we need to know the truth"
* "Thank you for teaching me not to feel guilty but to seek awareness instead" — 4/1993
* "Hope for the Future" — 4/1993
* "A most gentle and enlightening experience" — 4/1993

Some of the Aboriginal and other Indigenous visitors to the Camp have written such comments as,

* "Affirms my pride in being a Ngarrindjeri" — 4/1993
* "Great to see our material out of the museums and within our own Keeping Places" — 1/1997
* "Proud to be a Nunga" — 1/1996[11]
* "Deadly. Long live our struggle for cultural freedom" — 2/1996
* "Thank you very much, brothers and sisters — Nacho yungondalya yunkandalya — oh how we yearn for the voices of the past" — 2/1997

---

[11]Aboriginal groups in Australia use umbrella terms for regional groupings of Aboriginal nations. For instance, Nunga refers to many of the Aboriginal peoples in South Australia, Koori refers to Aboriginal peoples of Victoria and New South Wales and Murri refers to the peoples of Queensland.

- "I saw photos of my grandfather and father. Made me proud to be a Ngarrindjeri descendant" — 10/1994
- "Exactly what's needed for educating foreigners" — 1/1992[12]

  While most visitors to Camp Coorong seem to have valuable experiences there and this facility is recognised as an important place to conduct training for reconciliation,[13] reconciliation tourism has its challenges.

Constraints to Reconciliation Tourism: Tourism Industry Policies and Processes

In the current setting, the tourism industry is promoting tourism as a source of economic development but through private entrepreneurial enterprises and for profit motives. This can present significant barriers to the social aims and objectives of facilities such as Camp Coorong that are not capable of generating the profits expected by the mainstream tourism sector and have a social and political motivation behind their work.

  This uncomfortable disjuncture in aims was apparent at the 1993 *Indigenous Australians in Tourism Conference* held in Darwin, when the Pacific Asia Travel Association delegate, Robertson E. Collins, took the opportunity to counsel attendees:

> And now I speak to the Indigenous people in the room: if you go into tourism, you must be professional. There are plenty of examples where Indigenous people have been professional and highly successful. The Tjapukai Dancers are a classic example and there is an interesting theatre in Sydney.
>
> But I remind you of the real world out there: don't expect me to like you because you are black or white or brown or yellow; don't expect me to like you because you are an Aboriginal or an Indian. As a professional, you must meet my expectations of what I think is a professional performance, be it as a guide, dancer or hotel clerk. You have some advantages, but don't expect any special allowances.
>
> Don't mix your tourism goals with your political agenda. There is an old Hollywood cliché that bears repeating: '*if you want to send a message, use Western Union!*' Don't try to mix it into the script.(Collins, 1993, p. 35)

---

[12]While this is only a sketch of the many entries in the visitor books that have been collected since 1988, it is representative of some of the responses which indicate the profound impact of this small facility. However, it must be said the majority of entries are from the school children who visit and are more mundane or humorous in their content. It is striking that there is little negative comment in these books which may be due to the fact that many of the groups who visit the facility are already predisposed to appreciate the experience and also the fact that those who harbour negative views may be constrained in writing them in the visitors books because of the intimate nature of the interactions with the Ngarrindjeri.

[13]For instance, the author first became involved with this community by participating in fieldtrip to Camp Coorong as part of professional development training through the South Australian Department of Education's Aboriginal Education Unit which usually conducts fieldtrips there every year. Similarly, the Medical School of Adelaide University has held compulsory training at Camp Coorong for its students.

This statement reflects his perspective from a mainstream industry view and fails to acknowledge the roots of Indigenous tourism in a different political and social context, as clearly delineated in such documents as the NATSITIS. The dialogue conducted during reconciliation tourism is by necessity of a political and social nature but the tourism industry through governmental bodies such as the tourism commissions and the tour operators dealing with Aboriginal enterprises discourage such work because they may make the tourists uncomfortable and therefore damage business. However the reconciliation role of tourism requires the tourist to be made uncomfortable, to have their ideas challenged in order to affect the societal changes that reconciliation requires.[14]

Bridges That Divide[15] and Ferries That Heal

It would be remiss to discuss the Ngarrindjeri without addressing the effects of the Hindmarsh Island Bridge conflict. It has long-lasting effects that have implications for how the Ngarrindjeri view tourism and their engagement with the wider community. This controversy that emerged in the early 1990s resulted from a plan to build a marina and residential development on Hindmarsh Island that sought to capitalise on the area's proximity to Adelaide and tourism and recreational drawing potential. As part of the development plans, a bridge was required to replace the car ferry that served for access between Goolwa and the Island for the Marina development to proceed with expansion. Opposition emerged from environmentalists, community groups and trade unionists, but it was when some of the Ngarrindjeri[16] spoke out about opposition based on sacred sites and the spiritual significance of the Island[17] that the conflict achieved national and international attention. A Royal Commission called by the state government in 1995 found that the Ngarrindjeri proponents of sacred women's business connected with the Island were fabricators. However, this determination was undermined by a Federal High Court decision by Justice von Doussa in August 2001 in which he concluded, "I am not satisfied that the restricted women's knowledge was fabricated or that it was not part of genuine Aboriginal traditions" (Briton, 2001).

---

[14] Additionally, any discussion of the economic viability of Indigenous Australian tourism should acknowledge that a good deal of Australian tourism marketing internationally relies upon Indigenous imagery to create 'Brand Australia' in an intensively competitive market without yet providing returns to Indigenous communities for this service. This in effect is a valuable subsidy which remains hidden and needs to be exposed so that both the tourism industry and appropriate governmental bodies provide the legitimate support that Indigenous Australian tourism requires.

[15] It is one of history's ironies that bridges have come to represent reconciliation in the Australian national psyche following the bridge walks of 2000 (recounted in this section) in light of the meaning of the Hindmarsh Island Bridge (completed in 2001) for the Ngarrindjeri community and their supporters.

[16] The Ngarrindjeri community fragmented during this event, with the people advocating sacred sites and women's connections with the Island being labelled 'proponents' and those denying these attributes being labelled 'dissidents'.

[17] Anthropologist Diane Bell states "The Ngarrindjeri live in one of the most beautiful and complex parts of Australia, where the fresh water of the Murray River system which drains the southeast of Australia flows into the Southern Ocean. It is a land of long lagoons and brackish lakes; a land where wildlife proliferates, and where, not surprisingly the ancestral beings of the mythic past were busy laying down the foundations of Ngarrindjeri religion and law. It is the responsibility of the living to protect the sacred order. A number of Ngarrindjeri believed that a proposal to build a bridge … threatened this sacred order" (2001, p. 6).

Unfortunately for the Ngarrindjeri proponents, this finding came to late to stop the bridge which was officially opened on 4 March 2001.

The unfolding of this conflict has taken longer than a decade, 5 government inquiries and more than 30 legal cases and has had significant impact not only for the Ngarrindjeri and other locals, but also for the national scene on Native Title and Reconciliation as well as the international arena of Indigenous rights.[18] The diversity and multitude of sometimes contradictory conclusions that are drawn from these events are a result of the variety of perspectives and analytical lenses employed to comprehend this complex and momentous episode. However, within an analysis of Indigenous tourism, it would seem that Indigenous cultural beliefs, which are valuable marketing tools, are not to be allowed to hinder development and the insatiable spatial appetite of tourism and recreation.

Although deeply wounded by these events, the Ngarrindjeri have continued to run Camp Coorong and work towards reconciliation. Because they cannot cross the bridge in violation of their spiritual beliefs and therefore find it difficult to carry out their duties as custodians of the Island, they have sought support for the re-establishment of a ferry service to the Island. While the local council of Alexandrina has demonstrated support of Ngarrindjeri efforts to establish a ferry connection and have even concluded a protocol agreement with the Ngarrindjeri,[19] so far no meaningful state or commonwealth government support has been forthcoming. In an article entitled the *Politics of Surviving*, Bell (2001) emphasises the importance of the ferry to the larger project of reconciliation in Australia. She concludes,

> The Ngarrindjeri survivors plan the construction of another ferry to service the island [Hindmarsh]. They cannot use the bridge to visit their sacred places on the island. In my view, if we can't get this one right, there is no hope for the Reconciliation Movement in Australia. The Ngarrindjeri stories are a test case and thus far there are no winners.(Bell, 2001, p. 6)

In a way, the ferry is also a test case for the tourism industry. All of the players in tourism in this area utilise the Ngarrindjeri people's culture, history or physical presence manifested in the landscape as a drawcard to attract tourism to the area, including the South

---

[18]Two comprehensive resources which can be consulted for full insights into this complicated series of events are Bell's *Ngarrindjeri Wurruwarrin* (1998) and Simon's *Meeting of the Waters* (2003). The first is an anthropologist's exploration of Ngarrindjeri knowledges which are relevant to the bridge conflict and the latter is a journalist's account following extensive research into the events.

[19]This agreement had unusual origins. The unearthing of Ngarrindjeri ancestral remains during redevelopment of Goolwa's wharf (a site adjacent to the foundations of the bridge to Hindmarsh Island) led to a crisis. The resultant consultations between representatives of Alexandrina Council and representatives of the Ngarrindjeri Native Title Committee, the Ngarrindjeri Heritage Committee and the *Tendi* (a traditional Ngarrindjeri political body), led to an historic statement of apology from Alexandrina Council to the Ngarrindjeri community and establishment of a protocol agreement called the *Kungan Ngarrindjeri Yunnan Agreement* (Listening to Ngarrindjeri When they are Speaking). While this event has been explored in more depth elsewhere (Higgins-Desbiolles, 2004), for present purposes, the protocol agreement can be seen as a rare model of the kind of understandings that will need to be negotiated between Indigenous communities and tourism agencies, government agencies and other relevant organisations if tourism is to be an acceptable force for Indigenous communities. (See Williams, 2002).

Australian Tourism Commission, National Parks and wildlife of South Australia, local tour operators and regional tourism promotional boards (see Higgins-Desbiolles, 2003, pp. 249–250). Tourism and recreational demand are implicated in the tragic unfolding of the Hindmarsh Island conflict. Information released in the von Doussa court decision and in Simon's book (2003) indicates that the Ngarrindjeri proponents have been ill-served in the legal and political battles that comprise the conflict. Support for the ferry would go some way in mitigating the damages of this affair and fostering the reconciliation that took a severe battering in this episode.

The Wider Context of Reconciliation Tourism

Reconciliation remains as elusive as ever in Australia. Reconciliation tourism will be an important and on-going catalyst to its achievement, whether it receives the support of Australian governments and organisations or whether it remains within the people's movement indefinitely. Some of the recent initiatives contributing to reconciliation tourism include a wave of new travel guides to Indigenous Australia, festivals and events focused on reconciliation and as well as the tourism ventures such as Camp Coorong that continue the quiet, daily work of dissolving the barriers between Indigenous and non-Indigenous Australians.

There are a variety of publications that have been introduced recently to the travel guide market which are partly or wholly focused on reconciliation through tourism. Paul Kauffman (2000) has written *Travelling Aboriginal Australia: Discovery and Reconciliation* which includes, among other things, information about the reconciliation movement, Mic Dodson's *Always Ask — guidelines for visitors to Indigenous communities* and a description of places to visit by geographical areas of Australia (2000). Melinda Hinkson (2001) has written *Aboriginal Sydney*, which is described as a guide to the places of historical and contemporary importance to Aboriginal peoples in the Sydney region. Lastly, one of the world's largest publishers of travel guides, Lonely Planet, has produced *Aboriginal Australia and the Torres Strait Islands: Guide to Indigenous Australia* (2001). This book is valuable to reconciliation tourism on a number of levels, including its detailed content, the methodology pursued in its compilation and in the feedback loop established to inform all future Lonely Planet travel guides to Australia and its regions. This guidebook is over 400 pages in length and provides the reader with a comprehensive overview of the salient issues concerning Indigenous Australia before giving a detailed travel guide divided by geographical areas. More importantly, it was produced in a spirit of reconciliation as it took some three years in the making in order to commission Indigenous writers, provide them with professional development, consult with the appropriate elders in the locales and receive final clearance from Indigenous leaders Mic Dodson and Les Ahoy. Lastly, Lonely Planet embarked on its own journey of learning by taking the experience and advice gained from Indigenous contributors and advisers in this guidebook to improve the coverage of Indigenous issues in future Australia titles (2001, pp. 14–15).

Reconciliation has also been a theme for many important festivals and events held recently in Australia. The 2000 Sydney Olympics and its associated *Festival of the Dreaming* gave a primacy of place to Indigenous cultures that will have a long-term impact upon international demand for Indigenous experiences and which then may reverberate through the domestic market. Michelle Hanna (1999) has examined both of these events as potential sites for reconciliation in her work *Reconciliation in Olympism*. The Laura Dance and Cultural Festival held biannually in Queensland has attracted thousands of visitors to experience Aboriginal culture; in 2001 it featured reconciliation as its theme as it used art and culture to bridge the divide between Australia's peoples. The controversial Adelaide Festival of 2002 directed by Peter Sellars held themes of inclusivity, community, social justice and Indigenous presence. This festival made a space for reconciliation through several facets of its construct. First, Sellars' appointed two outstanding young Kaurna[20] professionals of the arts community of Adelaide, Karl and Waiata Telfer, to serve as two of ten Associate Directors of the Festival. The Opening Ceremony, called the *Kaurna Palti Meyunna*, was conceptualised through Kaurna spirituality as the spirit of the Dreaming ancestor, Tjilbruke, was invoked to bring peace and compassion, while all of the Indigenous peoples visiting from near and far were called upon to carry out seven days of ceremonies prior to the opening and to which the non-Indigenous were asked to respectfully stay away. This opening was followed by a series of free events in Victoria Square at the heart of Adelaide showcasing Indigenous performers from the local area, the state, the nation and the world who used the event to communicate with each other as well as perform for the non-Indigenous in the audiences. Finally the associated film festivals, *Shedding Light* and *Casting Shadows* featured films made by Indigenous directors and/or films with Indigenous themes that again reminded festival goers that Indigenous Australians should be included and their cultures embraced in all Australian events and festivals. Perhaps part of the controversy that dogged this Festival grew from resentment against this message and perhaps its source (a North American cultural industry leader).

Further Research

This chapter has addressed the topic of reconciliation tourism in a preliminary fashion by examining how one community uses the opportunity of tourism to work towards the attainment of reconciliation; therefore much remains for future research on this topic, as well as the broader category of tourism as a force for peace and understanding. Although the tourism literature is beginning to address Indigenous tourism in a focused way, only a few analysts have even superficially addressed the reconciliation motivation in Indigenous communities' engagement with tourism (such as Ryan, 1997, p. 273; Sofield & Birtles, 1996, p. 397; Zeppel, 1999, p. 24). This may reflect the current neo-liberal environment where value is conferred only on the economic dimensions of tourism. Yet the work of facilities such as Camp Coorong is contributing to social outcomes for Australian society which are of benefit in tangible and intangible ways; however, it may take recognition of consumer demand for this market niche for it to be accorded attention by the tourism industry, governments and analysts.

---

[20]The Kaurna people are the Aboriginal people of the Adelaide plains region.

In particular, future research will need to address the type of tourists drawn to reconciliation tourism, as modelled by Ryan and Huyton's work (2000a, 2000b) on demand for Aboriginal tourism experiences and as called for by Wearing (2000, pp. 161–172) in his outlining of a research agenda for volunteer tourism. However, a note of caution has also been sounded by Ryan about the ambivalence or perhaps even hostility that the domestic *pakeha* (non-Maori) market has to Maori tourism product in New Zealand, which in part appears due to societal tensions that could be directly relevant to the Australian context as well (2002, pp. 966–967). If non-Indigenous Australian participants in Indigenous Australian tourism experiences hold similar attitudes, this obviously curtails the possibilities for Indigenous Australian tourism to contribute to reconciliation. Another promising vein of research would be longitudinal studies to determine if, and how, exposure to reconciliation experiences lead to behavioural changes in tourists, such as involvement in reconciliation or other social justice movements. Another area ripe for exploration is how societal structures of government, industry and other organisations play a reactive, enabling or ambivalent role in these processes, as eluded to in the case of Alexandrina Council described above. Finally it could prove lucrative to make the macro–micro connections of tourism as an agent of global social movements, for instance by examining how the international Indigenous networks forged at Camp Coorong play out in the global arena.

Conclusion

As former Prime Minister Malcolm Fraser (2000) has observed, "… reconciliation is not something that will happen on one day in one particular year. It is an ongoing process which involves both government and people". As this chapter has demonstrated, tourism has had a detrimental role in the lives of the Ngarrindjeri people of South Australia and yet these same people have continued to use tourism as a tool to foster reconciliation between non-Indigenous and Indigenous Australians. This is because the Ngarrindjeri realise that tourism can be a force for understanding between non-Indigenous and Indigenous peoples and thus help to secure reconciliation, which they consider vital to their children's well-being. It is important for tourism planners and government agencies to realise that Indigenous tourism cannot prosper without acknowledging the vital importance of reconciliation in Australia and contributing to its achievement. Supporting the ferry to Hindmarsh Island would be one such initiative that would have invaluable impact. If the tourism industry and its supporters can meet this challenge, the potential of tourism as a social force in contributing to better societies seems much more promising.

Acknowledgments

This chapter is based upon an earlier work published in the *Journal of Travel Recreation Research* — Higgins-Desbiolles, F. (2003). Reconciliation tourism: Tourism healing divided societies? *Tourism Recreation Research*, 28(3), pp. 35–44.

The author wishes to thank members of the Ngarrindjeri community and Camp Coorong for their collaboration in this research project. In particular, Tom and Ellen Trevorrow, and Matt Rigney have provided the inspiration for this work. Vesper Tjukonai, Joan Gibbs,

Dr. Tanya Lyons and Dr. Olga Gostin have provided invaluable advice and support. However, any faults, inconsistencies and omissions are purely the responsibility of the author.

References

Aboriginal Australia and the Torres Strait Islands: Guide to Indigenous Australia. (2001). Footscray, Vic.: Lonely Planet Publications.

Beaumont, N. (2001). Ecotourism and the conservation ethic: Recruiting the uninitiated or preaching to the converted? *Journal of Sustainable Tourism, 9*(4), 317–341.

Bell, D. (1998). *Ngarrindjeri Wurruwarrin: A world that is, was and will be.* Melbourne: Spinifex.

Bell, D. (2001). The politics of surviving. *Off our backs,* March, 6 and 18.

Briton, B. (2001). Hindmarsh Island decision: Ngarrindjeri people yet to see justice. *The Guardian,* August 29, retrieved 3 March, 2002 from http://www.zip.com.au/~cpa/garchve4/1060hind.html

Brown, F. (1989). Is tourism really a peacemaker? *Tourism Management, 10*(4), 270–271.

Bull, A. (1995). *The economics of travel and tourism* (2nd ed.). Melbourne: Longman.

Collins, R. E. (1993). Indigenous cultures as a tourism attraction: An international perspective. *Indigenous Australians and tourism: A focus on the Northern territory* (pp. 32–7). Proceedings of the Indigenous Australians and Tourism Conference, June, ATSIC.

Council for Aboriginal Reconciliation. (2000). Retrieved November 10, 2002, from http://www.austlii.edu.au/au/other/IndigLRes/car/2000/16/appendices05.htm

Din, K. H. (1988). Tourism and peace: Desires and attainability. In: L. D'Amore, & J. Jafari (Eds), *Tourism — a vital force for peace* (pp. 75–81). Montreal: 1st Global Conference of International Institute for Peace.

Fraser, Rt. Hon. M. (2000). *Vincent Lingiari Memorial Lecture.* Retrieved August 24, 2000, from http://www.austlii.edu.au/au/other/IndigLRes/car/2000/2408.html

Hanna, M. (1999). *Reconciliation in Olympism: Indigenous culture in the Sydney Olympiad.* Petersham, NSW: Walla Walla Press.

Higgins-Desbiolles, F. (2002). Looking for the Noble Savage and Booking that Cannibal Tour: Tourism, Racism and Indigenous Peoples. *Sharing the Space* conference of the International Australian Studies Association, Flinders University, July 11–13.

Higgins-Desbiolles, F. (2003). Globalisation and Indigenous tourism: Sites of engagement and resistance. In: M. Shanahan, & G. Treuren (Eds), *Globalisation: Australian regional perspectives* (pp. 240–262). Adelaide: Wakefield Press.

Higgins-Desbiolles, F. (2004). Taming tourism: Indigenous rights as a check to unbridled tourism. *Local Frameworks and Global Realities? Tourism, Politics and Democracy conference.* Centre for Tourism Policy Studies, University of Brighton, UK, September 9–10.

Hinkson, M. (2001). *Aboriginal Sydney.* Canberra: Aboriginal Studies Press.

International Institute for Peace through Tourism (IIPT) (n. d.). Retrieved November 11, 2002, from http://www.iipt.org/backgrounder.html

Kauffman, P. (2000). *Travelling Aboriginal Australia: Discovery and reconciliation.* Flemington, Vic.: Hyland House.

Lanfant, M., Allcock, J. B., & Bruner, E. M. (1995). *International tourism: Identity and change.* London: Sage.

Lundberg, D. E. (1980). *The tourist business* (4th ed.). Boston: CBI Publishing.

Lundberg, D. E., Stavenca, M. H., & Krishnamoorthy, M. (1995). *Tourism economics.* New York: Wiley.

MacCannell, D. (1992). *Empty meeting grounds.* London: Routledge.

McGehee, N., & Norman, W. C. (2002). Alternative tourism as impetus for consciousness-raising. *Tourism Analysis, 6,* 239–251.

National Aboriginal and Torres Strait Islander Tourism Industry Strategy (NATSITIS) (1997). Canberra: ATSIC and Office of National Tourism.

Ngurunderi: a Ngarrindjeri Dreaming (1987). Director Max Pepper. Executive Producer John Dick. Pepper Studios for the South Australian Film Corporation and the South Australian Museum with the assistance of the Ngarrindjeri Community. Kent Town, SA.

On Our Own Terms (1996). Canberra: ATSIC.

Pilger, J. (2000). Australia's enduring disgrace. *Daily mail and guardian*, August 7. Johannesburg. Retrieved from http://www.mg.co.za/za/features/2000aug/07aug-pilger.html

Pizam, A. (1996). Does tourism promote peace and understanding between unfriendly nations? In: A. Pizam, & Y. Mansfeld (Eds) *Tourism, crime and international security issues* (pp. 203–213). Chichester: Wiley.

Rehn, A. (2003). The 'old people' return home. *The Advertiser*, May 6, p. 8.

Ryan, C. (1997). Maori and tourism: A relationship of history, constitutions and rites. *Journal of Sustainable Tourism*, 5(4), 257–278.

Ryan, C. (2002). Tourism and cultural proximity: Examples from New Zealand. *Annals of Tourism Research*, 29(4), 952–971.

Ryan, C., & Huyton, J. (2000a). Aboriginal tourism — a linear structural relations analysis of domestic and international tourist demand. *International Journal of Tourism Research*, 2, 15–29.

Ryan, C., & Huyton, J. (2000b). Who is interested in Aboriginal tourism in the Northern Territory, Australia? *Journal of Sustainable Tourism*, 8(1), 53–88.

Schmiechen, J. (1993). Paper on Camp Coorong. *Ecotourism: An aboriginal perspective*, South Australian Eco-tourism Forum, Adelaide, August.

Selling Australia (2001). The Brand. Sydney: Film Australia.

Simon, M. (2003). *The meeting of the waters*. Sydney: Hodder.

Smith, V. (1989). *Hosts and guests: The anthropology of tourism* (2nd ed.). Philadelphia: University of Pennsylvania Press.

Sofield, T. H. B., & Birtles, R. A. (1996). Indigenous peoples' cultural opportunity spectrum for tourism. In: R. Butler, & T. Hinch (Eds) *Tourism and indigenous people* (pp. 396–433). London: International Thomson Business Press.

Strong Business, Strong Culture, Strong Country (1996). Canberra: ATSIC and Northern Territory.

A Talent for Tourism (1996). Office of National Tourism. Retrieved March 7, 2001 from http://www.sport.gov.au/publications/talent/campcoorong.html

Turner, L., & Ash, J. (1975). *The golden hordes: International tourism and the pleasure periphery*. London: Constable.

Var, T., Ap, J., & Van Doren, C. (1994). Tourism and world peace. In: W. Theobold (Ed.) *Global tourism. The next decade* (pp. 27–39). Oxford: Butterworth-Heinemann.

Wearing, S. (2001). *Volunteer tourism: Experiences that make a difference*. Oxon: CABI.

Williams, T. (2002). Bone find triggers apology on bridge. *The Advertiser*, 8 October, p. 3.

WTO. (1980a). *The economic effects of tourism*. Madrid: WTO.

WTO. (1980b). Manila declaration on world tourism. Retrieved November 11, 2002, from http://www.world-tourism.org/sustainable/concepts.htm

WTO. (1985). Tourism bill of rights and tourist code. Retrieved November 11, 2002, from http://www.world-tourism.org/sustainable/concepts.htm

WTO. (1995). The charter for sustainable development. Retrieved November 11, 2002, from http://www.world-tourism.org/sustainable/concepts.htm

WTO. (1999). Global code of ethics for tourism. Retrieved November 11, 2002, from http://www.world-tourism.org/sustainable/concepts.htm

Zeppel, H. (1999). *Aboriginal tourism in Australia: A Research Bibliography*. CRC Tourism Research Report Series, No. 2. Gold Coast, QLD: CRC for Sustainable Tourism.

Chapter 11

Sustainable Tourism and National Park Development in St. Lucia

Janne J. Liburd

Introduction

National parks systems have grown incrementally throughout the world with little pattern to the spatial distribution. However, most appears to be established around the same principles and functions, which are very similar to the original American model (Butler & Boyd, 2000). Examining first the historical establishment of national parks, the conceptual and political context for present preservation efforts are discussed. National parks continue to play a significant role in areas of protection, conservation, economic potential for regional development, recreation and tourism. Current literature on the relationship between tourism and national parks make little attempt to distinguish between touristic, recreational and traditional subsistence use of national parks despite the potentially different individual needs, expectations and lived experiences. While acknowledging that this may be somewhat imprecise, it is generally argued that the problems caused by the impact from these kinds of utilisation are closely related and often dealt with in the same manner (Wahab & Pigram, 1997; Hall & Lew, 1998; Mowforth & Munt, 1998; Butler & Boyd, 2000).

However, to belong to a place is informed not only by particular modes of localised cultural knowledge, but shared through associated symbols and imaginations that inform social practice, which the analysis from St. Lucia will further illustrate.

Following a brief review of the main principles of sustainable development and sustainable tourism the much neglected issues of scale, equity and implementation are discussed. It will be argued that the sustainability of tourism and national parks is dependant upon decision makers, educators, NGOs and especially local stakeholders who adopt the principles of sustainable development into their management philosophy and daily

Tourism and Social Identities: Global Frameworks and Local Realities
Copyright © 2006 by Elsevier Ltd.
All rights of reproduction in any form reserved.
ISBN: 0-08-045074-1

practice. Moreover, the sustainability principles must be informed by the cultural context in which they are put into practice. Relatively few studies have focused on the operational and managerial implications of sustaining traditional economic activities within the national park boundaries, which represent significant challenges when the concept of preservation embraces a multi-use approach. Consequently, the many individual, ecological and socio-economic linkages that extend beyond the immediate park area must also be considered in order to facilitate a meaningful understanding of individual and shared participation in sustainable tourism and national park development.

In the island context of St. Lucia, the above-mentioned characteristics are clearly visible in the comprehensive proposal entitled *System for Protected Areas for St. Lucia* (Hudson, Renard, & Romulus, 1992). Based on the principles of sustainable development, the plan strongly advocates establishing a multi-use, co-managed national park in the south-east coastal region of St. Lucia. Funded by the United States Agency for International Development, a wide range of governmental and NGOs participated in the development of the plan. Undeniably, NGOs have played a significant role in national and international development since the 1980s as the limitations of state-sponsored and controlled development programmes became apparent. NGO involvement often fills or reduces the gap between the "top" and "bottom" of society by deliberately targeting the poorest population segments in their work. Advocating what Burns (1999, p. 3) has termed "participative development", the inclusion and diversity of approaches by the NGO sector also suggest that the development discourse is far from homogenous or fixed. On the other hand, rather than promoting radical, deep-rooted changes NGOs are often accused of preserving status-quo by setting up systems of patronage that not only undermines but also depoliticises social movements and other grassroots organisations (cf. Tvedt, 1995; Gardner & Lewis, 1996; Brennan & Allen, 2001). It will be argued that while NGOs at times may blur the larger issues at stake, in the present case the facilitation by CANARI did not at any point appear to depoliticise the national park project.

A closer examination of the approach to national park development in the south of St. Lucia will bring further light to this debate by focusing on the identity and traditional practice of a group of charcoal producers and a regional NGO, the Caribbean Natural Resources Institute (CANARI). The analysis will further illustrate that anthropological methods are well-suited and also unsettled when probing NGO involvement, identity, democracy and empowerment of local peoples. It is the overall intention of this chapter to investigate the unfulfilled potentials for a more dynamic understanding of sustainable tourism and national park development while challenging some of the issues we take for granted about local stakeholder participation.

Conceptualising National Park Development

Introducing the underlying conceptualisations and origin of national park development, the political and cultural constructions of nature is exposed in the following. Correctly noted by Hall (1998), the Western ideal of nature up until the late 1700s was one of order and control by man. Boundaries of the wilderness and the uncivilised were made apparent and demarcated as areas to be conquered. Representing the rational utilitarian spirit underlying

Western attitudes towards nature, human development was synonymous with taming "the waste and howling wilderness" (Wigglesworth, 1662 in Hall, 1998, p. 14). Only in a cultivated state did land acquire real value. The moral and ethical implications of this perception are manifested in evolutionary thought and enlightenment ideas of human progression in knowledge and society, and with that a well-established vocabulary of dualisms. With emphasis on man's rationality and supremacy, nature was separated from society in mind and fact.

During the 18th century Romantic Movement the same landscapes, wilderness and mountains became objects of admiration where man was acknowledged as part of nature. Nature and 'primitive' man were no less mysterious, wild or chaotic. But the spiritual values of the wilderness and ideas of preservation for its own sake found resonance in a growing recognition of the need for a balanced approach to man's use of nature. Dedicated conservation organisations took form, among them John Muir's *Sierra Club* whose California-based members were among those successfully seeking national park status for Yosemite in 1890 (Rothman, 1998, p. 18). Only surpassed by Yellowstone, the world's first national park in 1872, there are a number of important factors involved in the designation of these early parks. Moreover, traces of the rational scientific and romantic views and spatial imaginations of nature remain evident in present preservation and conservation efforts due to which they deserve further attention.

Recognising three essential characteristics, the widely acknowledged definition of a national park by the International Union for the Conservation of Nature (1969) are:

1. a relatively large area where one or several ecosystems are not materially altered by human exploitation and occupation, where plant and animal species, geomorphological sites and habitats of special scientific, educative and recreative interest of which contains a natural landscape of great beauty and
2. the highest competent authority of the country has taken steps to prevent or to eliminate as soon as possible exploitation or occupation in the whole area and to enforce effectively the respect of ecological, geomorphological or aesthetic features which have led to its establishment and
3. visitors are allowed to enter, under special conditions, for inspirational, educative, cultural and recreative purposes (quoted in Butler & Boyd, 2000, pp. 4–5).

Tourism and recreation have been among the motivating forces for land preservation since the earliest parks and reserves were established. In the US, the two million acre Yellowstone National Park was described by Congressional advisers as located on "worthless land unsuitable for lumbering, agriculture, cattle farming, mining and human settlement" (Hayden quoted in Hall, 1998, p. 17). In other words, the nature and spectacles offered within the national park areas added merit and real economic value to these sites. Due to their perceived worthlessness most of the early parks were located at a considerable distance from residential sites. Since visitors were required to stay overnight when *on route* to the national parks, all national park visitors could be classified as tourists irrespective of their travel motivations or pleasure use of the parks.

The year 1890 not only marks the designation of Yosemite National Park but also the closing of the American frontier. American was increasingly becoming an industrialised, urbanised nation where the finite nature of America's natural resources had to be recognised. Mandated by a wish to retain aesthetic and spiritual links with the wilderness Muir's *Sierra Club*, the formation of the *Wilderness Society* (1935) and kindred preservation organisations can be seen as a response to the loss of the frontier. Nature should be kept in unimpaired forms, either by adopting a hands-off managerial approach or restricting human activity deemed unsympathetic to the primitive nature of the wilderness areas (Hall, 1998, p. 19).

At the same time and primarily inspired by economic objectives a movement of progressive conservationists argued for the "wise use" of natural resources. To the conservationists, among whom President Theodore Roosevelt was found, the meaning of wise land use implied managing forest lands with emphasis on sustained-yield forestry that would continuously allow for timber harvesting, the building of dams for human water supply, selective mining and grazing. Rothman (1998, p. 34) ironically observes that the institutionalisation of progressive conservation in the US Government sparked the onset of "taming rivers as a favoured American sport and mission". Indeed following the extension of frontiers in America, not to mention in the New World, the renewed interest in nature arose as the loss of resources — real and imagined — intensified.

The predicament between strict preservation and progressive conservation resembles much of the debate over the meanings of sustainable development and sustainable tourism further discussed below. Evidently natural resource management continues to struggle with the dilemma of protection and utilisation. Also echoed in the National Park Service Act of 1916, the National Park Service (NPS) is authorised to:

> Conserve the scenery and the natural historical objects and the wildlife therein and to provide for the enjoyment of the same in such manner ... as will leave them unimpaired for the enjoyment of future generations. (quote from Zinser, 1995, p. 72)

The dual mandate of parks of conserving natural resources while providing for civic enjoyment is well established. Whereas the Yellowstone Act of 1872 had already set precedence for the political feasibility of designating vast amounts of land for the development of other national parks, the protection and enjoyment was now mandated at a national level to embrace a shared American heritage. Generally, national park development incorporates a national political aspect that involves legislation and governance as well as explicit interpretative acts of inclusion and exclusion. Endorsing specific historical events, places and environments to display a national heritage represents a highly selective, political act of place construction. It is selective because historical events include but a fraction of all happenings that have taken place in a particular time span, just as national park boundaries distinguish only a minor amount of land within the nation state borders. These selections become symbols used in the creation and recreation of a shared national identity, which in turn provides emotional legitimacy to the state. This is eminently illustrated in NPS' latest slogan: "Experience your America" (U.S. National Park Service, 2003). Represented as neutral or natural products of a shared, great American past, these selections can feasibly be read as a response to political requirements of the present. Still pivoting between romantic and rational notions of land use by the dawn of the 21st century, national parks, like nation-states, are modern creations even though they are commonly represented as old:

> Our national parks commemorate the historical and cultural events, social movements and people from which we derive our collective national heritage. Individual experiences can help people gain a sense of place and a stronger sense of history and national identity. Equally as important is the sanctuary that the parks provide for the mind and spirit. (U.S. National Park Service, 1999)

Visible in the quote above and in the NPS slogan the development of national parks is not only a political but also a cultural project. It is cultural because shared meanings and values are continuously attributed to specific natural areas and historical events as 'evidence', in this case, that the American culture is distinctive. The sole principle of inclusion and exclusion follows the boundaries of the nation, which is precisely the category of people defined as members of the same culture. While seemingly fixed and unchangeable, the continuous selection process signifies that all cultural and site selections are open to multiple interpretations, which accordingly may be contested and changed over time. Pointing out that national park boundaries are based on political concepts and cultural constructs rather than ecological divisions also calls for further inquiry into whether they are at all sufficient to protect for future generations the natural resources within the park boundaries. Furthermore, it demands attention to the use of park development as instruments of control over sites and exclusion of people who might have been inhabitants of the resource users in the area before it was turned into a national park.

In short, many of the early parks were established with a well-defined government mandate to preserve and provide for tourism and public accessibility that were compatible goals at the time. But the accommodation of larger numbers of visitors each year together with the rising pressures of financing national parks evidently poses other managerial challenges. Mirroring these developments was a growing support for a more symbiotic relationship between humankind and the natural environment, also visible in the effects of Carson's (1962) *Silent Spring* and Hardin's (1968) *Tragedy of the Commons*. Taking a closer look at current approaches to better, more balanced development and the application to tourism and national parks, the following section will investigate these managerial predicaments in further detail.

Sustainable Development and Sustainable Tourism

Current notions of sustainable development and sustainable tourism can be traced to a variety of antecedents, including but not limited to Western preservation and conservation movements. Recent international conferences and reports have helped frame interest, notably the 1972 UN Stockholm Conference on the Human Environment, the 1980 World Conservation Strategy and the three independent UN Commissions established between 1977 and 1984. The 1987 report by the World Commission on the Environment and Development, commonly referred to as the Brundtland Report, hinges on a holistic integration of economic, environmental and socio-cultural aspects. Sustainable development is presented as a more responsible and balanced form of development that allows for the conservation of natural resources and the environment while permitting it to be exploited in order to secure continued economic growth (Jurowski & Liburd, 2002). Few development proposals, if any, have been met with similar enthusiastic support — at least in the First World (Butler, 1998). Indeed, the widespread approval at multiple levels is established through the very generality of the concept, which is easily embraced as a positive approach to making things last, whether an ecosystem, an economy, a culture or an industry. Evident in the relation between tourism and national park development, tourism has vested interests in preserving the natural environment as its resource base and, as agued by progressive conservationists, as a significant means to economic growth.

While tourism is not mentioned in the Brundtland Report, the document provided the basis for the principles and policies defined in *"Agenda 21 for the Travel & Tourism Industry: Toward Environmentally Sustainable Development"* (WTTC, WTO & EC, 1995). The report emphasises the importance of partnerships between government, industry and non-governmental entities. Summarised in the guidelines and definition of sustainable tourism development posed by the World Tourism Organization (2001):

> Sustainable tourism development meets the needs of present tourists and host regions while protecting and enhancing opportunities for the future. Sustainable tourism is envisaged as leading to management of all resources in such a way that economic, social and aesthetic needs can be fulfilled while maintaining cultural integrity, essential ecological processes, biological diversity, and life support systems.

Lacking precision in conceptual meaning and especially in practice, a considerable amount has been written over the past decade on definitions and the imperative of implementing the principles of sustainable development in tourism. Predicted to reach 1.6 billion by 2020 (World Tourism Organisation, 1997), the volume of international tourism arrivals has caused well-known negative environmental impacts, some of which are currently facing national park systems around the globe. With mass-tourism crowned as the primary obliterating element in unsustainable tourism practices, 'greener' and small-scale forms of sustainable tourism continue to gain interest. Unfortunately, the issue of scale and context escapes critical attention in the fascination with everything small and green. As suggested by Butler (1998, p. 28):

> While some developments may have moved significantly towards sustainability, to claim that they are sustainable is clearly at best premature, and possibly completely inaccurate.

Butler & Boyd (2000, p. 162) correspondingly argues that conflict over park management is easily avoided on the basis that the type of tourism being encouraged is classified as 'sustainable', 'responsible' and 'environmentally conscious'. Moreover, tourism's impacts can only be assessed in the geographical region in which it occurs. Yet, the relations of those tourism activities and managerial ties extend far beyond the specific destination. Tourism cannot be seen as the single, external causative factor of change just as change does not automatically equal destruction. Sustainable tourism in a particular region does not denote a sustainable tourism industry, especially when the existing problems of the tourism industry lie in the unplanned tourism facilities of the past and in the growing number of tourists. This dilemma is easily detected in the development of national parks and sustainable tourism, which the analysis from St. Lucia will further illustrate.

In addition, the meaning and practice of sustainable tourism cannot be separate from the cultural values and the context in which they exist. Culture is about shared values, traditions, beliefs and meanings that exist between people in different contexts. Culture is reflected in notions of identity, language, integrity and feelings of belonging, which may change according to the context and situation at stake. However, not all cultural changes are conscious choices determined by those who identify with a particular culture. As the fundamental idea of sustainability and the system is to uphold balance, such a functionalist approach fails to acknowledge that elements of continuity and change are the norm for culture, environment and economy (Harrison, 1996). More constructively, a collaborative interpretation is needed of what is to be sustained for whom and how by the people whose habitat is, or may become the object of tourism and national park development. Charged with the opportunistic mandate to expose these much-neglected issues, attention will next be sensitised to the socio-cultural context of the Caribbean island of St. Lucia where the proposed Pointe Sables National Park is located.

The Making of Pointe Sables National Park in St. Lucia

A brief historical introduction will first serve to introduce the context for the NGO involvement and national park development in the south of St. Lucia. This moreover accentuates the connectedness of knowledge and power that extend beyond the immediate national park area where discourses on sustainable tourism, conservation and management of national parks are easily traced. The following account draws primarily on anthropological fieldwork using the method of participant-observation between August 1997 and January 1998. Follow-up research and personal correspondence have since been conducted via email, telephone interviews and use of online data.

With a population of 157,898 inhabitants the independent island-state of St. Lucia is located in the Eastern Caribbean chain of Windward Islands with Barbados to the southwest and midway between Martinique and St. Vincent (Government of St. Lucia, 2004). The town of Vieux Fort with 14,757 inhabitants is located to the extreme south of St. Lucia where the largest area of flat land is also found. During British and French colonialism, sugar cane was the primary cash crop produced in the Vieux Fort area. Following the British abolition of slavery in 1834 and emancipation 4 years later, approximately 13,300 former slaves were freed. The search for economic diversification commenced. Mainly due to the outbreak of World War II, sugar cane cultivation in the Vieux Fort area was significantly reduced in 1941 when the British agreed to a 99-year lease of approximately 1200 acres of land for a US military air base. Reflecting events like those experienced in other postcolonial Caribbean islands, this serves as evidence of how the Caribbean region has been fully integrated to the world economy for centuries (Mintz, 1985). The War brought substantial socio-economic and environmental changes to Vieux Fort. The installation of the US air base provided the town with most of its present physical infrastructure, including sewage systems, water and electricity supply, roads, an airport and a harbour. During the construction phase various ecological processes were altered. Rivers were diverged forcing local fishermen of the Savannes Bay to relocate and the Mankoté mangrove was used to hide planes and other military equipment. Despite very unsanitary conditions and recorded outbreaks of typhoid migration from the rural hinterlands to the town of Vieux Fort was significant. The military base remained in operation until 1949, after which 700 acres of land were returned to the Government of St. Lucia. The base was reactivated for a 2-year period, from 1955 to 1957, only to be closed down in 1960 by when the remains were handed over to the local government. Then the transition from US air base to international tourism appeared to be straightforward. The existing runway of the air base was extended to 9000 feet and the airport upgraded to international standards capable of handling jets. Yet, despite offering tax incentives and duty-free import of construction materials in order to invigorate investments in tourism in the south of the island, government legislation had little effect. With little or no regard to the destruction of natural resources or the socio-cultural context, other externally generated development schemes have since been introduced in the southern region. For various reasons, none of these ever fully materialised.

In contrast, the St. Lucian government and the British Development Corporation embarked on an ambitious project in 1970 to develop the Rodney Bay-Gros Islet area in the north of St. Lucia. Marina lagoons, 1 km of new sandy beach and over 160 hectares of land for the construction of hotels and tourism related facilities were created. Successfully attracting international investors, construction in the northern part of St. Lucia is still ongoing. This has further substantiated a perceived division in the island between the "developed North", where the main tourist facilities are located and the "underdeveloped South" where Vieux Fort's main street and open gutters literally ends in the ocean (Liburd, 2001).

In the early 1980s, the St. Lucia National Trust initiated preliminary research in the southeast coast region, which is home to some 15,000 residents. The St. Lucia National Trust is a quasi private/public agency mandated with responsibility to preserve and protect St. Lucia's natural and cultural heritage comparable to that of the US NPS. Primarily concerned with depletion of natural resources in the area, the St. Lucia National Trust sought assistance from two regional NGOs, the Caribbean Conservation Association and its then smaller affiliate, the Caribbean Natural Resource Institute (CANARI). As Cohen (2002, p. 268) correctly points out, local populations are frequently depicted as damaging the environment and the land it occupies as marginal, under-utilised or mismanaged, which was also the case here. Among the destructive practices listed by CANARI are: sand mining for construction, the use of dynamite for fishing and charcoal production in the mangrove, over-harvesting of lobster and sea urchin stocks (Renard, 1994, p. 2). CANARI subsequently designed and conducted a project for conservation, on-going testing and demonstration of good practice. The project obtained international funding from the World Wildlife Fund and was initiated under the auspices of the St. Lucia Ministry of Planning.

Clauzel (1997a) explains the how the World Wildlife Fund partnership elevated the issue of conservation to a more fundamental, yet ambitious approach of targeting the socio-economic problems of the south, home of approximately 30,000 people.

According to CANARI, the research process was managed by an Advisory Committee with representatives of "all relevant government agencies, non-governmental institutions and several members of the community" (Renard, 1994, p. 3). Indeed, NGOs *raison d'être* is often seen as the operating link between the state, international aid organisations and disempowered people at the 'bottom' of society. The importance of a "participatory planning" approach is stressed throughout CANARI's documentation (CANARI 1994, 1995, 1996, 2005). It is represented as having made especially government agencies and other NGOs aware of "community needs" (*ibid.*). In short, CANARI objective was to pursue a strategy of progressive conservation through multi-sited institution building with stakeholders that included international donors, national authorities and the local resource users. From 1985 to 1989, CANARI took on a more direct role from that of coordination to project implementation. This tacitly illustrates a change in the development discourse and practice from centrally top-down state-sponsored approaches. Critics of NGO involvement point to "unsubstantiated NGO myths" about direct involvement of poor people and the application of generalising notions of community needs and empowerment from 'below' (Farrington, Bebbington, Wellard, & Lewis, 1993; Gardner & Lewis, 1996, p. 109). Like other NGOs, CANARI is easily accused of preserving *status quo* through new structures of patronage and internationally directed sponsorships, which undermines and depoliticises social movements and other grassroots organisations. Evidently, NGO involvement is not unequivocal in scope. It can be argued that working from 'within' need not result in absorption or loss of cultural meaning and autonomy as it depends on the circumstantial strategies adopted and specific objectives pursued. Critical assessments on a case-to-case basis are clearly needed, which this chapter also sets out to provide a corrective against. Further comparative research is essential to substantiate the debates and facilitate qualitative understandings of NGO involvement in sustainable development (Liburd, 2004).

The St. Lucia National Trust launched another highly ambitious project in 1988 to prepare a comprehensive programme of conservation and development for the entire island. Planning and overseeing this were representatives from several government agencies, the Folk Research Centre, St. Lucia Tourist Board, St. Lucia Hotel and Tourism Association, the private sector and again, CANARI. Funded by USAID an extensive consultation process was carried out over several years. The documented outcome, *A System of Protected Areas for St. Lucia* (Hudson et al., 1992) identifies a total of 27 management areas comprised of 150 protected sites. It is the first official proposal to establish a national park on the southeast coast of St. Lucia. Interestingly, the area recognised as the Point Sables National Park is fully compatible with the original research and testing site of CANARI's. Undeniably this is directly attributable to overlapping project personnel, intersecting Board of Directors and Executive Committee memberships with notably the St. Lucia National Trust, and the NGO's close political affiliations with high government officials, including the Prime Minister.

Interestingly, the essential national park characteristics listed by the International Union for the Conservation of Nature's (1969) is only found in the particular landscape of "great natural beauty". The proposed Pointe Sables National Park consists of coral reefs, mangroves, seagrass beds, endemic species, archaeological sites, beaches, xerophytic forests, cliffs and off shore islands. Pointe Sables National Park is neither "a relatively large area", nor has "the highest authority of the country taken steps to prevent or to eliminate as soon as possible exploitation or occupation of the whole area". Local subsistence users continue to carry a range of potentially conflicting socio-economic activities inside the park boundaries.

During CANARI's involvement on the south-east coast, five groups have been formed according to the economic occupation strategy applied by the individual subsistence users. Two of the five groups, the fuelwood and charcoal producers, are identical in their membership of 15 individuals. The other groups include a total of 30 commercial seamoss cultivators, the fishermen's group with approximately 10 boats at the Savannes Bay, and lastly an undisclosed number of divers harvesting sea urchins at three different locations. It is my estimate that CANARI was working with an approximate total of 90 individuals with variable levels of engagement. Living outside the park area in Vieux Fort and surrounding villages, all of the resource users are poor landless individuals and families of the lowest social and economic levels in St. Lucia. Some of the land within the proposed park boundaries is still privately owned and under consideration for commercial exploitation. Among the most recent development proposals within the proposed park area are a golf course, marina and yacht club. And in 2004, a 254 room all-inclusive hotel and spa resort opened by the Savannes Bay. As CANARI advocates sustaining the traditional economic activities by acknowledging the locals-as-users in the park, the predicament of preservation and providing for enjoyment has not only been reproduced but significantly challenged in the process.

Following initial consultation between the St. Lucia Ministry of Planning, the St. Lucia National Trust and CANARI, a "Community Mobilisation Workshop for the Southeast Coast Project" was held in September of 1996 to formally present the idea of Pointe Sables National Park. Intending to bring together local stakeholders who were defined as the "subsistence users" of the area (Geoghegan & Smith, 1998, p. 4) the potentially conflicting utilisation and control of the area was addressed. Couched in terms of "locals-as-partners" frequently local populations are without any equitable representation in the development of national parks or new tourist enterprises, not to mention the distribution of benefits accruing from them (Cohen, 2002, p. 273). The workshop made it clear that issues of equity had to embrace the "locals-as-users" by maintaining equity of access to the park area.

Formalising issues of control and user rights of the proposed park area, the workshop initiative consolidated a group of locals who volunteered to work together as an interim park committee. Committee representatives were found among the three organisers of the workshop along with natural resource users, the private sector, education and a youth representative (Clauzel, 1996a). The interim committee was to generally oversee operations and the planning processes of the national park. Moreover, it was charged with a mandate to prepare the management guidelines for Pointe Sables National Park in accordance with which the park would be governed, once legislated.

In full correspondence with the number of diverse, socio-economic activities that continue to be the very livelihood of many people in the area, locals-as-users are acknowledged as stakeholders in the future conservation and management of Pointe Sables. The multi-use park concept is summarised by Clauzel (1996b, p. 1) as an attempt to:

- develop a management plan to sustain the various economic activities currently taking place in that area;
- encourage new entrepreneurial activities in that area which will be of economic, cultural or social benefit to the people of the south;
- streamline those activities along environmentally sensitive and sustainable development lines, thereby ensuring that the various resources are not exploited out of existence; and
- create possibilities for sustained employment for the people of that area.

In this context, preservation and protection are based on sustaining current economic practice and a sense of place and belonging. Benefiting the "people of the south", the category is made relevant through shared imaginations and maintenance of a long-standing opposition towards the "developed North" in St. Lucia. Resistance towards the north is also tied to a racial dichotomy dividing blacks and whites. Most of St. Lucia's land and sea-based tours are controlled from the capital of Castries by two families of colonial descent. While interracial marriages have long blurred the contrast between black and white they are still perceived as white as opposed to the people in the south of whom a majority is black.

Ordinarily classified as "outsiders", a term indiscriminately applied to tourists, expatriates or residents from the northern parts of St. Lucia, people who were not born in the Vieux Fort area were able to earn respect through participation in the park development process. Constituting a group of people in and of the south explicitly means exclusion of others who do not belong to 'us'. Tacitly a sort of cultural homogeneity, identity and democracy transpires, whether national or regional, where indeed there might be none. Yet, it is precisely through ongoing negotiations of diversified experiences in the Pointe Sables area that led to a shared cultural construction of place and belonging, which consequently are valued as important to protect and preserve. A closer look at some of the charcoal producers in the Mankoté mangrove of Pointe Sables and ongoing facilitation by CANARI will illustrate these identity processes in further detail.

A Group of Charcoal Producers Evolves

Focusing on how the group of charcoal producers evolved in the Mankoté mangrove, identity and place construction in the national park context will be further examined. Also the democratic implications of CANARI's involvement and notions of community participation are critically analysed.

Covering 63 ha, the Mankoté mangrove is an important wildlife habitat, a nursery, a source of nutrients for coastal systems, a place for recreation, fishing and seasonal crab hunting and production of fuelwood and charcoal (Renard, 1994, p. 6). Still a major source of fuel in St. Lucia like many parts of the Caribbean, charcoal production is an individual enterprise, only sometimes with help from family members. The production of charcoal requires hard physical labour: from the cutting of the woods using cutlasses inside the dense, humid mangrove; gathering of the sticks after which they are carried to a site where a pit is carefully prepared, packed and covered with dry grass and dirt before it is lit. The burning lasts from 1 to 4 days (depending on the producer's need of money), which influences the quality of coals produced. The coals are dug out from the pit, sifted and finally bagged before the product is ready for sale. Some of the producers literally raise their families on charcoal production, as they were themselves. High moral standards and individual respect are the only means by which a charcoal pit is protected. Unsurprisingly, mutual accusations of theft are commonly heard amongst the individual producers. Moreover, multiple occupation strategies are frequent, as charcoal production does not require full-time attention.

Charcoal production easily causes a significant depletion of the natural resource on which it depends. Using a participatory approach to natural resources conservation, the involvement by CANARI led to significant changes in the traditional harvesting techniques. Arriving at novel and improved practices, the resource base, yield rapid regeneration and increase in charcoal production were positively impacted (Renard, 1994, p. 6). In addition, ongoing monitoring activities were established in close cooperation with CANARI. Primarily designed to estimate the rate of exploitation and trends in the mangrove tree biomass all data are managed by CANARI. The results are disseminated to the producers through frequent meetings and discussions.

When the charcoal producers were first brought together by CANARI in 1986, this traditionally individual enterprise of charcoal production was transformed through a formal consolidation into a group: "*The Aupicon Agricultural and Charcoal Producers Group*" (the AACP Group). Constituted by 15 producers active at the time of consultation by CANARI, the AACP Group established individual memberships based on adherence to organisational rules and regulations. They instituted specific harvesting techniques and zoning of the area through which access to the mangrove became restricted. In other words, facilitated by CANARI and in cooperation with government institutions, exclusive user rights were authorised to members of the AACP Group alone. Effectively, other perhaps poorer charcoal producers from the Mankoté mangrove were excluded and some parts of the mangrove were fenced off. In other words, equity in access and benefits were restricted to a membership of 15. This is arguably a rather limited number when defining local "community needs" and if addressing issues of sustainable development and poverty alleviation in an area of 30,000 residents where many belong to the lowest socio-economic levels of society.

There are always multiple stakeholders involved in national park development and sustainable tourism. Aside from the narrow inclusion of the Pointe Sables "subsistence users" a stakeholder can be defined as any person, group or organization that is affected by the causes or consequences of an issue (Bramwell & Sharman, 1999). Stakeholder involvement is therefore not dependent on the size and maturity of the development project but applicable to all forms of sustainable development practices. Cognisant that consensus cannot be assumed in the local community, nor are the stakeholders a homogenous group of people living in harmony with Mother Nature, democratic processes of consultation and local stakeholder participation in decision-making are central to sustainable planning and policy-making in tourism and national park development. In this endeavour collaboration is of vital importance. Collaboration is defined as:

> a process of joint decision making among autonomous and key stakeholders of an inter-organizational domain to resolve problems of the domain and/or to manage issues related to the domain. (Grey in Robinson, 1999, p. 387)

Collaboration rarely takes place upon an even playing field, whether in economic, environmental, socio-cultural, local or global terms. Well known for producing unequal encounters between the destination population and visiting tourists sustainable development calls for cultural changes that are acceptable for the destination community as it determines what is to be sustained for whom and how by the people whose habitat is, or may become, the object of tourism and national park development.

Still, caution should be exercised to avoid making claims about locals as the best decision-makers where park development is involved. Assuming that the AACP Group operates as a small, democratic unit with culturally shared interests that makes them capable of reaching consensus is not only idealistic but also highly naïve. Smallness does permit relatively easy liaison building. However, it also intensifies face-to-face personalism, ethnicity and kinship ties of participating individuals, which *can* undermine objectives of sustainable development and inhibit the confrontation of disparate, serious issues. From a similar social background and many belonging to the same family, of the current AACP membership five of the most active producers have consolidated into a core and taken control of decision-making. While certainly not particularly democratic in scope, the social and cultural significance attributed to the place, ways of being together, talking and sharing is predominant.

To further illustrate, the AACP Group now organises several collective ventures that traditionally were only individual accomplishments. One example is the *Koud-men*, which is a practice of labouring for somebody who has a piece of work to do that requires some amount of labour. Usually on a Sunday, organising a *Koud-men* means that people are asked to show up with whatever tools needed and provide their labour free of charge in return for food and drinks. Not only does the individual traditionally hosting the *Koud-men* benefit but the socio-cultural values involved are of particular significance. Reputation and moral standards are built at *Koud-men* as are expectations of reciprocity (Samuel et al., 1992 in Clauzel, 1997a). The AACP Group has successfully organised *Koud-men* activities several times a year. Averaging about 20 persons working at various projects activities involve clean ups, rehabilitation of drainage patterns and trail maintenance in the mangrove.

Moreover, the AACP Group has taken on the responsibility of bringing a child of a diseased member through school, as the child's family has no means to afford tuition and fees. All income generated by the AACP Group are recorded and equally shared between its members, as are expenses. Spending more time at the mangrove than anywhere else, a single mother of eight continuously bring in flowers and plants in abundance to beautify the area whereby a sense of home and belonging is recreated. This careful experimentation with identity and place is made relevant through social situations, daily encounters and communication as a way of coping with demands and challenges of life in a meaningful way.

During my fieldwork the AACP group identity and sense of belonging were visibly reproduced, especially in the weeks prior to the official opening of the viewing tower in December 1997. In order to proudly display membership of the AACP Group badges with names were made to wear for the official opening celebration. Innovative practices and future projects took form with a common purpose of enhancing the area and increasing revenue-generating activities. Spinning of a local initiative to small-scale cruise development in the south of St. Lucia (Liburd, 2001), one of the charcoal producers became part of a vendor's group that produced traditional dolls made of banana leafs. Other ACCP members made miniature charcoal bags filled with tiny coal pieces that otherwise would have been discarded. These were sold at the Mankoté entrance as authentic local souvenirs to visiting cruise tourists. Again facilitated by CANARI, the AACP Group has successfully obtained several small and micro grants to pursue other development initiatives in Mankoté mangrove. Besides the construction of the above-mentioned viewing tower, information panels have been erected in pursuit of developing small-scale ecotourism. After a short tour guide training programme provided by a local entrepreneur and CANARI affiliate, the ACCP Group members interpret the guided tours themselves while generating additional income to the AACP Group. Eco-walks are conducted into the humid mangrove, which to most visitors appears somewhat dangerous as the swamps are muddy and "probably filled with all kinds of dangerous creatures", as one tourist remarked while on the tour. Another eco-tour is arranged by the St. Lucia National Trust in collaboration with the AACP Group and Savannes Bay fishermen to the park's off-shore islets. Among their near-future projects is the construction of an elevated boardwalk in order to entice visitation while limiting ecological impacts relative to the area's carrying capacity. This requires that tourism is continuously monitored in order to ensure that the ecosystem integrity is maintained. In addition to generating revenue and protecting the environment, the perceived benefits by the AACP Group include representation of their southern culture and ways of life to tourists. The guides also expressed interest in asking tourists about their culture and perhaps establish friendships. Following Meethan (2001, p. 162), these forms of local knowledge and social practices do not simply *reflect* differences, but they actually *create* differences through action. Consequently, the complexities of social and cultural practice in a globalised world cannot be meaningfully understood if isolated from other forms of internal and external change. Moreover, the key principles of sustainable tourism as a managerial strategy are given meaning by the local context in which they exist. The social, cultural, environmental and economic aspects are perceived as elements in ongoing processes to develop tourism, the national park and ultimately enhance their way of life while striving to prove a good experience for the visiting tourists. In other words, embracing locals-as-users is essential to the sustainable development of tourism and national parks.

The AACP Group at Mankoté has become an active network of people submerged in everyday life. Personal involvement in experimenting with and practising cultural innovation is evident. Whether build on religious notions of mutual respect and gratitude towards nature, or pragmatic utilisation of hours of hard labour invested in a specific task, the resource users are by no means a homogenous group of people who easily reach consensus. Within the AAPC Group the five core members are regularly accused of instituting new rules and projects without soliciting the remaining membership. The core members' counter argument is typically a request for more active participation in the production of coals and shared undertakings as revenue generated in the mangrove is equally shared between all 15 members.

Still CANARI's role as facilitator remains an umbilical cord to the AACP Group for mediating minor conflicts, continuous preservation, project funding, training and monitoring. Formalisation of management appears to be of pivotal importance in order to sustain the daily practice of the AACP Group and the development of the park at large. Further managerial and representational concerns are briefly discussed below.

Co-Management and Accountability

Research in community and collaborative management (co-management) generally focus on natural resources, problems of common property and resource-user groups (Berkes, George, & Preston, 1991; Pinkerton, 1993; Brown & Pomeroy, 1998; Berkes, Mahon, McConney, Pollnac, & Pomeroy, 2001). Extensive research on what co-management should be and are in practice has been well researched over the past two decades (Pomeroy, McConney, & Mahon, 2003). Discussions fall within a continuum of self-management and full jurisdiction to federal, territorial and local control in sharing of authority and responsibility. Arguably, these differences are not always well understood or disseminated to local stakeholders. Moreover, co-management research appears to have fallen short of addressing the contextualised benefits, identity and representation as well as the democratic and reconstitutional aspects. The latter implies that conventional administrative structures of governance are genuinely decentralised in order to make for better, more legitimate regulations that simultaneously reduce the need for comprehensive and costly programmes of monitoring and enforcement.

Based on CANARI's facilitation since the 1980s, co-management has become an integral part of the multi-use strategy to benefit the people in and of the south of St. Lucia. Legislation still pending, a management plan that designate the area as a multi-use and community managed national park have been drafted by CANARI in collaboration with relevant government ministries. Based on the diversity of stakeholders and their complexity of interests with the resource and one another, the proposed co-management strategy is feasibly rooted in the sustainability principles.

Unsurprisingly, the ecological and cultural boundaries are not identical with the park perimeters, which necessitate both formal and informal mechanisms to regulate the activities of insiders and the access of outsiders. And whereas issues of provisions of acceptable benefits by the surrounding community appear to be intangible and less apparent, outreach to resource users of the surrounding communities is noticeably underprovided. A stronger focus by CANARI and the AACP Group to further the dissemination of knowledge in the field of sustainable development to the nearby local communities remain to be comprehensively addressed. Nonetheless, CANARI's facilitation and the AACP Group's tireless efforts prove that co-management is *de facto* in effect in the mangrove, and that more sustainable production techniques are effectively applied.

Traditional resource-based practices and sustained livelihoods are often in the margins of production systems, which receive limited government attendance. Thirteen years after the initial proposal to establish protected areas in the island-state, the St. Lucian Government remains undecided about whether to move to strict protection of the Pointe Sables National Park, seize the exchange value of land for commercial development, or pursue an alternative strategy that permits delegation of management authority. Without legislation fully endorsing co-management strategically the state remains open to the feasibility of Mankoté as a co-management testing site for the national park at large. Visible in the display of CANARI's factual results of their 2002–2005 Programme (http://www.canari.org/2002-2005programme.html), the reference to government practice in parentheses is unequivocal:

> An improved policy environment for participatory resource management (although this has not yet translated into the implementation of new policies).

While it is undoubtedly premature to attempt to evaluate the co-management experience, or to elevate the case onto a level of recognisable good practice, two notable learning experiences from CANARI and the AACP Group in Pointe Sables National Park deserve further recognition. First, the traditional subsistence users have successfully implemented sustainable harvesting and production techniques to help preserve the very resource base on which they and tourism depend. They currently provide an estimated 30% of all charcoal sold in the southern town of Vieux Fort (Samuel & Smith, 2000). Secondly, by inclusion of experiential and cultural aspects of place construction, co-management have effectively help bridge potentially conflicting operations as new local leaders have emerged in the process. One of the present challenges is to ensure accountability and responsibility for managerial actions, especially when they are not based on a democratic mandate.

In due course, a few reflections over my own anthropological representation and methodology are appropriate. Drawing on (Markowitz, 2001) this entails that explorations of compassionate relations, including personal/anthropological affiliations are made transparent in research and representation. Applying the traditional anthropological method of participant-observation, my fieldwork included participating in the dubious exercise of fencing off the mangrove. In the process I was observing how the relations of the AACP group was defined and perceived by people; how they talk and think about their own group as well as others, including CANARI, and how particular world views are maintained or contested (cf. Eriksen, 1993). Exchanging ideas and communicating values can also encapsulate normative elements, such as prescribing the appropriate ways to act in certain places and at certain times, while a sense of identity and belonging to the group is probed. Personally, I was presented with a membership badge at the tower opening ceremony to symbolise my close affiliation with AACP Group from the very outset of fieldwork. Moreover, the relatively limited time spent in St. Lucia did not allow for more in-depth understandings of other resource user groups within Pointe Sables, nor did those perhaps poorer charcoal producers excluded from using the Mankoté mangrove figure among the list of people systematically interviewed.

Working with CANARI also mirrored common anthropological concerns with knowledge and power relations at interconnected micro and macro levels of global society. While initially cautious of my research that included conducting fieldwork among the CANARI staff in order to gain an understanding of their values and motivations, these NGO employees were fellow social scientists. They were critical of, and well versed in anthropological literature, which was unsettling at times. Participant observation involved hanging out in their office, reading in their library, copying documents, jolting about in pick-up trucks to various meetings and encounters with resource users in the national park, talking politics, swapping stories over a beer or the AACP Group's favourite homebrew, *Crème de Mint*. Unanswered questions about funding but access to classified documents in confidentiality further complicate matters of representation and accountability. This adequately reflects the shifting and interconnected sites of anthropological fieldwork as well as the socio-political terrain of NGOs in general. Their practices are subject to shifts within global relations of power and knowledge and decisions taken in distant donor offices. Commonly NGO accountability appears to be vested in a continuum between the project beneficiaries and donor agencies. Unless they are able to establish a level of credibility with relevant stakeholders involved, their operations may have a limited impact and frame of existence.

This is in sum a simple representation of how NGO workers, local stakeholders, decision makers, tourists and anthropologists are continuously engaged in the processes of modifying their situations and negotiating identities, albeit within limitations and in varying contexts (Meethan, 2001).

Conclusions

The dilemma between conservation and providing for public enjoyment in national parks has a long-standing trajectory traceable to the establishment of the world's first national parks in America. I have argued that perceptions of nature and management are far from neutral constructs. Political and cultural acts of inclusion and exclusion are integral to the processes of site selection of areas considered worthy of preservation and enjoyment for present and future generations. Sustainable development and the application to tourism similarly hinge on a long-term holistic maintenance of economic, environmental, social and cultural aspects. The much neglected issues of scale and equity were critically examined in the context of tourism and national park development. In order to avoid prioritisation of environmental sustainability over cultural and economic equity it was argued that sustainable development must be informed by the cultural context in which it is adopted into the management philosophy and daily practice of all stakeholders. The highly general concept of making things last, whether an ecosystem, a culture or an economy is thereby attributed real value and meaning by those habitat become the object of national park and tourism development. Simultaneously avoiding romantic and homogenising notions of "the local community" and "local needs", local residents do not automatically qualify as the best managers of natural resources. Nor are efforts necessarily democratic in scope. The analysis from the south-east coast of St. Lucia illustrated how local traditional harvest practices in the island's largest mangrove significantly had depleted the natural resource, which was among other unsustainable local practices listed by the NGO, CANARI, along with utilisation of dynamite for reef fishery and sand mining for construction purposes.

One of the notable traits of NGOs is their participatory approach to development, which deliberately targets the poor and marginal segments of society. Issues of NGO involvement were discussed and attention cultivated to the context and a group of resource users within the proposed national park area. It was argued that the making of the Aupicon Agriculture and Charcoal Producers Group (AAPC Group) effectively excluded other marginal people from their subsistence base. Seemingly not practicing social, cultural or economic equity and inherently undemocratic, any claims towards sustainability in the national park or eco-tourism operations are easily rejected as unsubstantial. Furthermore, CANARI is easily accused of setting up systems of patronage that created unwanted relations of mutual dependency between the NGO and the local social movements of the south-east coast. On the contrary, CANARI's engagement in national park development also demonstrated that NGOs can provide a real alternative to moving beyond the empty rhetoric of locals-as-partners towards equitable acknowledgement of locals-as-users. While providing no corrective against the lack of democratic participation and exclusion of many perhaps poorer people from the park area, the complexity of democratic participation was addressed through meaningful personal commitment by the AACP Group and their cautious experimentation with identity and place of belonging. Moreover, based on the principles of sustainable development the management plan developed for Pointe Sables National Park embraced the extensive ecological and cultural knowledge of traditional users and provided for a multi-use, co-managed park. CANARI had previously evaluated their stake in protective measures as "too great to dismiss" and that failure to involve stakeholders would likely have led to active resistance toward national park development and tourism (Geoghegan & Smith, 1998, p. 13). In other words, CANARI's facilitation had by no means depoliticised the park development project. The collaborative process gave the project legitimacy and credibility through a coherent development and management strategy, as opposed to the many failed development schemes in the south. *De facto* in effect, co-management furthermore implicates ongoing political engagement as new managerial changes or potential violations of park regulations are subject to penalties instituted and executed by the relevant government ministries in collaboration with the local resource users. In spite of organizational weaknesses and continuous reliance on CANARI the AAPC Group of charcoal producers proves to build continuous confidence and sense of responsibility toward more efficient execution of co-management.

While emphasising the need to ensure accountability, transparency and responsibility for actions taken by NGOs, local stakeholders and anthropologists alike, I have deliberately not attempted to provide a comprehensive evaluation of the effectiveness and motivations of CANARI's involvement in St. Lucia. Rather my anthropological analysis in the south-east coast of St. Lucia was designed to investigate the unfulfilled possibilities for a more dynamic understanding of the *processes* of place and identity construction that are integral to co-management, sustainable tourism and national park development. Whether the Pointe Sables National Park in St. Lucia becomes an example of good practice in the future remains to be seen.

References

Berkes, F., George, P., & Preston, R. J. (1991). Co-management. The evolution in theory and practice of the joint administration of living resources. *Alternatives, 18*(2), 12–18.

Berkes, F., Mahon, P., McConney, P., Pollnac, R., & Pomeroy, R. (2001). *Managing small-scale fisheries: Alternative directions and methods.* Canada: International Development Research Centre.

Brennan, F., & Allen, G. (2001). Community-based ecotourism, social exclusion and the changing political economy of KwaZulu-Natal, South Africa. In: D. Harrison (Ed.), *Tourism and the less developed world* (pp. 203–221). Chichester: John Wiley & Sons.

Burns, P. (1999). Tourism NGOs. *Tourism Recreational Research, 24*(2), 3–6.

Butler, R. W., & Boyd, S. W. (Eds). (2000). *Tourism and national parks. Issues and implications.* New York: Wiley.

Butler, R. W. (1998). Sustainable tourism — looking backwards in order to progress? In: M. Hall, & A. Lew (Eds), *Sustainable tourism* (pp. 25–34). London: Longman.

Bramwell, B., & Sharman, A. (1999). Collaboration in local tourism policymaking. *Annals of Tourism Research, 26*(2), 392–415.

CANARI. (1993). *Management Agreement for Mankoté Mangrove* (draft only). Wallingford: CABI Publishing.

CANARI. (1996). *Strategic plan 1996–2005*. Panos Institute.

CANARI. (1995). *Caribbean Park and Protected Areas Bulletin, 5*(2). Panos Institute.

CANARI. (1994). *Caribbean Park and Protected Areas Bulletin, 5*(1). Panos Institute.

CANARI. (2005). *2002–2005 Programme*. Retrieved from http://www.canari.org/2002-2005 programme.html, July 25, 2005.

Carson, R. (original 1962, 1994) *Silent spring*. Boston: Houghton Mifflin.

Clauzel, S. (1996a). *Report on a Community Mobilisation Workshop for the Southeast Coast Project*. St. Lucia National Trust.

Clauzel, S. (1996b). Pointe Sable National Park Planning Project. *Conservation News, 5*(4), St. Lucia National Trust.

Clauzel, S. (1997a). *Status information on natural resources and their management on the southeast coast of St. Lucia*. Pointe Sable National Park Planning Committee, Vieux Fort. St. Lucia National Trust.

Cohen, E. (2002). Authenticity, equity and sustainability in tourism. *Journal of Sustainable Tourism, 10*(4), 267–276.

Eriksen, T. H. (1993). *Ethnicity and nationalism*. London, UK: Pluto Press.

Farrington, J., Bebbington, A., Wellard, K., & Lewis, D. J. (1993). *Reluctant partners? Nongovernmental organisations, the state and sustainable agricultural development*. London : Routledge.

Gardner, K., & Lewis, D. (1996). *Anthropology, development and the post-modern challenge*. London, UK: Pluto Press.

Geoghegan, T., & Smith, A. (1998). *Conservation and sustainable livelihoods: Collaborative management of the Mankoté Mangrove, St. Lucia*. Case study series by the Caribbean Natural Resources Institute.

Government of St. Lucia. (2004). Statistics Department. Retrieved January 28, 2004 from http://www.stats.gov.lc/pop22.htm

Hall, C. M., & Lew, A. A. (1998). *Sustainable tourism. A geographical perspective*. Longman, Malaysia.

Hardin, G. (1968). The tragedy of the Commons. *Science, 162,* 1243–1248.

Harrison, D. (1996). Sustainability and tourism: Reflections from a muddy pool. In: L. Briguglio, B. Archer, J. Jafari, & G. Wall (Eds), *Sustainable tourism in islands and small states: Issues and policies* (pp. 69–89). London: Pinter.

Hudson, L., Renard, Y., & Romulus, G. (1992). *System for protected areas for St. Lucia*. St. Lucia National Trust.

Jurowski, C., & Liburd, J. J. (2002). A multi-cultural and multi-disciplinary approach to integrating the principles of sustainable development into human resource management curriculums in hospitality and tourism. *Hospitality and Tourism Educator, 13*(5), 36–50.

Liburd, J. J. (2004). NGOs in tourism and preservation — Democratic accountability and sustainability in question. *Tourism Recreation Research, 29*(2), 105–110.

Liburd, J. J. (2001). Cruise tourism development in the south of St. Lucia. *Tourism, 49*(3), 215–228.

Markowitz, L. (2001). Finding the field: Notes on the ethnography of NGOs. *Human Organization, 60*(1), 40–46.

Meethan, K. (2001). *Tourism in global society. Place, culture, consumption*. Hampshire and New York: Palgrave.

Mintz, S. (1985). *Sweetness and power: The place of sugar in modern history*. New York: Viking.

Mowforth, M., & Munt, I. (1998). *Tourism and sustainability. New tourism in the Third World*. London and New York: Routledge.

Pinkerton, E. W. (1993). Social management efforts as social movements. *Alternatives, 19*(3), 33–38.

Pomeroy, R., McConney, P., & Mahon, R. (2003). *Comparative analysis pf coastal resource comanagement in the Caribbean*. Barbados: Caribbean Conservation Association. Retrived on June 26, 2005 from http://cermes.cavehill.uwi.edu/publications/ComparativeAnalysis.pdf

Renard, Y. (1994) Community participation in St. Lucia. *Community and the environment: Lessons from the Caribbean.* London: Panos Institute.

Rothman, H. K. (1998). *The greening of a nation? Environmentalism in the United States since 1945.* Fort Worth, Texas: Harcourt Brace College Publishers.

Samuel, N., & Smith, A. (2000). Popular knowledge and science: Using the information that counts in managing use of a mangrove in St. Lucia, West Indies. *CANARI Communication, 278.* Retrieved on June 25, 2005 from http://canari.org/278samuel.pdf

Tvedt, T. (1995). *Non-Governmental-Organisations as a channel in development assistance: The Norwegian system.* Report to Norwegian Development Agency by the Centre for Development Studies, University of Bergen (mimeo).

U.S. National Park Service. (2003). Retrieved on July 31, 2003 from http://www.nps.gov/parks.html

Wahab, S., & Pigram, J. J. (Eds). (1997). *Tourism, development and growth. The challenge of sustainability.* London: Routledge.

World Commission on the Environment and Development. (1987). *Our common future.* Oxford: Oxford University Press.

World Tourism Organisation. (1997). Tourist arrival to reach 1.6 billion by 2020. *WTO Newsletter,* Spain.

World Tourism Organization. (2001). Concepts and definitions. Retrieved March 22, 2001 from http://www.world-tourism.org/frameset/frame_sustainable.html

WTTC, WTO & EC (1995). *Agenda 21 for the Travel and Tourism Industry: Towards Environmentally Sustainable Development,* World Travel and Tourism council, World Tourism Organization, and Earth Council, London: WTTC.

Zinser, C. I. (1995). *Outdoor recreation: United States national parks, forests and public lands.* New York: Wiley.

Chapter 12

Identity and Interaction: Gazes and Reflections of Tourism

Patrícia de Araújo Brandão Couto

Introduction

This chapter presents the interim findings of an ethnographic study entitled "Itacaré: a new meaning for paradise found through eco-tourism". The general theme is the process of social change taking place in the small town of Itacaré and surrounding area in the state of Bahia, Brazil. The interaction between local associations and the Environmental Protection Area (APA) Itacaré — Serra Grande Management Council, when created as public forums (Cefai, 2002) makes up the central theme of this analysis, since it helps us to understand the composition and redefinition of the social identity of the inhabitants and groups that populate this town, both spatially and culturally, through their questions and tendencies.

The following topics converged on the theme of the project. First, tourism as a way of symbolically and materially reorganizing the town; second, the environmental issue, due to the impact of its legislation and regulatory action instituted by local, state, and federal governments on the social and economic life of the town; and third, the relationship between local and global, by making it possible to comprehend the process of interaction between local reality and external factors that have been contributing to this town's transformation.

In this chapter, I reflect on the processes of interaction that take place between different social segments that currently make up the town of Itacaré, based on the new identity categories created by the inhabitants to express this conflict. As a variant of this theme, I intend to discuss what the local traditional population — cocoa growers, farmers, fishermen, and "ribeirinhos" [riverbank dwellers] — thinks in relation to tourism, tourists, the environmental rules imposed by the creation of the APA Itacaré — Serra Grande

Management Council and the new inhabitants who have settled in the municipality seeking economic opportunity. The following section places the research problem into context.

The Research Context

Located 530 km from Salvador and 70 km from Ilhéus, the Itacaré and surrounding area currently have a population of 18000, distributed in an area of 746 km^2; 55% of the population lives in the rural area, while approximately 8000 inhabitants are concentrated in the urban area of the town. An old port town once dedicated to the cocoa trade, Itacaré today lives off of fishing and tourism.

In summary, we can divide the history of the town of Itacaré into two phases: before and after construction of the highway (1996–1998), a consequence of the creation of the APA Itacaré — Serra Grande environmental district (1993). Before that time, although relatively isolated due to difficult overland access, the town once stood out as an important cocoa shipping port[1] in the south of Bahia,[2] mainly from 1920 to 1960, when it began to lose importance as a port.

Its original social classes were comprised of fishermen, river-bank dwellers, small subsistence farmers, and large land owners linked to the cocoa economy, who went bankrupt in the 1980s due to the spread of a fungus known as "Vassoura de Bruxa" (the witch's broom) among the plantations and the subsequent fall in the price of cocoa on the international market. Then, the town entered a process of unbridled decadence, accentuated by its difficult access and consequent isolation.

The so-called cocoa crisis affected not only Itacaré but also the entire state of Bahia. The low cocoa prices dictated by the international market caused plantation owners to go into debt and left many rural workers unemployed. The search for alternative economic activities stimulated the already growing lumber business in the 'Atlantic Forest' region and the expansion of cattle-raising activities. At the same time, the high unemployment rate[3] triggered a great rural exodus and a significant increase in the Agrarian Reform Movement.

Among the strategies utilized by the government to restructure the state's economy was the creation of a state tourism development plan known as PRODETUR/BAHIA in 1991, whose purpose was to restore the state's tourist industry to national ranking. This plan established a series of goals and redesigned the state's tourist map by dividing it into seven areas: Costa dos Coqueiros (the Coconut Coast), Costa do Dendê (the Dendê Coast), Costa

---

[1] According to Falcon (1995) cocoa cultivation in the south of Bahia developed in three cycles: 1746/1820 — plantation and domestication of the region followed by stagnation without consequences; 1820/1895 — renewed planting with initial exports reaching 100 thousand sacks; 1895/1930 — affirmation of cocoa as the economic basis of the southern region of the state.

[2] According to local information, "the ships would anchor outside because the Rio de Contas current was too strong. The sailors would go up the river in smaller vessels to Correia Ribeiro, where all the region's cocoa production was stored. There, they got the sacks of cocoa, went back down the river and hoisted the cocoa aboard the ship, which went on to Salvador (IESB Report/January 2001).

[3] According to IBGE census data (1991) more than 200 thousand people were laid off in the cocoa region.

do Descobrimento (the Discovery Coast), Costa das Baleias (the Whale Coast), Costa do Cacau (the Cocoa Coast), and Chapada Diamantina (the Diamond Plateau). For each of these regions, a basic destination was selected, but the political environmental-protection strategy linked to ecological tourism was considered the future common basis of support for the different developmental areas (Gaudenzi, 2004, p. 1).

As a result of that planning in 1993, decree 2186 created, in the town of Itacaré, which is located in the so-called Costa do Cacau (the Cocoa Coast), the APA of Itacaré — Serra Grande for the purpose of "preserving what remained of the beautiful landscape and scenery of the Atlantic Forest region, in addition to encouraging sustainable development of its natural resources via tourism".[4]

In 1996, through the project known as BID/Prodetur, work began on paving the "Parque Ilhéus — Itacaré" Road.[5] Then, in 1997, work began on implementing Plano Manejo (the Manejo Plan) under the auspices of the APA Itacaré — Serra Grande Management Council, to define zoning[6] and land-use guidelines as well as new environmental rules to be followed. The establishment of land use and occupation restrictions for the region has created conflict between the traditional local population (Little, 2002), the new inhabitants and those who determine the instruments of control. To make this picture even more complex, the road, which was concluded in 1998, and the new tourism movement gave rise to factors of irreversible change.

Implemented with *a priori* economic purposes, the highway quickly achieved its objective. Formerly frequented by a few in-state summer vacationers, alternative travelers and surfers in search of paradise, Itacaré has now become a domestic and international tourist attraction. Easy access, besides enabling the presence of seasonal visitors, has led to a wave of migration to this region both by neighboring populations in search of new economic opportunity and small entrepreneurs and large real estate speculators from southeastern Brazil. In addition, five settlements have been built in the region since the 1990s.

As one can see, a more complex social, economic, environmental, and spatial distinction has resulted, when compared to the period prior to the creation of the APA and construction of the road, when the town was relatively isolated. Many superimposing interests have arisen, expressed through diacritical signals coming from more than 100 associations that have sprung up in the area as well as the social-identity categories created to establish distinctions between the old and new residents, which will be discussed further on. This description and analysis above can be thought of as a snapshot of Itacaré, when I began my fieldwork in 2002.

---

[4] See on the Internet web site www.itacare.com.br/itacare/apa/guia.php

[5] The new road was given this name because it was the first Brazilian highway to have environmental monitoring during the entire construction phase. This monitoring was performed by an interinstitutional group made up of representatives of nongovernmental organizations, the Bahia State Highway Department, engineers of the various contractors involved and the various municipal governments in question.

[6] This APA has 17 Zones with guidelines and planning: 1 Wildlife Preservation Zone; 1 Rigorous Protection Zone; 1 Permanent Preservation Zone; 1 Agro-Forest Zone; 1 Ocean Coastal Zone; 1 Visual Protection Zone; 2 Tourism Zones; 1 Special Tourism Zone; 1 Tourist Village Zone; 1 Diversified Use Zone; 1 Agriculture Zone; 1 Controlled Occupation Zone; 1 Rarified Occupation Zone; 1 Priority Expansion Zone; 1 Urban Support Nucleus Zone; and 1 Consolidated Urban Nucleus Zone (Eco-tourism Inventory/2002).

Methodology for Distinguishing Identity Categories

At that time, I had not yet chosen the type of approach I would use as the central mode[7] of analysis. That indecision was certainly the result of the constant surprises, paradoxes and conundrums I encountered as I tried to understand the astonishing dynamics of the tourist phenomenon. However, since it is often in the field and in permanent observation that one discovers what it is precisely that needs to be investigated in this initial phase of research, I was already able to notice in individual discussions the recurrence of a marked difference between those who were considered "insiders" and those who were considered "outsiders" in Itacaré.

Signaled by the constant repetition of these classifications, I tried to penetrate the meaning of these attributions that, in a cumulative process, became more and more consolidated as the fieldwork progressed between 2002 and 2004. In this period I was able to conduct a series of 30 interviews in which various identity distinctions were explained in conversations with my informants. Thus, the classifications I will present can be considered individual evaluations, but ones that reflect collective beliefs and attitudes.

In other words, at certain times I was able to accomplish some group dynamics and discuss the different categories found with different local groups. Also notable was the fact that the various groups and/or individuals were not aware of how much these classifications had penetrated into their mode of conversation and, when confronted with them, often denied they even used them.

To present the categories that make up this identity distinction, I use as a reference the principle that

> "all the elements of a classification, with their respective properties, are only what they are by virtue of the position they occupy within it. Thus, the analysis or separation of elements is merely temporary in a research procedure that requires supplemental input from others in order to integrate or summarize the elements, just as the latter need supplemental input from the former. Here the dialectic movement between analysis and synthesis has neither a beginning nor an end" (Elias & Scotson, 2000, p. 58).

Distinction of the Classifications

Over the period of participant observation, documentary research, and interviews, I encountered the following identity categories used by people in the town to label different population segments: native, *forasteiro* [stranger, outlander], local, *ficante* [literally one who stays, or is a "stayer"], son of the land, son of Itacaré, outsider, settler, tourist.

1. Native: fruit of the process of interaction with visitors, mainly tourists and alternative travelers, this category was incorporated by the traditional local urban population to

---

[7]To recall, I refer to the processes of interaction between the local associations and the APA Itacaré — Serra Grande Governing Council, when created as public forums (Cefai, 2002).

identify those who were born and raised in the municipality and who also recognize themselves as "sons of the land or of Itacaré".

2. *Forasteiro* [stranger, outlander]: has a pejorative connotation, used to identify those who are staying in Itacaré temporarily and have not established any worthwhile relationship — friendly or economic — with the local population. It is necessary to explain that the "tourist" does not fit in this category, due to his/her economic importance for a large portion of those who are established in Itacaré.

3. Local: those not born in the municipality but who have been given this title of status due to the many years they have been in Itacaré, where relationships of trust are essential to being recognized as someone "from there".

4. Ficante [literally, one who stays, a "stayer"]: is someone who arrives as a tourist or alternative traveler, falls in love with the place and begins to postpone his/her departure, establishing ties of friendship, ephemeral or not, with the town. These people are in a transitory stage and, precisely for this reason, this category has an ambiguous connotation because it serves both to qualify and disqualify them. The qualification is due to the friendships established, whereas the disqualification is linked to factors of an economic nature, since they have better professional qualifications and can find jobs in local establishments, taking opportunities away from the permanent population of the town. We can say that this category combines, in its own ephemeral state, a time of illusion with the possibility of "living in paradise".

5. Son of the land: is an old expression employed by inhabitants born in the region to identify themselves. It is currently still in use in rural regions.

6. Son of Itacaré: was also originally used by the traditional local population to describe themselves. However, this expression lost its collective and unifying meaning of the origin of the residents when it was adopted by some bankrupt cocoa growers and members of the local middle class. The latter joined forces with the purpose of confronting the new residents that arrived to exploit Itcaré touristically. Since this collective action was characterized as an action by the local elite, the expression "sons of Itacaré" lost its integrating power and assumed a more ambiguous meaning, referring to the privileged rather than being used with the same frequency and connotation by the other residents.

7. Outsider: a generic expression referring to all those who are neither from the rural nor from the urban regions of the municipality and who are somehow a threat to the local population.

8. Settler: the name attributed to the rural population of the state of Bahia that settled in the municipality during the 1990s, after the conflicts generated by the high unemployment resulting from the fall in the price of cocoa in the international market. They are looked on with reservation and kept at a distance by the local population.

9. Tourist: I use here a phrase I heard in the field "The tourist is our daily bread!" Therefore, in the case of Itacaré as well as many other places in Brazil, the tourist is seen as a necessary reality and, for that reason, is treated well by the local population because the tourist is the source of income for the majority of the local families.

Some Reflections on the Distinctions Found

As one can see, all these identity categories encountered allow us to reflect on the space–time relationship among the inhabitants of this territory, where mobility, a characteristic of the tourism phenomenon, began to imprint a transitory aspect on everyday life. In spatial terms, these classifications express the feeling of belonging, exclusion, and inclusion in relation to the place, whereas the time factor, in the sense of duration, measures the relationship one develops with that space, affective or otherwise.

If we establish a distinction scale of these classifications, we are able to observe that while "native", "son of the land", and "son of Itacaré" can be grouped unconditionally as categories of belonging, on the other extreme, the categories "outsider" and "stranger" (*forasteiro*) and "tourist" epitomize the ephemeral nature of one's presence and transitory condition. This condition is observed both in the negative aspects attributed to the "outsider" and the "stranger" (*forasteiro*), due to the very obscurity of their identities, and in the positive aspects of one who is seen as the generator of economic "foreign exchange", as in the case of the tourist.

Situated between these extremes of distinction are the categories "local" and "stayer" (*ficante*), as expressions of a state of latency for the attribution of belonging. But the category of "settler" alludes to someone who came to stay but, at the same time, is a reflection of an uncontested imposition.

To analyze the distinctions found in Itacaré, I used as a reference the "principle of antiquity" of the classic distinction between "the established and the outsiders" of Elias and Scotson (2000). In this study about a place in England referred to fictitiously as Winston Parva, the authors distinguish the different distinctions of the networks of social relationships that were woven in the process of interaction between old and new residents and describe the general properties of all the relationships of power, explained in the pairs: moral and social superiority — inferiority; self perception — recognition; exclusion — belonging.

However, some distinctions between the theoretical model of reference and the context analyzed in this research must be clarified. Elias and Scotson (2000) encountered a homogeneous social-economic reality where the moral superiority of the older residents stands out as an element of explicit conflict due to the arrival of new residents.

As I attempted to demonstrate when describing the context of the place under study, I did not find, like the authors referred to above, a homogeneous reality, composed of urban workers distinguished by their different lengths of presence in relationship to the place, but rather, a reality that was quite complex due to the arrival of the road and tourism and the formation of new social groups in Itacaré. Even in the context prior to the factors of change studied, the degree of group cohesion already indicated a social fragmentation between the traditional population — the riverbank dwellers, fishermen, and farmers — and the big landowners, the cocoa growers. Therefore, the focus of analysis takes place in an environment of heterogeneous composition, accentuated by the dynamics and mobility of the tourist movement.

In addition, if the principle of antiquity in Itacaré is the basis for the categories of identification that developed, serving to legitimize the older residents in relation to their "right to the place", it is not characterized by a moral superiority on their part, but rather, a certain resentment on the part of the older residents in relation to the economic, technical, and intellectual superiority of many of the newcomers who have settled in Itacaré. In other words, the older residents feel threatened by the power differential with which they were confronted and try to legitimize their rights in relation to the place via a discussion of belonging.

Therefore, the advent of tourism did not position the traditional local groups as the holders of authority and influence, due to the fact that many of the traditional local segments have not succeeded in inserting themselves in a dominant way in the tourist industry, which those groups had thought of before as a kind of economic salvation for the town.

In principle, the wealthier local social segment, namely, the bankrupt cocoa growers began to believe that tourism would be a new way to reaffirm the former power they once held when they were big cocoa producers. However, a large part of this segment has not succeeded in participating in the economic dynamics of tourism. They therefore began to resent the "invasion" of the town so much that they founded the Association of Sons of Itacaré to defend themselves from the new "conquistadores" (conquerors).

But the fishermen, riverbank population, and farmers, although always deprived of local power and authority, via the identity classification, never fail to express their frustration in relation to the expectations they had about the road and tourism. In fact, they remained in the same position or lost their land to real estate speculators who arrived in the region. In every-day life, they maintain a cultivated rivalry (Leitão, 2004) with the tourist operators' middlemen and with the neighboring populations, which, in a seasonal flow, arrived and continue to arrive in Itacaré in search of work.

For clarification purposes, the economic opportunity generated by tourism has caused many families from the interior of Bahia to relocate to Itacaré during the high season, to increase their family incomes by exploiting tourism. Those who have a better education try to obtain employment at hotels or in the local stores, but most of the migrants participate in the "informal economy", as is the case of street vendors in the urban sections of town. In many situations, this transitory fixation ends up becoming effective. It is important to say that in addition to the fact that pendular migration does not take place only on the state level, but also on the interstate level, if not international. Many persons coming from the southeastern and southern regions of Brazil, especially the states of São Paulo and Minas Gerais, have settled in the town, as well as Frenchmen, Italians, Swiss, and Germans.

As a counterpart to the identity categories used by the local population, the large, medium, or small businessmen who arrived in the town have also cultivated this rivalry and resent being referred to as "foreigner" (Simmel, 1999) in moments of conflict between the parties in question — from inside and outside. One could say that they act with a certain variation in their attitude toward the local population. Many of the businessmen adopt a conciliatory mode of conversation and allege that they are trying to integrate the so-called natives to the work market generated by tourism. However in daily practice, they justify the importing of manpower or their preference for employing "outsiders" by an alleged lack of qualifications on the part of the natives for the new job market required by tourism. The data on this issue has not yet been properly analyzed, but I was able to verify in the field phase of the study the preference for hiring persons from outside the region.

Another factor worthy of observation is that the confrontation between old and new residents is not explicit. It reveals itself in the subjective nature of conversation and in the logic of implied friendships in the processes of individual and collective interaction. Therefore, we cannot say that there is a rigid logic of friendships, because tourism, like the extremely dynamic phenomenon it is, implies a certain reflexive agility in the process of collective interaction imposed by the seasonal mobility of the town. The thermometer for measuring this is in the following statement: "let's see who stays, what they do and how they act". We can say then that, excluding the identity categories of origin (native, son of the earth, and son of Itacaré), the passage from one category to another depends on whether or not a person remains in a given position in this relationship of forces.

Conclusion

One can conclude that in the situation under examination, there is a permanent state of conflict but one that does is not unidirectional. Sometimes the conflict is explicit, via verbal outbursts of anger, and other times it is jocular, when the different segments meet. Thus, the rivalry expressed in the discussion of identity categories is governed by a logic of friendships as fluid as the mobility implied in the tourism activity.

Unfortunately, given the complexity of the subject matter, it is difficult to adequately discuss the repercussions of the creation of the APA Itacaré — Serra Grande Management Council on the daily life of the local population and what they think about it. However, I would like to point out some relevant aspects to be developed in future discussions.

Since this region was classified as an "Area of Environmental Protection", removal of the traditional population from the Atlantic Forest is not required, provided the land-use and environmental protection criteria are respected. However, these criteria interfere directly in the traditional habits of the population, creating a feeling of resentment due to the imposition of many restrictions, such as, for example, the prohibition against planting manioc, which has been a basis element in the local diet for many generations.

Affected by the restrictions imposed on it, the traditional population has been divided in relation to its procedures and perspectives. While one part is trying to incorporate the environmental issue in its daily existence, participating in classes on environmental management or transforming their lands with the minimal resources available to them into areas focusing on activities more compatible with the development of eco-tourism, another part refuses to accept the new ecological precepts, maintaining their traditional habits or selling their lands to real estate speculators.

Thus, while we can note a obvious effort on the part of the local population to adapt to the new environmental criteria, at the same time we can perceive that the imposition of the restrictions, accompanied by a lack of adequate assistance, has been producing an asymmetric relationship between the rights and obligations of the traditional local population and those of the Environmental Protection Management Council, made up mainly of "outsiders".

It is necessary to emphasize here that there is neither an overt refusal to respect the environmental precepts nor a rejection of the tourist activity. On the contrary, the inhabitants recognize the benefits that these activities can bring them, generated largely by the "outsiders".

Thus, the identity categories described and discussed herein reflect the need for understanding on the part of the local population in relation to the expansion of the networks of sociability (Urry, 2005b) produced after the occurrence of the three factors of historically material and symbolic change distinguished here, namely, the creation of the APA, the construction of the road, and the development of tourism. Prior to the construction of the road, Itacaré was relatively isolated, but its completion has resulted in new copresences (Urry, 2005a), due to greater access and mobility, thus generating new modes of hierarchy, value scales, and social networks in the town, distinguished by their various levels of status.

I would like to emphasize that even though I have not dwelled on the intrinsic conflict of those categories, these new relations of closeness do not produce only strife and frustration among the residents of Itacaré, but also greatly expand the possibility of communication between different worlds, revealing the social need to classify to comprehend this new reality. We can only wait and see what happens.

Acknowledgments

The author acknowledges M. Marco Antonio da Silva Mello (thesis chair/PPGA-UFF) and M. Daniel Cefai (thesis chair/ParisX-Naterre).

References

Cefai, D. (2002). *Qu'est-ce qu'une arène publique? Quelques pistes pour une approche pragmatiste.* In: D. Cefai & I. Joseph (org). *L'heritage du pragmatisme. Conflits d'urbanité et epreuves de civisme.* Paris: Presses Universitaire de France.

Elias, N., & Scotson, L. (2000). *Os estabelecidos e os outsiders* [*The established and the outsiders*]. Rio de Janeiro: Jorge Zahar.

Falcon, G. (1995). *Os Coronéis do Cacau* [*The colonels of Cocoa*]. Salvador, Brazil: IEMANJÁ.

Gaudenzi, P. (2004). *Evolução da Economia do Turismo na Bahia* [*Evolution of the tourism economy in Bahia*]. http://www.bahia.ba.gov.br/sct/parte3.htm. Downloaded on 1/12/2004.

Leitão, W. M. (2004). *Rivalidade Cultivada, conflito e unidade social num bairro carioca* [*Cultivated rivalry, conflict and social unity in a Carioca neighborhood*]. Revista Comum Rio de Janeiro: FACHA.

Little, P. E. (2002). *Territórios sociais e povos tradicionais no Brasil: por uma antropologia da territorialidade* [*Social territories and traditional peoples in Brazil: By an anthropology of territoriality*]. Série Antropologia. Brasília: UNB.

Simmel, G. (1999). *Sociologie: estudes sur les formes de la socialisation.* Paris: Presse Universitaire de France (PUF).

Urry, J. (2005a). *Mobility and proximity.* http://perso.wanadoo.fr/ville-en-mouvement/interventions/John_Urry.pdf. Downloaded on 4/25/2005.

Urry, J. (2005b). *Mobility and connections.* (http://www.ville-en-mouvement.com/telechargement/040602/mobility.pdf. Downloaded on 4/25/2005.

Chapter 13

Television Travels: Screening the Tourist Settler

David Dunn

> No, you cannot return to an island
> expecting that the dances will be unchanged,
> that the currency won't have altered,
> that the mountains blue in the evening
> will always remain so. (Iain Crichton Smith, *No Return*)

Television is ubiquitous. As the medium has moved from what John Ellis (2000, p. 61ff) has called its 'age of scarcity' to its present age of availability, the need for new stories and formats has brought about new influences on culture and identity. It is no longer a single authoritative broadcasting voice which is heard but a multiplicity of 'ordinary' voices which allow viewers to work through a variety of more casual and varied messages. Deregulation and globalisation have been matched by the development of unobtrusive lightweight equipment which can easily be transported and deployed and is not dependent on a studio. Televisual geographies are thus, as David Morley and Kevin Robins (1995, p. 11) have suggested, 'becoming detached from the symbolic spaces of national culture, and are realigned on the basis of the more 'universal' principles of international consumer culture'. Producers have both increasing access to any location in the world which takes their fancy and, in addition, increasingly voyeuristic access to the stories of 'ordinary' people.[1] Where once broadcasters worked within national boundaries, Morley and Robins (1995) argue, 'new conditions of mobility make local attachment not a matter of ascribed and determined identity but increasingly a question of choice, decision and variability' (*op. cit.,* 1995, p. 41).

---

[1] See Bonner (2003) and Dovey (2000).

There is a parallel here with the new mobilities of the lives of viewers, for whom increasing leisure and disposable income along with changing work patterns have meant increased opportunities for travel; travel-as-work and travel-as-dwelling as well as travel-as-leisure. If, as Chris Rojek (2000, p. 3) maintains, leisure has replaced religion as the user-up of surplus energy and resources, then travel-as-self-discovery offers, as many commentators attest,[2] its own opportunities for secular pilgrimage; for recreation and re-creation. This chapter is about television as both a travelling and a colonialising culture. It examines what John Urry (2000, p. 66ff) has described as the medium's 'imaginative mobilities' through discussion of two series, *Castaway 2000* (BBC1, 2000) and *A Place in Greece* (C4, 2004). Both are evidence of television's ability to construct its own geographies as well as narratives of mobility. In both, place becomes a colonised *locus* for a journey of tourist-like desire, transgression and consumption. *Castaway 2000*, a precursor of more populist 'reality' shows, offered its participants the opportunity to cross boundaries on a metaphorical journey of self-realisation, documenting their year's sojourn of self-sufficiency as tourist settlers on the depopulated Scottish island of Taransay. It appropriated a 'real' place, but constructed a generically liminal space for recreation and re-creation which made scant reference to the lives and community of the island's earlier inhabitants. *A Place in Greece*, an eight part lifestyle series about two couples' struggle to build their 'dream house with a view' in Crete, chronicled the obstacles which they encountered as tourist settlers, including lack of finance, no proper planning permission and inactive local builders, while reflecting an ethnocentrism highlighted by the inability of any one of the four to speak Greek.

Castaway 2000

If conventional holiday programmes have needed to find new first person narratives to engage both with audience and tourist destination, lifestyle television's focus on makeovers has witnessed a growth of 'escape to the sun' programmes. In these the tourist destination is represented as the setting for a new life, or as an opportunity for extended holidaymaking through the purchase of one's own holiday home. John Urry (1995, p. 141ff) has suggested that the democratisation of tourism has meant its 'de-differentiation' from leisure, and given what had been the essentially conservative nature of the holiday programme, it is perhaps not surprising that the discourse of re-creative consumption first appeared not within the genre itself but in programmes such as BBC1's 'experiment for the twenty first century' *Castaway 2000*, in which a year's sojourn of self-sufficiency on the island of Taransay offered its tourist settler participants the opportunity for crossing boundaries on a metaphorical journey of self-realisation; a clear enough example of how the specific of tourism and the general of increasingly mobile private lives increasingly overlap (Dunn, 2001).

Measuring three miles by two and lying off the west coast of Harris, Taransay combines peat moor, long stretches of sandy beach and a rugged coastline with spectacular views to

---

[2] See, among others, Turner (1973), Graburn (1978) and Nash (1996).

sea and to the mountains of Harris. It is a depopulated Hebridean island, with once tenanted land given over to sheep and deer, and houses disappeared or in ruins. It is also a symbol of an ever increasingly marginalised Gaelic culture where for some empty landscape connotes the economic and social inevitability of clearance,[3] for others a lost past[4] and a fading language, the discourses of Improvement and its dark familiar Celtic Twilight existing in symbiotic tension. In his short account of Taransay, local historian Bill Lawson (1997) reflects the latter, chronicling the departures of its inhabitants over the centuries, and evoking his own memories of the last family to leave the island in 1974, the MacRaes. Although all three MacRaes have since died, in his mind's eye they still inhabit the island and regale him with stories of the past.

> And that to me is the real beauty of Taransay, to see it along with the memories of the MacRaes. The visitor who sees it now, empty, sees only a small part of Taransay. (Lawson, 1997, p. 43)

In contrast, by choosing an empty, MacRae-less and, to all intents and purposes, history free Taransay as the location for the television series *Castaway 2000* the BBC and Lion Television, however unwittingly, joined the ranks of the island's improvers, presenting it as the *locus* for a filmed experiment in which some 30 people would leave their everyday lives for a year to create a new community 'for a new millennium'[5] under the gaze of the camera, with new buildings and a new infrastructure and the advice of the Centre for Alternative Technology, but with scarcely a reference to its previous communities improved out of existence.[6] The text accompanying *Castaway 2000*'s Application Form asked

> Have you ever dreamed of living on an isolated island? Does the prospect of the millenium bug give you an itch to get away from it all? Would you like the power to take decisions about how your life runs and make up the rules as you go along? Would you like to be part of an exciting BBC experiment looking into the way we live in the future? (cited in McCrum, 2000, pp. 20–21)

Almost from the start the discursive tensions implicit in a project which presented Taransay as televisual *tabula rasa* rather than as Hebridean palimpsest came to the fore. In a discussion with the Director of *An Comunn Gàidhealach*[7] on BBC Radio 4's *The Word*

---

[3] See Chapman (1978), Kidd (1993), Withers (1992) and Womack (1989).
[4] See Agnew (1996, p. 37).
[5] These words formed part of the opening commentary of Episode One (18.i.00).
[6] Hunter (2000, pp. 1–30) places great emphasis on 'a history-from-below' which foregrounds the dispossessed and their suffering over the dispossessors, while acknowledging that his critics find this implicitly sentimental and lacking adequate historical evidence.
[7] *An Comunn Gàidhealach* is the Gaelic Language Association charged with maintaining and promoting the language within and beyond the Gaeltachd.

(14.i.00: 16.30) before the first programmes were transmitted, *Castaway 2000*'s Executive Producer Colin Cameron[8] argued that the series was not about stereotyping the Hebrides as a primitive place, and that the producers had considered a number of islands, not all Scottish, and would have been prepared to set the experiment in the middle of Dartmoor if they could have isolated the participants effectively there. The Director of *An Comunn*, Donald John MacSween, countered that had the departed population of Taransay had the support systems put in place by programme makers for their castaways, the island would never have been depopulated in the first place.

The title of John Urry's book *Consuming Places* (1995) is deliberately ambiguous. Places are sites of consumption. They can be consumed. They can consume people's identities. They can be exhausted by use. Taransay had, perhaps, already been exhausted by use when it could no longer support a traditional crofting community. *Castaway 2000* makes scant reference, however, to why the island's population departed. Rounded timber framed houses, or 'pods', far removed from the vernacular styles of stone built black house[9] or of croft were built, and, being wood framed, were reliant on materials not readily to hand on treeless Harris. The lobster fishing of the last inhabitants of the island[10] was replaced by the polytunnel cultivation of, amongst other things, kohlrabi, a vegetable rarely found on supermarket shelves in Stornoway. Thus the series emphasised, if only to those familiar with the Hebrides, the appropriation and consumption of island space to create its own temporary televisual place.

As soon as the advance party of Castaways arrived on the island (Episode Four, 26.i.00) they claimed it as their own. It had, of course, already been claimed by the programme makers. Flanked by a shot of a sunrise over a 'typical' beach, Julie, emerging from the helicopter which brought her across exclaims, 'Just look at this. Just look at the sky. And it's ours for a year.' *Sub specie aeternitatis* a year is not, in itself, over long; certainly shorter than the time lived through by any previous sustained inhabitations. But television producers have to be wary of overtiring their audiences, or indeed their protagonists. Julie's pleasure was in sharp contrast to her return to the project proper when, like a disconsolate tourist finding herself in the back of beyond she says, 'For me it started to go wrong at the Kyle of Lochalsh hotel when a bath plug didn't fit' (Episode Five, 23. iv. 04).[11] The message is clear enough; here is a place to be consumed for a time, and visually at that. Michael Cronin (2000) suggests that

> the experience of travel in a country where the language is unknown to the traveller will be heavily informed by the visual. If you cannot speak, you can at least look. Sightseeing is the world with the sound turned off (Cronin, *op. cit.*, p. 82).

---

[8] The series had two Executive Producers, Colin Cameron of the BBC which commissioned it, and Jeremy Mills of the producing company Lion Television.

[9] The black house, or *tigh dubh*, was for centuries the traditional Hebridean dwelling, built of a low double wall of stone, the cavity insulated by earth and stones, the turf or thatched roof attached to the inner wall to allow some protection from the wind (Nicolson, 1960/2000, p. 29).

[10] See Lawson (1997, p. 41).

[11] Episode Five (23.iv.00).

On Taransay where the locals are conveniently departed, and their Gaelic voices remain unheard, let alone understood, by the Anglophone incomers sightseeing is about as much translation between cultures as is possible.

This had been underpinned in a previous Episode (Episode Two, 19.i.00) when two of the series' experts, Dr Cynthia McVey, a psychologist, and Lucy Irvine, on whose experience of living on a desert island the film *Castaway* had been based, had visited the island to discuss the restoration of the schoolhouse, a foursquare building open to the elements with one ruined gable end. The sequence begins with a wide shot looking up from a foreground of beach to the shell of the building silhouetted on a ridge. The picturesqueness of ruins and the pleasure of gazing on them are seldom in doubt.[12] The shot cuts to McVey and Irvine inside the building where the intention is that the open gable will be filled in with a wall of glass. Irvine says, 'This is just an amazing position – for a *school* [emphasis in the original] house — just to think that the kids are going to be looking out on this, you know. I know that sometimes it's going to be pouring with rain, but you can make this so cosy as well.' During this the camera pans through the open wall to a wide shot of the beach, the sea and the mountains of Harris. It could have lingered on the ruined gable end or on the remains of the fireplace that once warmed schoolchildren who studied without the benefit of a glazed vista, but the discourse of visual consumption from a position of comfort, a commodified temporary gaze, is favoured here over the discourse of place exhausted by consumption. Here the distinction made by Urry (2000) between land and landscape is clearly articulated, the former 'a place of work that is conceived of functionally (rather than aesthetically)' while 'the notion of landscape emphasises leisure, relaxation and visual consumption by visitors' (*op. cit.,* pp. 137–138).

However problematic the subsequent attempts to combine function and aesthetic, at the heart of *Castaway 2000* was the construction and representation of a Heimat culture,[13] set in opposition to encroaching globalisation. While the needs of dramatic conflict on screen demanded a disparate group of tourist settlers, the group stood, in theory at least, united against the outside. In Taransay, of course, the 'real' inhabitants had been reduced to a Celtic cultural memory withheld from castaways and viewers alike. Instead the castaways united against the producers, challenging their representations, escaping from the island in protest at broken or unfulfilled promises about living conditions.[14] There were other, cultural, subversions occasioned by the castaways' mobility. The previously carefully made up and groomed secretary Tammy Huff is seen hard at work on a building site. 'At home, being in society, it's how you look ... what I wear ... make sure things don't clash. But here and now it just doesn't matter, even though you've got the cameras on you. What matters is keeping warm and dry'. By the end of the year many castaways were reflecting on their changed attitudes towards hair care and hygiene.[15] Rosemary Stephenson, the doctor's wife, and one of those initially not prepared to travel to the island until issues of cleanliness

---

[12] See Lowenthal (1985, pp. 127–140) on the *schadenfreude* of gazing on ruins.
[13] See Morley and Robins (1995, p. 20).
[14] See McCrum (2000) throughout, with the proviso that his is the 'official' book of the series.
[15] *Castaway Diary Three* (8.xii.00).

and sanitation had been addressed admits that 'Here I can easily go for a week without a shower. I haven't washed my hair for ... probably now about five weeks', while management consultant Liz Cathrine tells viewers, 'I don't think there's anyone who washes daily in the same way as they do at home'. Accompanying such inverted makeovers[16] was an increasing scatological interest bordering on the obsessive[17] in the functioning and maintaining of the compost lavatories. The camera observed in close up the process of 'peak knocking' whereby the rising pile of recently deposited material was smoothed out with the aid of what looked like a wooden trowel attached to a pole to the accompaniment of much laughter on the part of the castaways fortunate enough to be on latrine duty.[18]

Such transformations were perhaps to be expected, as was the way in which some castaways coped with the ritual of slaughtering animals, even to the extent of 'putting on a show' for visiting friends and relatives.[19] In this instance, however, the camera, in the thick of things so to speak in the latrines, maintained its distance, as did most of the castaways, and apart from a close shot of the pistol being loaded showed only the backs of a shadowy group of men in a darkened slaughterhouse, concentrating on the reactions of the visitors to the sights and sounds off camera.[20] This transgressive ritual, with its carnivalesque ambivalence towards pig sticking (Stallybrass & White, 1986, p. 45ff) was seen, perhaps, as a ritual too far for the sensibilities of viewers.

In Taransay's history a year is a short time. For the castaways who lasted the course it was a stage in their lives which subsequent media follow-ups tried to prolong. In what they styled 'a rescue archaeology' Hayden Lorimer and Fraser MacDonald (2002) reflected on the speed with which the traces of television's occupation were disappearing, yet found meaning even from the ephemeral. They use an appropriately visual metaphor for the new televisual mobility incarnate in Lion Television's 'experiment'.

> Discarded in the quagmire, we find a business card. It's saturated, the contact details are decomposing. Reality TV's short dalliance with Taransay is indeed coming to an end. (Lorimer & MacDonald, *op. cit.,* p. 101)

A Place in Greece

A Place in Greece (C4, Spring 2004) is just one of an increasing number of series which offers evidence of a blurring of the distinction between holiday programmes and lifestyle makeover, reflecting a key feature of what Frances Bonner (2003) terms 'ordinary television'.

---

[16] Most programmes featuring makeovers go under the generic title of 'lifestyle' and are about a perceived improving of appearance in such a way as to increase the individual's cultural capital (Moseley, 2000).

[17] The subject recurred in all four *Castaway Diaries* (24.xi.00, 1.xii.00, 8.xii.00, 15.xii.00).

[18] *Castaway Heaven and Hell* (18.xii.00).

[19] MacDonald (1997, p. 110) discusses the contrasting attitudes of locals and visitors towards semi-public slaughter in a crofting community in Skye.

[20] Episode Twelve (21.ix.00).

> Ordinary television appeals to its audience not only by showing them themselves and their own mundane domestic activities, but also by asserting that there is a better, more exciting ordinary to be had by simple methods, and showing how this is to be achieved. As a matter of course, it overstates the ease, the accessibility and longevity of the transformations, healings and achievements it vaunts [...] (Bonner, *op. cit.,* p. 216)

'Ordinary' lives on screen increasingly reflect 'ordinary' mobilities, and this eight part series is about two couples' struggle to build their 'dream house with a view' overlooking Souda Bay in Crete. In the light of the number of obstacles which they encounter, including lack of finance or proper planning permission, inactive local builders, the inability of any one of the four to speak Greek and consequent scant prospect of employment, it is on the face of it hard to accept Bonner's claims about the ease of their transformation; and when one couple plot behind the other's back to do them out of their share of the completed project, the prospects for healings and positive achievement seem remote. On the other hand the narrative needs to reflect, or indeed manufacture, such obstacles[21] and it is fair to assume that it is at least in part due to the agency of the producers that the project got off the ground in the first place.

At the heart of the series is Brian Saunders' obsession with installing a vast picture window, which will replace one wall of the first floor sitting room, sinking into the floor to allow an uninterrupted view plus access to the terrace. He and his partner Andrew Sutton are the prime movers in this drama, and in the course of the series they decide to leave their home and jobs in Coventry to live permanently in Crete. The other couple, Pete and Lesley Cardey, intend only prolonged holidays in their half of the house. The emphasis on the view offers a vindication of Urry's (1990, 1995) belief in the primacy of the gaze in tourism, and in the importance of scopic consumption, but there are other discourses at work, especially that of travel as an extended secular pilgrimage. In *A Place in Greece*'s geography of mobility, transgression and consumption of place are all part of that greater whole; a shared journey of re-creation to what Victor Turner (1973) termed 'the centre out there', a centre with its own rules and anomalous behaviour. The parallel with pilgrimage is not, of course, exact. Conventionally, pilgrims returned home, wiser and made whole. The newly mobile Brian and Andrew do not intend to do so, at least in the immediate future, but will maintain their anomalous identity as tourist settlers in their Anglophone house with a view of a foreign land.

As the national identity of broadcasters is eroded by increasing globalisation, there is also, as Morley and Robins (1995, p. 107) argue, 'the danger of a fearful refusal to translate: the threat of a retreat into cultural autism and of a rearguard reinforcement of imperial illusions'. In the penultimate episode Brian decides that in the absence of any income he and Andrew can save on car hire by buying a second hand car. He has heard of one for sale and is shown in an unnamed bar talking to an unnamed Greek woman who assures him, 'My cousin Kostas has a very good car for you. A very good price.' Brian asks about its condition and is assured that it is very good. There is a cut to a deserted village square identified in the commentary as 'the sleepy village of Kephalos'. This is illustrated conventionally enough by a long shot

---

[21] See Todorov's (1977) account of how narrative is posited on the overcoming of obstacles.

of an old man walking slowly with the aid of a stick plus a group shot of old men on a bench, typical tourist brochure material of the sort that signifies 'the real Crete'. Brian and Andrew are sitting at a café, and to build up narrative tension they provide a running commentary on every car that is seen to drive up. Each seems an acceptable possibility until a battered white pickup rattles in. There is a shot of the old men's eyes appearing to follow it. Brian, playing up to the camera says, 'This can't be it. This cannot be it. Tell me this isn't it ... It is'. Kostas introduces himself and his pickup. They examine the rust, the dents, the bald tyres, all shown in close up. Brian, patronisingly polite for the benefit of the camera, says, 'I don't think so, no.' Andrew adds, over a shot of a dent in the bonnet, 'It's aerodynamically shaped at the front.' After a test drive in which Brian and Andrew play up the dangers of what they believe to be a death machine Kostas asks, 'So, do you like my Toyota?' Brian struggling to open the door and get out replies archly, 'Yes, it's not quite the right colour that we were looking for.' Kostas indicates that at €700 it is a good deal, but Brian and Andrew demur, wordlessly declining his offer. Kostas shakes hands and departs. Brian, walking in the opposite direction with Andrew offers a cool and dismissive, 'Yes thank you,' and then adds in a stage whisper to camera, 'We won't be ringing you. My hands are shaking. It needs to be scrapped.'

It is hard in a transcript to give an adequate sense of the patronising and knowing tone of this sequence or of its cynical construction, using stereotypical shots of 'the sleepy village' and its inhabitants to create an ambivalent representation of a subaltern culture,[22] which is nice for visiting Brits to live off as long as they maintain a wary contempt for the *dolce far niente* of the Mediterranean and a suspicion of the motives and values of the locals. Underpinning this is the narrative opening in which Kostas' cousin offers assurances about the excellence of the deal, a status quo whose equilibrium[23] is, as viewers are likely to anticipate given the series' representations of Cretan life, quickly challenged by the dramatically built up arrival and the detailed close ups of the Toyota. The English couple's inability to speak Greek, coupled with the way in which they are encouraged, either by their own sense of performance or by the accompanying film crew, to provide a running commentary on their hosts to the latter's disadvantage may offer a more accurate documentary account of the paradox of British mobility and British culture of insularity than the producers had intended.

Conclusion

Overcoming cultural distance is difficult, and *A Place in Greece*, in common with *Castaway 2000*, makes little attempt to meet the challenge, preferring instead to colonise for whatever time the unfamiliar and to represent it as a place of ambivalent pleasures and narrative tensions. The final image of the former is of both couples at least temporarily reconciled and toasting their good fortune in their newly built eyrie from which they can look down, physically and metaphorically, on a Crete reduced to a blur of twinkling lights and distant lives. Given the precariousness of their reconciliation, hinted at in a series of close ups as each

---

[22] See Shurmer-Smith and Hannam (1994).
[23] See Todorov (1977).

responds to the other, and their anomalous status as tourist settlers, there exists the possibility that living happily ever after in paradise is not the message which its makers, ever open to the possibility of a follow-up, wish to inscribe in the series. When Paul exclaims at what he describes as 'the ephemeral view' he is, perhaps, unaware of the appropriateness of his solecism.

References

Agnew, I. (1996). Liminal travellers: Hebrideans at home and away. *Scotlands, 3*(1), 32–41.

Bonner, F. (2003). *Ordinary television: Analyzing popular TV*. London: Sage.

Chapman, M. (1978). *The Gaelic vision in Scottish culture*. London: Croom Helm.

Cronin, M. (2000). *Across the lines: Travel, language, translation*. Cork: Cork University Press.

Dovey, J. (2000). *Freakshow: First person media and factual television*. London: Pluto.

Dunn, D. (2001). A place of recreation: The island of Taransay as tourist destination in the television series *Castaway 2000. Media Education Journal, 30*, 23–27.

Ellis, J. (2000). *Seeing things: Television in the age of uncertainty*. London: I. B. Tauris.

Graburn, N. (1978). Tourism: The sacred journey. In: V. Smith (Ed.), *Hosts and guests: The anthropology of tourism* (pp. 17–31). Oxford: Blackwell.

Hunter, J. (2000). *The making of the Crofting community: New edition*. Edinburgh: John Donald.

Kidd, C. (1993). *Subverting Scotland's past: Scottish whig historians and the creation of an Anglo-British identity, 1689–c.1830*. Cambridge: Cambridge University Press.

Lawson, B. (1997). *The Isle of Taransay: A Harris island in its historical setting*. Northton: Bill Lawson Publications.

Lorimer, H., & MacDonald, F. (2002). A rescue archaeology, Taransay, Scotland. *Cultural Geographies, 9*, 95–102.

Lowenthal, D. (1985). *The past is a foreign country*. Cambridge: Cambridge University Press.

MacDonald, S. (1997). *Reimagining culture: Histories, identities and the Gaelic renaissance*. Oxford: Berg.

McCrum, M. (2000). *Castaway: The full, inside story of the major TV series*. London: Ebury Press.

Morley, D., & Robins, K. (1995). *Spaces of identity: Global media, electronic landscapes and cultural boundaries*. London: Routledge.

Moseley, R. (2000). Makeover takeover on British television. *Screen, 41*(3), 299–314.

Nash, D. (1996). *Anthropology of tourism*. Oxford: Pergamon.

Nicolson, N. (1960/2000). *Lord of the Isles*. Acair: Stornoway.

Rojek, C. (2000). *Leisure and culture*. London: Macmillan.

Shurmer-Smith, P., & Hannam, K. (1994). *Worlds of desire, realms of power: A cultural geography*. London: Edward Arnold.

Stallybrass, P., & White, A. (1986). *The politics and poetics of transgression*. London: Methuen.

Todorov, T. (1977). *The poetics of prose*. Ithaca, NY: Cornell University Press.

Turner, V. (1973). The center out there: Pilgrim's goal. *History of Religions, 12*, 191–230.

Urry, J. (1990). *The tourist gaze*. London: Sage.

Urry, J. (1995). *Consuming places*. London: Routledge.

Urry, J. (2000). Sociology beyond societies: Mobilities for the twenty first century. London: Routledge.

Withers, C. (1992). The historical creation of the Scottish highlands. In: I. Donnachie, & C. Whatley (Eds), *The manufacture of Scottish history* (pp. 143–156). Edinburgh: Polygon.

Womack, P. (1989). *Improvement and romance: Constructing the myth of the highlands*. London: Macmillan.

Author Index

Subject Index